AMAZING
FAITH

AMAZING

FAITH

*How One Man Spent
His Life Taking God
at His Word*

THE AUTHORIZED BIOGRAPHY OF BILL BRIGHT
Founder of Campus Crusade for Christ International

BY MICHAEL RICHARDSON

WATERBROOK
PRESS

Cover captions (left to right):
- Bill joins Billy Graham and Joon Gon Kim at Graham's 1973 Crusade in Seoul, South Korea.
- In 1983, President Ronald Reagan signs the "Year of the Bible" proclamation. Behind him, Bill Bright is flanked by U.S. Senator Bill Armstrong (left) and Congressman Carlos J. Moorhead, the leaders who promoted the law.
- In 1983, then–Vice President George Bush greets the Brights, thanking Vonette for her work as the National Chairperson for the Day of Prayer.
- This photo of Campus Crusaders on the march in the 1960s is representative of the current size of the ministry, totaling 25,000 full-time staff and 500,000 trained volunteer staff in 196 countries.

AMAZING FAITH
PUBLISHED BY WATERBROOK PRESS
2375 Telstar Drive, Suite 160
Colorado Springs, Colorado 80920
A division of Random House, Inc.

Scripture quotations are taken from the King James Version (KJV) unless otherwise indicated. Scripture quotations marked (TLB) are taken from *The Living Bible* copyright © 1971. Used by permission of Tyndale House Publishers, Inc., Wheaton, Illinois 60189. Scripture quotations marked (NASB) are taken from the *New American Standard Bible*®. Copyright © The Lockman Foundation 1960, 1962, 1963, 1968, 1971, 1972, 1973, 1975, 1977. Scripture quotations marked (NIV) are taken from the *Holy Bible, New International Version*®. NIV®. Copyright © 1973, 1978, 1984 by International Bible Society. Used by permission of Zondervan Publishing House. Scripture quotations marked (NKJV) are taken from the New King James Version. Copyright © 1982 by Thomas Nelson, Inc. All used by permission. All rights reserved. All italics in Scripture quotations are the author's.

ISBN 1-57856-561-8

Printed in the United States of America
2001—First Trade Paperback Edition

10 9 8 7 6 5 4 3 2 1

To my family, elders and youngers,
and the One who keeps us together.

Contents

Contents

APPENDIXES

Foreword

Ifirst met Bill Bright in Los Angeles in the spring of 1949 where he was planning major events for the advancement of the gospel. He was a visionary then and he still is. Over the years, Ruth and I have enjoyed beautiful and strategic times together with Vonette and Bill. Often, in international leadership circles, theirs have been the hands who held high the Christian's challenge to fulfill the Great Commission in our lifetime. I do believe if that is fulfilled, it will be due in significant measure to the vision and obedience of Bill Bright.

I was so pleased he received the Templeton Prize for Progress in Religion. It recognizes Bill's worldwide impact on the hearts and minds, not only of young people but also of political leaders, executives, and persons of influence from all walks of life.

I know Bill did not seek this book. He is a humble man of God. The author said it took four years to persuade Bill just to begin the project. But it is a good thing that this particular record of the acts of the Holy Spirit in modern days has been compiled to encourage the next group of leaders to help communicate the gospel to the world.

This account can only tell part of what God has done through the heart and mind of Bill Bright. It's a little bit like John the Beloved said: "No book could contain the whole" of the Lord's work, in this case, through the Brights and their thousands of trained staff and volunteers across scores of nations of the world.

Let me add my challenge to the one implicit in this book: If God could so grip the heart of Bill Bright to see the gospel preached to all the nations in one man's lifetime, why cannot He do so with you? Let this man's story put you in greater touch with the Greatest One of all history, our Lord Jesus Christ. Let Him make you another who would join Bill Bright in helping change the world for Christ's sake!

—Billy Graham
Montreat, North Carolina

Introduction

On a brilliant May day in London in 1996, a former American businessman stood in Buckingham Palace as Prince Philip placed a silver medallion around his neck. He was neither athlete nor statesman nor general. He was a diminutive man from Oklahoma and something of a curiosity of the moment. In the China Room of the palace, the prince said, "Tell me about your journey."

But neither the man nor his wife could tell the tale. Time did not permit to explain how a young couple in 1951 made a radical change in their careers and proceeded to build an organization operating across the world. The story of Bill and Vonette Bright reaches from the prairie of Oklahoma to the palace of Queen Elizabeth to the provinces of every continent. It is the story of a couple whose vision and touch have been felt in the hearts of leaders in the nations' capitals, of students on campus, and of youths on a beach.

It is a trail of tears, squabbles, perils, setbacks, frustrations, numerous critics, and a few painful messes. His is no rocketed career, but a winding road, full of terrible traps and heartaches as well as successes that seem to belong in the *Ripley's Believe It or Not* collection. Virtually every big idea he has had was opposed in his own ranks, criticized by religionists, and scorned by secular mockers.

"It would be difficult to name another individual whose contribution to the spiritual progress and growth of mankind can be more suitably described as original, innovative, and dramatically effective," wrote Dr. James C. Dobson, founder of Focus on the Family, in a letter regarding the Templeton Prize.

"Every time I am with him he has a new idea, another way to advance the cause of religion and the Christian faith in the world," said Chuck Colson, founder of Prison Fellowship.

"Bill is a gentleman who has for a lifetime exemplified personal integrity and lived out moral values which govern his life," commented Ted W. Engstrom, president emeritus of World Vision.

"There is no one else I know in this world who has lived the Spirit-filled life so consistently," observed former Dallas Cowboys football coach Tom Landry.

"Bill Bright has an ingenious way of seeing a need and finding God's way to fill it," said U.S. Senate Chaplain Lloyd John Ogilvie.

Within days after being in a royal palace in London, Bill Bright was in his native Coweta, Oklahoma, wearing a guayabera and serving tables at a family reunion.

In 1951, Bill began signing his letters, "Yours for fulfilling the Great Commission in this generation." Where did he get that idea? How did he expect to be a part of such a program? "Small plans cannot enflame the minds of men," he says. After serving with Bill Bright for forty-six years, one of his ministry associates, Roe Brooks, described him with these words: "He cares enough to cry, and he cares enough to try."

CHAPTER 1

Unlimited Horizon

I t was 1921, and America was a boiling cauldron of conflicting philosophies—communism, socialism, pacifism, and various other political theories that had come ashore from Europe to clash with values and beliefs that had made the nation great.

Great ponderings about life and liberty were part of the continuing aftermath of World War I in the United States, along with a heavy national debt and fierce social unrest. Already these postwar years had seen an anarchist bombing on Wall Street that killed thirty persons and injured four hundred. There had been dozens of race riots, including one in Chicago in which thirty-eight died. Scores of African-Americans had been lynched in various locales in the South. Who could know, in this restless year of 1921, what the future would bring?

Into this uncertain world, on October 19 of that year, William Rohl Bright was born in a rambling, white, two-story house five miles outside the town of Coweta in northeast Oklahoma. The house was on a five-thousand-acre ranch belonging to Bill's father, Forrest Dale Bright, whose own father, Samuel, had been the first Bright to come to the Oklahoma Indian Territory decades earlier.

Bill's mother was Mary Lee Rohl Bright, who together with her husband had far more urgent worries that year than the current political and social upheavals. Mary Lee had lost a previous son at childbirth, and while pregnant with Bill, she was told that her own life was at risk. The doctor gave her little hope that both she and the baby could make it. So she prayed, not for her own life but that she would be able to give a healthy birth to the child within her. She promised God that her child would be dedicated to His service. Not until twenty-four years later, when Bill announced his own decision to follow Christ, would Mary Lee Bright tell her son of this contract with God regarding his life and destiny.

Although his mother was silent about this matter during Bill's childhood, in many other ways her life spoke to him—and to all those around her—of her devotion to her Lord. She read from her Bible each morning and evening and sang hymns as she went about her work.

"She lived a very selfless life," Bill later recalled. "Our neighbors would turn to her when they were ill, when they needed anything. She was very sensitive about literature, poetry, art, and those finer qualities. She brought that spirit to the community.

"She lived for her husband and seven children. She worked hard, but she always had time for us. She came out of a German tradition where the mother always waits the table and then eats later.

"At the end of the day—after we had all gone to bed, because we worked hard and we worked long hours—she was up reading her Bible and praying. I remember that vividly."

The story was different for Bill's father. Known as Dale to friends and family, he took no part in religious matters as Bill and his siblings were growing up, believing that such things were for women and children. On Sunday mornings, while Mary Lee took their children to church, Dale typically joined several townsmen a few blocks away to talk business and politics.

Bill's father was never abusive, but when he raised his voice, Bill knew he was to obey without question. Dale Bright never spanked his children, leaving that discipline to their mother, but he could be hard-driving, set in his ways, and inexhaustibly determined to prevail when in the thick of any struggle. Both family and friends learned it was not a good idea to cross him. In his youth and early manhood, Bill was very much his father's son.

Bill remembers him in those early days as "the typical macho rancher. He could ride the wildest broncs and the wildest steers, and he had a gift with livestock. He could go into a corral of wild horses and they'd tremble." Bill, too, learned to ride broncs—one of the rites of manhood in Oklahoma—while also adopting his father's view of religion, although he was baptized at age twelve in the Methodist church.

Another strong influence on young Bill was his grandfather. Samuel Bright, a former schoolteacher, was one of the brave souls who had "made the run"—those who saddled up for the great land-grant rushes between 1889 and 1895 that had so transformed the Indian Territory. Bold and popular, Sam Bright was elected mayor of Beggs, Oklahoma, and moved later to the larger town of Okmulgee, some fifty miles from Coweta. His new house there, although not a mansion by today's standards, nonetheless stood out to young Bill, who had never before seen bearskin rugs and floors so polished "you could see your face in them."

Grandfather Bright was a bold, impressive figure. "He was my hero and my idol," Bill would recall. "His appearance was regal, his voice was like music, his manner was stately." He was also warm and benevolent and fun. A particularly unforgettable memory for Bill was of the day his grandfather purchased for him what was then a modern marvel, store-bought ice cream. "It made me feel so special."

Summers brought treasured visits to Grandfather Bright's "mansion" for Bill and his siblings and their cousins. A widower, Sam Bright had remarried by the time Bill was born, and his second wife—the only grandmother Bill ever knew—likewise made a lasting impression on the boy. "She was always so vibrant, so vivacious, and she had a remarkable gift of making everybody feel wanted. Grandmother Bright was like a combination of elegance and a warm heart. Her hair was light brown and always beautifully groomed. I remember how she went to such great lengths to entertain us. She would treat me as if I was so very important."

The time spent with these grandparents would be a source of profound and refreshing memories in Bill's later life, like rivulets on the dry Oklahoma prairie after a welcome shower.

As Bill grew up, he watched wide-eyed as his grandfather and father transacted deals with other men of the region involving large sums of money, then sealed the agreement with nothing more than their word and a handshake.

He also discovered what quality of man his grandfather was. Once, Bill learned, an investment in an oil property failed to work out as Sam Bright had expected and as he'd led several partners in the endeavor to believe. He refunded their money from his own pocket, although he was under no legal obligation to do so and his partners had been well aware of the risk.

On another occasion, a judge ruled in his grandfather's favor in a lawsuit he'd felt obligated to file regarding another business dealing. But when the judge awarded him $150,000—three times the $50,000 damages his grandfather had requested—Sam Bright announced that he would accept only the smaller amount.

With such a grandfather, Bill knew he had a strong name to fall back on and to live up to. His was a rich heritage of fair play, total honesty, and the absolute value that a man's word was as good as any bond.

Meanwhile, in more easygoing moments, young Bill rode his horse—named Pet—on the rolling ranch land owned by his father and grandfather. He recalls galloping "lickety-split across the prairie toward what seemed to be a totally unlimited horizon."

CHAPTER 2

"My Unusual Record"

W hen his years of upbringing were over, Bill Bright gave an
enlightening appraisal of them in a brief autobiography he
wrote as an assignment for a freshman college class in the fall
of 1939, when he was just turning eighteen. The paper, discovered sixty years
later in the Bright family archives, reveals the complexity and diversity, the
humility and the intellect, that pulsed through the young man from Coweta.

After recounting his birth on the family ranch, Bill wrote:

> It was there that I learned the things that are synonymous with
> farm-ranch life, which I believe will be an asset to me wherever I
> go or whatever I do. I learned to work and work hard, to chop
> corn when the sun was so hot that weeds withered and wilted as
> soon as they were cut down. I learned what it is to get up at 4
> o'clock in the morning and work until dark.
>
> But farm life is not all drudgery. I learned to love the smell of
> new mown hay, the sight of budding fruit trees and the acres of
> waving wheat fields of golden grain.
>
> No, farm life was not drudgery. To me the farm is one of the
> most fascinating places in the world.

Although Bill's work ethic was molded largely during the Great
Depression—Wall Street's fateful crash occurred only days after Bill's eighth

birthday—the Bright family's resources and hard work kept economic disaster at bay. There was no opulence, but the family never missed a meal. For others nearby who did experience hardship and want, the Brights stayed true to their culture's neighborly code of taking care of one another. For Dale Bright, that meant sharing his pride and joy—a relatively new threshing machine—with other farmers and ranchers whenever the need arose. A commitment to community sharing of resources and to mutual respect was ingrained in Bill.

For his first seven years of formal education, Bill attended a one-room schoolhouse. "I remember quite distinctly the first day that I entered grammar school," the autobiography continues, "how I cried when I left my mother (whom I have always loved dearly) and how happy I was to return at night."

Most of his school-day memories were more positive.

> I spent some very memorable and exciting times at the old
> white frame rural school building. I remember the winters when
> snow and ice covered the ground. I delighted in skating on the old
> frog pond located behind a grove of trees out of sight of the
> teacher, but close enough so that we might hear the warning bell
> and make it back to class without being tardy.

The same boyish tendencies show through in his remembrance of life at home:

> While only a lad I enjoyed slipping out behind the old
> corncrib and rolling me a cigarette of corn silks or brown peach
> leaves. (You can imagine how it tasted.) Perhaps this is the reason
> I have never had any desire to smoke or drink. I am a teetotaler
> in every way.

Bill's mother, a former schoolteacher in her native Indiana and a cousin of the widely popular poet James Whitcomb Riley, remained a strong influence in Bill's education. She read to her children from the *Iliad,* the *Odyssey,* and other classics, giving Bill a lasting appreciation for literature.

"I think that perhaps I am my mother's child in many respects," Bill sur-
mised in the autobiography.

> Like her I love the wonders of nature and am inclined to be some-
> what of a dreamer.... Like her I love to read. Many are the times I
> would come in to dinner, grab up the daily book or a magazine,
> and become so interested, Mother would find it necessary to call
> me several times.... One of my greatest pleasures comes from read-
> ing my favorite poems out loud to myself.

His acknowledgment of a special bond to his mother naturally led him
to mention his father, revealing a mix of Bill's humility and sense of achievement.

> But I'm not altogether like my mother who is usually so kind
> and gentle. Like my father I have a temper, but have succeeded in
> curbing it to a certain extent.

Repeatedly in the autobiography, the same mix of humility and bravura
appears. "Upon entering high school," he wrote, "I was merely another student. The only thing bright about me was my name. I excelled in nothing,
but was and still am a lover of all kinds of sports." He went on to list several
truly notable accomplishments at Coweta High School, then quickly added:

> Please don't think that I say this in a braggadocian manner,
> because it has never been my policy to brag about anything that I
> have done, and I never intend to in the future.

Then came more acknowledged weaknesses:

> I have the peculiar habit of forgetting where I put things.
> Often times I will spend an hour of fruitless search for something
> I have misplaced, and...someone will find it right under my
> nose....

> So often when I am writing a letter or any kind of an essay I find myself thinking a long ways ahead of my writing, which often results in some very poorly constructed sentences.

But he knew his strengths as well.

> Being always of an energetic nature and not wishing to idle away my spare time, I helped to organize a 4-H Club in Coweta, of which I was elected president. This started me on my unusual record. This gave me confidence in myself, and I worked harder than ever.

He was also confident of his oratory abilities:

> It was during the eighth grade graduation, when I gave the class oration, that I learned that I could speak. Or at least I received so many fine compliments to that effect that I assumed as much. It was this that induced me to take up debating [in high school], in which I did very well....
>
> As my father was bitterly opposed to my participating in any kind of athletics, I turned to dramatics and speech work. In my senior year I had the lead in the two high school plays and won first in Original Oration and Extemporaneous Speaking at the Interscholastic Meet at Tahlequah, Oklahoma.

His father's opposition to his athletics sprang from an injury Bill sustained as a freshman on the football team. One day Bill decided not to give an inch to an imposing 250-pound, six-foot fullback who was bearing down with the intensity of a freight train. At five-foot-six and 125 pounds, Bill was determined to tackle the Goliath in his tracks—and did. But the resulting collision of the fullback's hard-driving legs with the left side of Bill's head resulted in a burst eardrum, an injury that would later change his life. At the time, however, he felt no significant ill effects, although his father insisted he play no more football.

Bill obediently turned to other pursuits for success. His public speaking abilities and his love for sports led him to become the public address announcer at home football games, the community's dominating events each fall.

His father, meanwhile, had become chairman of the Republican Party of Waggoner County. As candidates for public office came through the area, Dale Bright arranged for them to speak in Coweta. Bill often acted as the master of ceremonies, introducing the candidates in meetings at the high-school gym or in the open air on Main Street. He found himself proclaiming the virtues of people of importance, including candidates for governor and Congress.

Dale Bright's political prominence also meant that the Bright home became the rural entertainment center for the community, and at mealtimes Mary Lee was typically serving others in addition to her family. Politics was a subject Bill often heard his father discuss with their guests. Bill came to understand how politics and government worked to provide for the betterment of the community, whether through a school, a library, or a road. He perceived that leaders could get people together, present the vision of the work, engender a "barn-raising" spirit, and actually see the vision become reality.

Among the regular guests in the Bright home were J. J. and Alice Woolman, who owned the weekly *Coweta Times-Star*. Bill read the newspaper voraciously and soon began reporting on high-school activities for the paper, his articles sometimes appearing on page one.

The autobiography recounts his particularly busy senior year of high school. He tells of winning "a nice sum of money at livestock judging contests throughout the state, taking many of the highest honors," and being awarded an out-of-state trip for taking first prize in an Oklahoma public speaking contest.

> Maybe it was because I tried to be friendly to everyone, or
> because I worked hard; anyway, I was elected president of the
> Epworth League, president of the Future Farmers of America,
> local chapter and Northeastern Oklahoma. I was president of
> 4-H Club, vice president of the H-Y Club, business manager

of [the] school paper, and business manager of the high school annual.

But the crowning point of my school career came the night of graduation from high school after I had given the class oration.

This oration, entitled "The Hope of Democracy," was described in the next edition of the *Star-Times* as having been "well prepared and exceptionally well presented." The newspaper also reported Bill's "crowning point"—he was given a medal for the Security National Bank Award as the "best all-around student" in the senior class of thirty-three members.

Seated near the back of the auditorium on that graduation night in May 1939 was a member of Coweta's seventh-grade class named Vonette Zachary, whose father, Roy Zachary, owned and operated the town's main service station. Looking up to the stage as the Security National Bank Award was announced, Vonette thought Bill Bright would go on to be a great man someday—just like the kind of man she hoped to marry.

That fall Bill began his studies forty miles away at a state college (now Northeastern State University) in Tahlequah. He took with him several goals, all of which he would eventually meet: to be elected president of his class, to become editor of the school yearbook, to be elected president of the student body, and to be selected as the college's most outstanding student.

The mix of humility and self-confidence coming through in his assigned autobiography that freshman year genuinely reflected his personality and approach to life. "I was introverted," he would later remember, "yet I felt like I could do anything." He continued to meet opportunities for public speaking and service, but found himself sometimes battling with shyness. He really didn't like crowds or being put on the spot, unless he was in charge of that spot—as in a play, where he seemed to come alive, knowing exactly what to say and do.

Once, during a break in a basketball game in the college gymnasium, Bill—then president of the student body—was supposed to come to the microphone to make an announcement. It was a forty-foot walk across the gym floor to the microphone. But Bill couldn't force himself on this occasion to walk that distance in front of everybody. Instead he stepped out and went around the building so he could reenter from a side door closer to the microphone. The nervousness vanished the moment he began to speak, and he made the announcement with aplomb and professionalism.

Although he studied oration, debate, and drama in college, his natural shyness never really left. "Unless I was there for a purpose," he observed, "I always felt self-conscious."

In the autobiography, the freshman Bill had written about career goals:

> I believe that any person of average intelligence can accomplish much if they have the determination and the desire to do so. I desire to become a great doctor, and I find it necessary to work my way through school. At present I wash dishes and scrub floors. I have been taught it is no disgrace to work and that success comes only through effort.
>
> I have no desire to be wealthy or famous, but only to serve my fellow men and to achieve the things in life that I know are worthwhile.

By the time of his college graduation, he had abandoned the short-lived consideration of a medical career. Instead, his plan for life included these objectives: to be a rancher, to obtain a law degree, to own a newspaper, then to run for Congress. With such credentials, he believed, a person like himself could help change the world.

At this stage of his life, the true spiritual state of William Rohl Bright could probably be best described as that of an unbelieving, social churchgoer and hedonist. Despite his mother's godly influence and his religious upbringing, "I had never received Christ," he later recalled. "When I went away to college I left all that behind and was basically a humanist.

"I was never exposed to a godly man. My father was not a Christian, and my grandfather whom I practically idolized was not a Christian. I'd never met a man who, to my knowledge, really loved Jesus Christ, and frankly I didn't know that many women who did....

"I set my goals as a humanist, materialist, self-sufficient person—no God, no Savior, and no Bible."

CHAPTER 3

From Frustrated Warrior to Happy Pagan

B ill Bright was almost halfway through his junior year in college when the attack on Pearl Harbor plunged the United States into World War II. Bill joined others from his campus in going immediately to enlist in December 1941, but at their local Selective Service office they were told that college students were not yet being taken.

Resolved to fight for his country, Bill pushed through his last year and a half of college as if it were the morning's last chores on the farm—just so he could get on with real living and participate in the defense of his nation. He carried on with his many student responsibilities and kept his goals in sight. Twelve months after Pearl Harbor, in the middle of Bill's senior year, a front-page *Times-Star* story back home in Coweta noted:

> Mr. Bright is president of the student body at Northeastern
> State College; is president of Sigma Tau Gamma fraternity; was
> editor of the college yearbook, '41-'42; president of the Oklahoma
> Federation of Student Councils '42-'43; president of Haskell Hall
> for men '42; member of student council '40-'41; is at present a
> member of Rho Theta Sigma honorary fraternity, Delta Psi
> Omega dramatics fraternity, Debate Congress and International
> Relations Club. In addition to these offices of trust Mr. Bright has
> won state and national recognition as a speaker and debater.

After trying unsuccessfully to wangle an appointment to West Point or the Naval Academy, he went through his senior final exams like an Olympic hurdler headed for the gold. The May 6, 1943, edition of the *Times-Star* headlined Bill's selection as the college's Outstanding Senior and included a handsome photograph of a young man with piercing dark eyes and square-cut face.

Now he was ready as a college graduate to join three brothers, a brother-in-law, and many of his college fraternity brothers in the global struggle for freedom. But his frustration was only to grow. He failed his physical because of the perforated eardrum from the football injury eight years earlier.

Bill had long ago learned not to take no for an answer when pursuing a heartfelt dream. There had to be a way around this obstacle. He appealed the decision, but the appeal was denied. He then prevailed upon friends at his local draft board to try getting him in through the Tulsa draft board. When that failed, he arranged to get a physical exam in Oklahoma City, figuring his injury might get overlooked in a bigger shuffle. But everywhere he heard the same response: "No."

Would political influence help? With his Dad's assistance, he tried Washington. He wrote to national Republican leader Wendell Willkie as well as to Democrat Harry Truman, who was then chairman of a special Senate committee evaluating the country's war effort. But it led only to further disappointment. "They were fighting the war," he would recall, "and they didn't have time to fool with a kid who was brokenhearted."

With so many off to war, Bill went home to help his father by assuming a heavy share of farm and ranch duties. But the inner frustration ate at him. Being deprived of military service cut him to the core. He was out of the mainstream. The military was highly respected, and he had no part in it. Envy grew inside him as he read of a Coweta man coming home from thirty-one bombing missions in Europe with a Distinguished Flying Cross, four oak leaf clusters, and a Purple Heart. "Hero Mustered Out," the local headline read. Bill had friends who were actually returning from a war he still could not enter.

He decided to seek a job at the local radio station as a disc jockey and announcer. That way, at least, he could report about the war. He was in the application process at the radio station when a surprising opportunity came to him. He was invited to join the "faculty in the field" of Oklahoma's higher education system. As assistant county agent of Muskogee County, his job was to help train young men and boys at their places of work—farms, factories, and shops—for maximum productivity to support the war effort.

Teaching was honorable, but it bothered his ego to know he'd probably gained the job only because others more qualified were off to war. And although the pay was better than what some professors made, it didn't buy him the lifestyle he wanted. "I was a very materialistic young man," he would later recall. "I accepted my check, which was more than I was worth, but it wasn't enough."

A year later he decided to try again to enter the military. He would apply the fast-shuffle theory on a grander scale by going to Los Angeles. With so many guys enlisting there, surely any warm body would get through; they couldn't possibly be as picky as the local Oklahomans over something as minor as a burst eardrum. And, while he was at it, if he had to spend time gaining California resident status, he could try using his proven talents by getting involved in the theater.

As Bill prepared to head west for the war, for his nation, for a career, for the theater—for something bigger, anything bigger—Mary Lee Bright saw to it that a new Bible was packed among her son's things when he left Coweta. Bill barely noticed at the time and had no plans for making use of it.

On his first evening in Los Angeles, Bill paused for a stoplight at Sunset Boulevard and Figuerora Street. He noticed a young man looking for a ride, clean-cut and decently dressed. Bill thought, *Why not?*

"Where you going?" the young man queried as he climbed in. He seemed affable and intelligent.

Bill mumbled something about enlisting for the war and being en route to visit the Pasadena Playhouse.

"Where are you staying?" the rider asked. Bill didn't know; he had just hit town.

"Why don't you spend the night where I live?" responded the young man, who explained he was with the Navigators, an evangelistic ministry.

May as well, Bill thought. The guy was well-spoken and well-mannered, and he knew the city.

Bill drove him to what turned out to be the home of Dawson Trotman, founder and director of the Navigators. At the Trotman family dinner table, several Navigators quoted Bible memory verses and took part in a lively conversation.

After dinner, it was announced that a birthday party for a certain Dan Fuller, home from the U.S. Navy, was being held at his parents' home nearby. Bill was asked to join the party, and he went along with the crowd. The sailor's father was radio evangelist Charles E. Fuller, featured speaker of *The Old-Fashioned Revival Hour* (and later founder of Fuller Theological Seminary). That meant little to Bill at the time. He gave not an instant's thought that perhaps his mother's prayers were keeping up with him twelve hundred miles from home.

The Trotmans and the Fullers did not press Bill about his faith. They were hospitable, and Bill was struck with their intellect and polish—something he'd never noticed among Christians. He talked with Dan Fuller about college life and the war. After the party Bill spent the night with the Trotmans and went his way.

When he appeared before the Los Angeles draft board, he found that he'd flunked his physical again because of that pestering eardrum. He appealed. He put on his best dramatic efforts, recounting the war commitment of his brothers and friends, his prior rejections, and his unwillingness to settle for less than military service. He would sign any waiver to clear Uncle Sam's liability for any medical costs due to the eardrum. He virtually begged: "Doctor, I came all the way out here from Oklahoma to get involved in the war and help defend my country. You simply cannot turn me down."

Only for a moment did the veteran physician seem willing to relent. "If it were entirely up to me," he said, "that would be one thing; but even if I pass you, somebody else down the pike is going to find you out. You'll only be rejected later." The issue was clear-cut for the military: Poison gas could penetrate a perforated eardrum, and the results almost certainly would be fatal.

Bill had never known depression, but this was a pit for him. A life marked by opportunity, performance, achievement, success, and recognition was now met with unremitting rejection.

Staying in Los Angeles, he went to work as close to the war as he could get. He became an electrician's helper for a contractor building ships for the navy. The pay was good, but Bill quickly saw that it was all out of proportion to the work done at the shipyard. There was no apparent commitment to craftsmanship, only an attempt to look busy. *If the ships they were building actually ever floated,* he thought, *it would be a miracle.*

After a few weeks Bill discovered that the disproportionate pay was no accident. It appeared that the contractor was corrupt. Little work was being performed and yet billings were made. This was make-work.

So he was employed in the war effort, but it put dirty money in his hands. What was the proper response? Look the other way? Use the money for good ends? Quit? The newshound in him determined to learn more before deciding. He began checking into the company's administration. What he found confirmed his suspicions. He perceived that hours of work were being reported that did not, in fact, take place. Personnel were reported who did not exist. Kickbacks were flowing from top to bottom to keep this corruption quiet.

He confronted first his supervisor, then the manager. He said if they didn't change things he would go to the newspaper with his information on their scandal. They offered to promote him and increase his pay to keep him quiet, which was even more repugnant to Bill.

He pondered his responsibilities and his options. He was not, in fact, an official investigator. And perhaps the company was fulfilling its obligation to the government for how many ships it produced; if the government didn't care, what could a young fellow from Oklahoma do about it? Besides, this wasn't Coweta, and he didn't know a soul at the newspaper. He might even get drawn into some long legal process that would keep him from making money.

Meanwhile, one of his new friends had an enterprise that held some promise—a specialty foods company—and invited Bill into the business as a partner. Bill decided simply to walk away from the shipbuilding sleaze and plunge himself into his own endeavor.

Within a few weeks, however, it became clear to Bill that his new partner was not the working kind. Bill was performing all the labor, making the products and the sales, and supervising the deliveries. He confronted his partner with a choice: Either work or buy me out or let me buy you out. The fellow sold out, and Bill began his own business, known first as Bright's Epicurean Delights and later as Bright's California Confections and Bright's Brandied Foods. Brandy was the chief additive in his thirty-two-product line of fancy foods, and richness was their chief distinction.

Now he was blazing his own trail. Bill worked hard; eighteen or twenty hours a day was not unusual. His confections were a delight with the rich and famous who could afford them. His products were being carried by the best-known stores—such as J. W. Robinson, Bullock's, and Wilshire in Los Angeles; Nieman-Marcus in Dallas; and B. Altman in New York—and he met with specialty buyers from leading department stores and epicurean shops throughout America. Business boomed, and soon his merchandise was even being exported to different countries.

He had the good fortune of meeting Martin Cornman, the dean of buyers for many fancy-food stores across America, as well as R. B. Curl of the Farmer's Market in the heart of Los Angeles, who helped Bill learn the export trade to certain exclusive stores overseas. Neither Cornman nor Curl had a son, and both, in a business sense, "adopted" Bill and became his mentor.

Bill also found time for studying drama at the Hollywood Talent Showcase under Cosmo Morgan as well as doing an amateur radio program on Sunday mornings and going horseback riding in the Hollywood hills on Sunday afternoons.

He was full of himself, and now he had money for clothes and cars and good times. Looking back he would observe, "Frankly, I was a happy pagan."

CHAPTER 4

Who Art Thou?

T he landlords of Bill's Hollywood apartment were a friendly, elderly couple who quickly took an interest in him. They repeatedly invited Bill to attend their church, Hollywood First Presbyterian, not far down the street. They spoke highly of their pastor, a man named Louis Evans Sr. "You'd love Dr. Evans," they told Bill, who couldn't imagine loving any preacher.

Late one Sunday afternoon Bill returned from riding horses in the hills of Hollywood. He smelled like a horse, but on an impulse and without changing clothes, he decided to drop in on the Hollywood Presbyterians. The evening service had begun. He slipped in unobtrusively, sat on the back row by himself, then left before the service ended "so no one else would see me—or smell me. "So much for church, or so I thought."

Meanwhile, his landlords had also put Bill's name on the prospect list for the church's well-organized visitation program, which operated under the direction of a precise woman, Dr. Henrietta Mears. Bill soon received a telephone call from a young woman of the church's college and career department. Her voice was like velvet. Bill was impressed and thought meeting her would be a good idea. She invited him to a party being held at the ranch of a movie star member of the church, and Bill agreed to go.

Nothing had prepared him for what he encountered at the party. "Gathered together in a big, play-barn were three hundred of the sharpest college-age men and women I had ever seen. They were happy, they were having fun, and they obviously loved the Lord. In one evening, my notion that Christianity is appropriate only for women and children was really shaken. I had never met people like these before."

The group included actors and actresses, students, and young professionals. They were people of Bill's age and ambition—much like him and how he wanted to be. They were articulate, attractive, goal-oriented, and friendly. They knew where they were going and how they were getting there.

Bill, now twenty-three, began attending the church's evening meetings for young college and career-minded people as well as the meetings for young business people. They would sing and give testimonies, after which Dr. Mears or others would give a Bible message. Each evening ended with a social time.

Sometimes the young people gathered for parties at the home of a church elder, Elwain Steinkamp, a developer and homebuilder in the prestigious Bel Air community. The spacious and magnificent Steinkamp home with its huge swimming pool was a place of delight to a young man alone in Hollywood.

The Steinkamps befriended Bill. One day, Mr. Steinkamp was talking with him beside the pool. Bill was eager to hear of his business success, but the man had other things to say. "Material success is not where you find happiness," he said. "There are rich people all over this city who are the most miserable people you'll ever meet. Knowing and serving Jesus Christ is what's really important. He's the only way to find happiness. And Christ said: 'What does it profit a man to gain the whole world and lose his own soul?'"

That perspective was far from what Bill came to California thinking. Why was he working night and day if not to earn the money to be happy?

But it was hard to quarrel with the facts of Steinkamp's success. To Bill, he seemed to have it all—family, wealth, fancy home, clothes, cars, friends. Yet here was the successful elder debunking the material and exalting the spiritual. Who else did Bill know who thought like that? One person, his mother, definitely. She lived her life the way Steinkamp was talking, but she didn't verbalize it so plainly. The difference to Bill was that Steinkamp and most of these attractive collegians and young business professionals not only lived for Christ, but they communicated it clearly.

And Steinkamp wasn't the only successful Christian businessman Bill encountered. "I'd never met a Christian businessman whom I admired.... Now I suddenly found myself face to face with some of the most prominent business and professional leaders in Los Angeles who were Christians."

Bill was also attending worship services at Hollywood Presbyterian, always sitting on the back row and not risking direct involvement. What he heard was intellectually challenging. Senior Pastor Louis Evans was indeed a compelling speaker. Eloquence was something Bill had studied, pursued, and appreciated, and Evans eloquently portrayed Jesus Christ "in an attractive way I had never known before."

Back at his apartment, Bill opened that never-used Bible from an unemptied box. As a matter of intellectual integrity, he felt compelled to begin an in-depth study of the life of Jesus, an exercise that quickly bore fruit. "I became convinced that Jesus was truly the most remarkable person who ever lived, no one like Him in all of history.... The months passed and the more I learned about Him, the more excited I became."

Bill began to realize something was missing in his life. He remembers: "I wasn't aware of sin particularly.... I thought I lived a pretty good life. My mother had instilled those qualities into me. But now, I became aware that I needed Jesus Christ."

The teaching of Henrietta Mears would be instrumental in helping Bill find fulfillment for that need. Dr. Mears was not a Presbyterian but a Baptist from Minnesota who had been recruited to direct education and training activities at Hollywood Presbyterian. She was called "Teacher," and although she was single and in her fifties when Bill met her, she was no dull spinster.

This woman commanded attention. She was a dynamo, a seemingly tireless worker with a radiant personality. It was as if everything she did and everything she said had a purpose. She spoke with authority, in flat, definite declarations bolstered by facts and her experiences. She had traveled the world several times and seemed to have a tale to tell from every land, always with a purpose—as an illustration of a Bible truth, a parallel with the life and teachings of Christ, or a manifestation of what Christian principles could produce. She had a global view of life and a fully integrated philosophy, mined by her study, refined by experience, and molded and tooled for her life's purpose: introducing others to Jesus Christ and teaching them to introduce still others to Him, and in the process influencing the world for Christ.

Dr. Mears struck Bill as loving, bold, wise, and articulate. She smashed all his caricatures of Christianity. Cutting through the staid, dead rituals he had known and conjured, she presented a living, personal God, Creator of the earth, a patient Father who had creatively and at great cost to Himself restored His wayward children to His family through the sacrifice of His Son and who wanted to fill the inner longings of every human being on earth. This was captivating language to Bill.

One Wednesday evening in the spring of 1945, Dr. Mears was speaking to the young adult group on the conversion of the apostle Paul. She focused on what Paul asked Jesus in Acts 9 after encountering Him in a blinding light from heaven: "Who art thou, Lord?" and "Lord, what wilt thou have me to do?" These were, she said, among the most important questions anyone could possibly ask God, even today.

"The happiest people in the world," she explained, "are those who are in the center of God's will. The most miserable are those who are not doing God's will. Paul deceived himself into thinking he was doing God's will by persecuting the Christians. In reality, he was pursuing his own ambitions. So God set him straight, through this dramatic experience on the road to Damascus."

Bill shifted in his seat. He had specialized in self-directed ambitions. He had always enjoyed life and considered himself happy. But Dr. Mears was talking about an inner happiness he had not known. It made him ask himself: *Where was this "center" of God's will?*

"Now," Dr. Mears continued, "not many of us have dramatic, emotional conversion experiences as Paul did. But the circumstances don't really matter. What matters is your response to that same question: 'Who art Thou, Lord, and what wilt Thou have me to do?'"

She did not leave the questions dangling rhetorically. She specified the steps for her listeners to take that night, one-two-three: They were to go home, get down on their knees, and ask God those very questions.

Teacher had spoken. It was authoritative and gripping.

"As I returned to my apartment that night," Bill would remember, "I realized that I was ready to give my life to God.... What attracted me most was God's love, which had been made known to me through my study of the Bible and through the lives of the people I had met at Hollywood Presbyterian Church. I knelt beside my bed that night and asked the questions with which Dr. Mears had challenged us. 'Who art Thou, Lord? What wilt Thou have me do?'

"In a sense, that was my prayer for salvation. It wasn't very profound theologically, but the Lord knew my heart and He interpreted what was going on inside me. Through my study I now believed Jesus Christ was the Son of God, that He had died for my sin, and that, as Dr. Mears had shared with us, if I invited Him into my life as Savior and Lord, He would come in."

Bill wasn't aware of anything dramatic or emotional that happened when he prayed. But he had crossed over from death to eternal life in Jesus Christ.

Asking those questions that night "didn't seem very dynamic at first, but as I began to grow in my new commitment and love for the Lord, I became more and more aware of what a sinner I am—and what a wonderful, forgiving Savior He is."

CHAPTER 5

Walking in the Light

One of the first Scripture passages Bill Bright memorized as a new Christian was 1 John 1, which challenged him to "walk in the light as He is in the light." From this passage he determined what such a "walk" included: No unconfessed sin; control of the Spirit; meditation on the Bible; prayer—listening as well as talking; sharing of one's faith; and obedience to the commandments of God. This chapter became a guiding beacon, reminding Bill that the only reason a person did not live constantly in God's light was that at times he sinned.

Until now, Bill had tested his actions in life by whether it produced recognition or fortune; now he began testing his experience with whether it was relevant to Jesus, and whether it required faith in Him.

Bill soon was elected president of Hollywood Presbyterian's Sunday school class for college students and young professionals, which meant he was meeting regularly with Henrietta Mears to ponder the truths of the Bible and to plan and pray for ways to reach others with the love of God. This was an exhilarating endeavor, allowing Bill to do so many things he liked to do—survey, analyze, study, synthesize, create, write, speak, debate, organize, and lead.

Working closely with Dr. Mears, who was more than twice his age, Bill found her to be "an exceptional woman...colorful, exuberant, and remarkably courageous." He listened to her carefully and quickly began to "catch" her priorities, as expressed in her own "ten commandments" as a teacher:

1. I will win the personal allegiance of every student...to the Lord and Master by talking, writing and prayer. I will expect a decision on the part of each one and I will make sure that decision is based on facts.

2. I will not think my work over when my pupil has made his decision for Christ. I will help him realize how necessary daily Bible reading and prayer are. I will also put helpful books in his hands and will encourage him to unite with God's people. I will show him the importance of church work.

3. I will see that he finds a definite place in some specified task. I will not rest until every student is an out-and-out aggressive Christian, for God has a place for each one to serve.

4. I will bring Christianity out of the unreal into everyday life. I will show my students the practical things they should be doing as Christians. The ministrations that the world needs so much today—meat for the hungry, drink for the thirsty—are judgment-day tests of genuine Christianity (Matthew 25).

5. I will seek to help each one discover the will of God.

6. I will instill a divine discontent into the mind of everyone who can do more than he is doing, not by telling him the pettiness of his life, but by giving him a vision of great things to be done enthusiastically, passionately.

7. I will never let anyone think I am disappointed in him.

8. I will keep the cross of Christ central in the Christian life. It is great to be out where the fight is strong, to be where the heaviest troops belong and to fight there for God and man.

9. I will pray as I have never prayed before for wisdom and power.

10. I will spend and be spent in this battle. I will not seek rest and ease.

The objectives Dr. Mears articulated for her program were no less direct and energetic: "Canvass your neighborhood, teach the Word, win people to Christ, enlist for service....

"Study your program," she taught, adding that plans for reaching such objectives "must be sound...definite.... Balance your program, don't run to extremes.... See if you are putting due emphasis on attendance, worship, teaching, stewardship, missions, social life, and evangelism.... Strive always for a successful program, remembering nothing succeeds like success.... Everyone likes to belong to a growing concern."

Henrietta Mears exuded total trust in Christ. No matter what problem one might bring to her, she would quote Psalm 37:5—"Commit thy way unto the LORD, trust also in him; and he shall bring it to pass." Relentlessly, she poured it on: You can always trust God. Whatever your problem, cast all your cares upon the Lord because He cares for you.

Almost before realizing it, Bill found that he, too, could canvass, teach, win people to Christ, and enlist them for service. Bill became a spark plug in the Mears ministry machine. He gained confidence as the roots of the Bible's promises grew deeper in his life. He was afire, and when it came to forging ahead with ways of pressing the message of Christ, Bill would try almost anything.

An example at this time of Bill's visionary impulse was his thinking about capturing the authentic life and message of Christ on film—after all, here he was in the motion picture capital of the world. He was aware of only one major film about Jesus, Cecil B. DeMille's 1927 epic, *The King of Kings*. So he went to visit the famous producer. DeMille, a Christian, told Bill and others that if he had the money, he would produce nothing but Christian films. Bill thought perhaps his own business success might one day provide the revenues to finance the project he himself was envisioning. And thus the seeds were sown for a project that would reach fulfillment more than three decades later.

Bill was trying to absorb all of life with an intensity he had never known. Besides his new ministry involvement, he was still working long and late at his business, which was booming. He had expanded his product line and gained more accounts across the nation and overseas. For further expertise, he picked the minds of several of the experienced businessmen at Hollywood Presbyterian.

Soon there was even more on his mind. When his sister Joann was visiting from Coweta, he took her one evening to the famous Coconut Grove at the Ambassador Hotel to celebrate her birthday. Diana Lyn, a young starlet of the day, happened to walk by their table. She not only was beautiful but she also reminded Bill of Vonette Zachary back home in Oklahoma. Joann and Vonette were friends, so Bill asked his sister about "the Zachary girl." She was now a student at the Texas State College for Women (now Texas Women's University) in Denton, near Dallas.

The next day he dropped Vonette a note on his fancy business stationery.

> Joann and I were at the Coconut Grove last night. We saw Diana Lyn. She reminded me of you. Trust you are having a good summer.
> Sincerely, Bill

It was the first of a barrage of communications by mail and telephone. Vonette, five years his junior, received his calls and letters warmly. She still considered Bill a winner. He was going somewhere and always had been.

Eventually he arranged to see her on an upcoming business trip to Dallas. Finally they would have their first date.

As Bill drove eastward, visiting accounts in Phoenix, El Paso, and Dallas, he was preoccupied with Vonette. He was considering whether to ask her—on this, their first date—to marry him. Their calls and letters had indicated many commonalities. Moreover, he and Vonette had known each other for fifteen years, their families were good friends, and Bill assumed she was a godly woman since she'd been active in church all her life. Of course, having already surrendered his own life to the lordship of Christ, he dared not marry anyone but a true believer.

But he was unsure if the thought of proposing to Vonette was from God. He asked God to lead him, and in fact to stop him if marrying her was not His will. Eventually, a settled inner peace came upon him. Yes, this was of God; he would marry Vonette Zachary.

Thinking this way was foreign to him. He had dated many young women, but never had the thought of matrimony surfaced. Most of his life he had focused on business success. Discovering the love of Christ had moved God to the top of his priorities, and now he was amazed at the very thought that God would be involved in his marriage planning. Vonette seemed a logical choice, but even more his prayers seemed to be answered with the impression that God Himself wanted him to marry her.

Vonette, meanwhile, had concluded before seeing Bill that if he proved to be everything she remembered him to be—and that his letters and phone calls had reinforced—she was in love.

The dashing Bill Bright now had a mustache and looked uncannily like Clark Gable. When he picked up Vonette at her campus, she appeared every bit as beautiful to him as the starlets he saw in Hollywood, and a good bit like Diana Lyn in fact.

Bill had always seemed to be a man with a plan, so over dinner Vonette asked what he had in mind for the future. He had definite plans, he answered—business success, marriage, travel—and they all depended on her! Before long, he leaned forward and asked: "Will you marry me?

"We'll live in Bel Air," he added, "and go horseback riding in the Hollywood hills, and travel to Europe and around the world. You'll have the finest of everything—a home, clothes, a car…"

Vonette flushed. "Bill, I'm flattered," she told him. She paused. "But this is so sudden; let's have a good time this weekend and then see how we feel before you leave."

She added: "I do believe I'm in love with you."

"Take all the time you need to think it over," he suggested. "But as for me, my mind is made up." In fact, he said, he wanted to visit her folks that Monday when he drove on to Coweta.

By Sunday, Vonette's mind was made up as well. That evening she wrote a letter to her parents, to be delivered the following morning, preparing them for Bill's arrival.

As Bill drove into Oklahoma, his mind was racing: Yes! Vonette Zachary was the woman he was to marry. She was beautiful, she was smart, she was ambitious and able. And they had the same roots and similar dreams. They would be a sparkling couple. What a bride he would have to take back on his arm to Hollywood one day!

Vonette's parents had been totally surprised by their daughter's letter and had barely collected their composure when Bill arrived to discuss the possibility of the engagement. Though they thought highly of Bill, they had no idea of the romantic interest Vonette and Bill had in each other.

At the conclusion of their meeting with Bill, the Zacharys gave their approval of the relationship but pleaded for time. Vonette should finish college and have time to mature and to be certain that she had not merely been swept off her feet. Bill agreed that they should wait.

Mrs. Zachary had volunteered to chaperone Vonette to California to visit Bill for two weeks that summer in 1946. The ensuing two-week visit confirmed that Bill and Vonette wanted to spend the rest of their lives together.

Meanwhile, as Bill's knowledge of the Scriptures grew, a divine discontent had come over him about the use of his time. Wanting to know more about God and to grow in his theological understanding, he decided to go to seminary. Within the Presbyterian circles in which he now was involved, Princeton Theological Seminary in New Jersey was regarded as the best. The school was all the way across the nation, but his sporty new maroon Ford would be up to it. He would commute to New Jersey, while running his fancy-foods business through trusted employees.

He'd met a businessman in his church who had then invested in Bill's expanding enterprise. Bill then made a fateful decision to hire the businessman's son to handle the day-to-day responsibilities of the business. Bill's goal was to gain more time to study and serve the Lord. It seemed a reasonable strategy, but it would later be a source of unrelenting pressure. For the moment, though, it gave him a sense of freedom that allowed him to be a seminarian and a businessman simultaneously.

Bill and Vonette's engagement proved to be informal, as their romance continued primarily by correspondence. Bill's letters were humorous, adventurous, romantic, and inspiring, and Vonette's were lively too. The couple caught none-too-frequent dates mostly on Bill's travels between Hollywood and Princeton.

Meanwhile, the relationship with Vonette forced a vital issue to the surface: her salvation. Bill told her that God would have to be first in their marriage. Vonette responded, "I always thought a man should put his family first." In their letters and phone calls, the issue kept coming up, bringing agony to Bill.

He would remember it as "one of the greatest conflicts of my life." Here he was in seminary, heading for a life of total commitment to Christ, and Vonette wasn't at all sure about religion outside of church attendance. In fact, by the time she graduated from Texas Women's University in the summer of 1947, she expressed doubts about the Bible's relevance to daily life. Bill wondered: Was she a Christian? Mentally he prepared thorough explanations of the gospel for her, but he decided against presenting them when he was with her; he wanted to be sure no romance was mixed up in her decision.

As a student at Princeton, meanwhile, Bill was a sponge, soaking up everything. He would look back on his short time there as "a fabulous, fabulous experience.... Every day was an adventure." In addition to classes, he began the morning and ended the evening with a prayer group, and in the course of a typical day joined one or two other groups, praying with students from all over the world. On weekends he went out with fellow students to witness and to minister in various churches.

His quest for spiritual reality led him on several occasions to visit the seminary's president, Dr. John A. MacKay. "He was a scholarly old Scotsman and greatly beloved. He was a godly man. I would drop by his office and ask if he had time to pray with me. This great man would get on his knees with me.... I always felt, through his prayers, that I was lifted into the heavens.

"Here I was just a first-year student, but he was such a humble, gracious man who always made me feel welcome."

It was during this period that Bill came upon *The Strong Name,* a book by New Testament scholar Dr. James Stewart of Edinburgh, Scotland. This masterpiece thoroughly challenged Bill to a fuller understanding of forgiveness and peace as well as the issue of communicating one's faith clearly. It spoke persuasively of life with Christ as "an incredible adventure." That perspective on Christianity—adventure, not passive asceticism—was where Bill decided to live.

He was especially affected by these words from Stewart:

If we could but show the world that being committed to
Christ is no tame, humdrum, sheltered monotony, but the most
thrilling, exciting adventure the human spirit could ever know,
those who have been standing outside the church and looking
askance at Christ would come crowding in to pay allegiance, and
we might well expect the greatest revival since Pentecost.

This declaration seemed to summarize Bill's own experience; he had seen
the humdrum in the church and in the secular world around him, and he
had been captured by the contrasting excitement of the spiritual, intellectual,
and social brilliance of the people at Hollywood Presbyterian and Princeton
Seminary.

These words from Stewart became a foundation upon which Bill would
build his personal ministry and upon which he challenged others to build
theirs. Later, when Bill was criticized in theological circles for gospel presentations that assumed people had a hunger for Christ, Bill would reply that
Christ is so very appealing and attractive that most people would say yes to
Him if He were properly and authentically presented.

Bill was later inspired along the same lines by this observation from New
Testament translator J. B. Phillips:

There is a vast difference between the first believers and those
of the twentieth century. To those first-century Christians, it was a
new quality of life altogether, and they did not hesitate to describe
this life in this way: Christ in you, the hope of glory. Perhaps, if we
believed what they believed, we could achieve what they achieved.

While he respected his professors, he didn't agree with all of them. One,
a specialist in the art of preaching, taught that sermons should never last
more than twenty minutes and should include three well-honed points. But
Bill had been weaned and matured on hourlong sessions from Henrietta
Mears and Louis Evans, and a half-century later he would still maintain that
"mini-sermons merely produce mini-Christians resulting in mini-churches."

Because Bill had excelled in oration, a better and more piercing challenge at Princeton for his public speaking ministry was when he heard the question, "When you step down from the podium, will people say, 'What a great preacher he is,' or, 'What a great Lord he serves?'" Bill resolved at once that in his own speaking, teaching, and preaching, whatever his audience, he would so speak that listeners would be impressed not with him but with his Lord.

The first time Bill commuted cross-country, his stopover in Coweta occurred at the same time as a series of revival meetings at the local Methodist church. Bill had been praying for his father's salvation since the day of his own conversion, and he urged his parents to attend one night. They agreed.

Bill would remember the preacher as a "frontier-type" evangelist. "He loved Christ and knew how to preach the gospel.... He wasn't sophisticated, but I sensed he was a man of God."

The revival meetings had already been going on for two weeks—with another seven nights scheduled—but no one had publicly accepted Christ as a result. Tonight, once more, there was no response when the evangelist gave his invitation. Then he said, "If you have loved ones for whom you've been praying, go put your arm around them and bring them to the altar."

Bill thought how well known and respected his parents were in the community. He didn't want to embarrass them. "So I was waiting and praying, 'Lord, what shall I do?' and the Lord said, 'Go put your arm around your father and invite him to go to the altar with you.'" Bill walked across the sanctuary. (He and Vonette were seated on the opposite side from his parents, because of the large crowd attending that night.) He put his arm around his father and asked if he wanted him to go to the altar with him.

His father stood and walked forward, accompanied by Bill, Mary Lee, and Vonette. But he did not make a decision for Christ. "I'm just not ready," he said.

The following night the Brights attended again, and the same situation developed. No decisions. The evangelist gave the same pointed invitation for persons to stand with loved ones. Again Bill put his arm around his father, who went forward once more, followed by his wife and son and Vonette, and kneeled at the altar.

"Are you ready, Dad?" Bill asked.

"Yes," his father said. Suddenly Dale Bright got up from the altar and went back and put his arm around Bill's brother Glenn, who had recently returned from military service, and invited him to come to the altar with him. It was a moving experience for the Bright family and the church, although Glenn did not receive Christ until later.

"From that night," Bill remembered, "my father was a totally different man."

CHAPTER 6

Burning Hearts

After several months at Princeton Seminary and thousands of miles of driving, Bill was questioning the wisdom of stretching himself from coast to coast. He realized his business in Hollywood needed more of him. Fuller Seminary was being established in Pasadena, and he had the opportunity to be in on the ground floor of that endeavor as a student. So in 1947 he left Princeton and plunged into seminary study at Fuller with renewed fervor.

In one class at Fuller, Bill took an exegetical tour of Romans 6 that so impressed him, he never forgot its four points: know, reckon, yield, obey. *Know* your position in Christ as dead to sin, risen in power. *Reckon* or account yourself dead to the old sin nature; behave by faith as if it were dead and don't respond to it. *Yield* your body as an instrument of righteousness. *Obey* God's commands by faith. Bill absorbed these truths and sought to apply them throughout his life.

Earlier in 1947, Henrietta Mears had traveled to Europe and witnessed firsthand the destruction and lingering upheaval caused by the war. She was devastated by the human tragedies she saw. Back in Hollywood, she spoke with a new urgency about the world's desperate need for the healing message of the love of God in Christ. But she hadn't understood exactly what was to be done.

In June, Bill was present as Dr. Mears spoke at a teachers' training conference at Forest Home Conference Center in Southern California's San Bernardino Mountains. She declared that the seeds of decay—atheism and moral expedience—had long before created a putrid garden where Hitler and Nazism had grown. "The same is taking place in America today," she warned.

> God has an answer. Jesus said that we must make disciples of all men. We are to take His gospel to the ends of the earth. We must become evangelists, even though evangelism is not recognized in our day as a valid program. We must present the full doctrine of Christian truth.
>
> God is looking for men and women of total commitment. During the war, men of special courage were called upon for difficult assignments; often these volunteers did not return. They were called "expendables." We must be expendables for Christ....
>
> If we fail God's call to us tonight, we will be held responsible.

The phrase "expendables for Christ" was riveted in Bill's mind and heart. Later that evening, he joined Louis Evans Jr.—the pastor's son and now president of the college department at Hollywood Presbyterian—for a visit to Teacher's cabin at the conference center.

The three of them began to talk and pray. Suddenly they were enveloped in a profound experience. "We were overwhelmed with the presence of God," Bill remembered. "It was one of those things I had never experienced, and I didn't know what to do. I just got on my knees and began to praise the Lord."

They were quickly joined by another young man who came to the cabin door and saw Bill and the others on their knees in prayer. His name was Richard Halverson, pastor of a small church in Coalinga, California. He had become disenchanted in his ministry, and like so many other pastors over the years, he had come that night to seek counsel from Dr. Mears.

Halverson was drawn into the others' experience. "Suddenly he was changed, and he began to praise God with us. It was a dramatic, marvelous experience....

"We knew the living God had come to take control. And we were so excited we were like intoxicated people." Bill would call it "my first real encounter with the Holy Spirit."

As never before they sensed the awesome call of God. Yet they felt helpless. They wanted to be used of God. What could they do? Where could they begin?

"While we were all carried away with the sense of the holy presence of God, our minds were racing with creative ideas." While praying, they saw before them in their minds the nation's teeming college campuses, where an army could be recruited for God.

A specific first step for implementing that vision came to their minds and hearts. Later that summer, the collegians of Hollywood Presbyterian were to hold their annual summer conference right there at Forest Home. Could they dare to expand that conference to include hundreds of collegians from all over the nation and to share tonight's vision with them? It seemed quite impossible—with less than two months' time—but they determined to set out to accomplish it.

Out of their experience that night was birthed what came to be called the Fellowship of the Burning Heart, a name derived from John Calvin's seal showing a hand offering a heart afire with the inscription: "My heart I give Thee, Lord, eagerly and sincerely." That very night the three young men—Bright, Evans, and Halverson—decided to record in writing the commitment each of them was making:

> I am committed to the principle that Christian discipleship is sustained solely by God alone through His Spirit; that the abiding life of John 15 is His way of sustaining me. Therefore, I pledge myself to a disciplined devotional life in which I promise through prayer, Bible study, and devotional reading to give God not less than one continuous hour per day (Ps. 1).
>
> I am committed to the principle that Christian Discipleship begins with Christian character. Therefore, I pledge myself to holy living that by a life of self-denial and self-discipline, I may emulate those Christlike qualities of chastity and virtue which will magnify the Lord (Phil. 1:20-21).
>
> I am committed to the principle that Discipleship exercises itself principally in the winning of the lost to Christ. Therefore, I

pledge myself to seek every possible opportunity to witness, and to witness at every possible opportunity, to the end that I may be responsible for bringing at least one to Christ every 12 months (Matt. 28:19; Acts 1:8).

I am committed to the principle that Christian Discipleship demands nothing less than absolute consecration to Christ. Therefore, I present my body a living sacrifice, utterly abandoned to God. By this commitment, I will that God's perfect will shall find complete expression in my life; and I offer myself in all sobriety to be expendable for Christ (Rom. 12:1-2; Phil. 3:7-14).

In the Fellowship of the Burning Heart they recognized their calling to a life of expendability—saying no to self and yes to Christ, wherever that might lead.

The following night Bill returned to Hollywood and spoke at a midweek prayer meeting at his church. About 250 collegians were there, and Bill challenged them to be expendable for Christ—to make a no-holds-barred, absolute, irrevocable surrender to the lordship of Christ. When he invited anyone there to stand who wished to give his life in that way to Christ, the entire group rose to their feet at the same time.

The meetings of the college and career group at Hollywood Presbyterian would never be the same. Dr. Mears and the three Burning Heart brothers gave testimonies of what they had experienced and told of their plans to expand the upcoming August conference at Forest Home. They had decided to call it a "Briefing Conference"—just as soldiers are briefed before they go forth to battle. Teacher again spoke of her vision for seeing the world reached for Christ. The hundreds listening agreed to plunge themselves into efforts to make the Briefing Conference ready for hundreds more beyond themselves.

As the weeks went by, sins were confessed and turned from and new devotion to Christ was manifest in lives turned over to Him for His use. They were sharing Christ with hundreds who were deciding to follow Him.

Dr. Mears, Bright, Evans, and Halverson were ablaze and in one accord, pressing themselves beyond reason and expecting God to honor their faith.

In July, these four drove to the historic Mount Hermon Conference Center near Santa Cruz, which was under the direction of one of Teacher's disciples, Cyrus Nelson. With Nelson and his fellow Mount Hermon leaders, they shared the vision God had given them, the commitments they had made, and the plans they were laying. Nelson and the others were so struck that they invited Teacher and her men to give testimonies about all of it to about a thousand youth who were attending camp there at the time. When they did, hundreds of youth publicly dedicated their lives to be expendable for Christ.

Bill and his Burning Heart brothers felt as if they were being propelled from one situation to the next. They began receiving invitations to speak to youth, college, and professional groups. "We moved from city to city, church to church, and that same spirit of revival was everywhere.

"I spoke at one church, a very fashionable church where the gospel hadn't been preached in current memory. But when the invitation was given, the whole congregation came forward, including the pastor, to surrender to Christ.

"Such was the result of that visit—that divine, supernatural visit of the Holy Spirit—at Forest Home in Dr. Mears's cabin. The Spirit of God was working in the lives of people, and in my own life."

That summer Bill wrote:

> The tragedy of our times is that we live in a militantly pagan world. Social, economic, political and spiritual chaos has over-whelmed world leaders, and the urgency of the hour has brought God's people to their knees in one last plea. God, in His tender mercy and loving kindness, has granted a revival.

It was a revival, he judged, that would stave off the threatened annihilation of civilization, now that the Cold War was revving up on the heels of World War II.

Teacher's countenance during these days glowed with a new radiance and ebullience. She spoke firmly, lovingly, and often. She worked hours into the night, every night. She wrote letters, made calls, organized and held meetings, deputized, delegated, and trained. She had the distinct ability to integrate vision and task, not only to see but also to plan and to execute those plans.

All this was not lost on Bill. He realized he was in harness with someone special—a visionary, an organizer, a synthesizer, a mobilizer. Not only was she a master from whom to acquire leadership skills; she also was a disciple from the throne of God to labor with and learn from.

So many of the things Dr. Mears said were becoming ingrained principles in Bill's thinking as well:

> There is no magic in small plans. When I consider my ministry, I think of the world. Anything less than that would not be worthy of Christ, nor of His will for my life.

> The greatest of a man's power is the measure of his surrender. It is not a question of who you are or what you are, but whether God controls you.

> Are you proving that the Christian life is a joyful, happy thing? Do you look glad that you are a Christian? Make the Christian life contagious.

> Enthusiasm starts a hard job; determination works at it; only love continues until it is finished.

> Serving God with our little is the way to make it more.

> Kindness has converted more sinners than zeal, eloquence, or learning.

> You teach a little by what you say. You teach most by what you are.

> An efficient leader may, through his knowledge of his job and the magnetism of his personality, greatly increase the efficiency of others.

> All that I see teaches me to thank the Creator for all I cannot see.

You must decide what you want to build and then proceed
with the plans.

What you are is God's gift to you. What you can become is
your gift to Him.

Bill was riding a wave of renaissance such as he had never before experienced. And as he sensed more and more that Vonette was not as excited about the Lord Jesus Christ as he was, his letters changed from fun and romantic to very serious. He was advising her what to read and to pray about. He also urged her to come west to attend the Briefing Conference at Forest Home.

Vonette agreed to come, but with her own agenda in mind. Before departing for California to visit Bill and "his group," she told a friend in Texas, "I'm either going to rescue him from this religious fanaticism or come back without a ring."

As the Briefing Conference began, Vonette met Bill's friends, who indeed were attractive people, exuberant about what she understood to be "their religion." But as she walked with Bill on the grounds of Forest Home, she made it clear to him that she didn't feel as he did about God; she didn't want to stand in his way, she told him, so maybe the best thing was for them to break the engagement. Bill knew a crossroads in their relationship was imminent.

Forest Home could accommodate only five hundred persons for lodging, but hundreds more came from eighty-seven different colleges and universities. They slept in their cars, in tents, and out under the stars. What they encountered that week at Forest Home was decidedly different from a typical church conference. Although Dr. Mears believed in detailed planning, and had invited Louis Evans and two other pastors as speakers for the week, she intentionally announced no definite schedule.

She told the conference leaders that she had brought them together for the expressed purpose of waiting on God to set the agenda. To carry this out, they held a prayer march around an open portion of the grounds that they called Victory Circle. They claimed the ground for Christ and prayed that disbelief would be rebuked and that stubborn hearts would be melted.

The leaders also committed themselves to work in prayer to decide who would speak when. No one would give a message until all knew from the Lord who it was. God would set the schedule.

On the conference's opening night, when all the attending students gathered for the first time in the Victory Circle, they heard the testimonies about the movement God had begun. Some of the students stood and confessed their desire for God; some who were unbelievers immediately responded to Christ and were converted.

As this furnace of faith was burning into the night, Teacher slipped out with the conference leaders to her cabin and prayed. When she returned to the Victory Circle, she stood in the center and spoke of sin, confession, and the filling of the Holy Spirit.

The testimonies during that first Victory Circle meeting—there was no singing—lasted four hours, in accordance with the desires of Dr. Mears and the conference leaders. They wanted everyone to have time—and for God to have time—to deal with human hearts.

Later that night, Vonette met with Dr. Mears in Teacher's cabin while Bill remained outside, pacing and praying. He had told Dr. Mears that his fiancée did not know Jesus personally and asked her to meet with Vonette in person.

Dr. Mears quickly found common ground between them: Vonette was minoring in chemistry in college, and Dr. Mears had been a chemistry teacher back in Minnesota. In fact Vonette, with her mind for science, recognized that "everything had to be very practical and workable to me. This was one of the reasons I had questioned the validity of Christianity."

But Teacher said she could understand how Vonette was thinking. "As she explained simply to me from God's Word how I could be sure that I knew God, she used terminology very familiar to me. She explained that, just as a person going into a chemistry laboratory experiment follows the table of chemical valence, so it is possible for a person to enter God's laboratory and follow his formula of knowing Him and following Him.

"During the next hour, she lovingly proceeded to explain to me who Christ is and how I could know Him personally.

"'Dr. Mears,' I said, 'if Jesus Christ is the way, then how do I meet Him?'"

The older woman shared with her Christ's words in Revelation 3:20—"Behold, I stand at the door, and knock: if any man hear my voice, and open the door, I will come in to him, and will sup with him, and he with me." She also repeated John 1:12—"But as many as received him, to them gave he power to become the sons of God, even to them that believe on his name."

"Receiving Christ," she told Vonette, "is simply a matter of turning your life—your will, your emotions, your intellect—completely over to Him."

Vonette thought she had nothing to lose and everything to gain if what Dr. Mears had told her was true. She bowed her head and prayed, asking Christ to come into her heart.

Looking back, she says it was at that moment that her life began to change. "God became a reality in my life. For the first time I was ready to trust Him. I became aware that my prayers were getting beyond the ceiling. I found that I had control of areas of my life that I had not been able to control before. No longer did I have to try to love people. There just seemed to be a love that flowed from within that I did not have to create.

"God had added a new dimension to my life and I found myself becoming as enthusiastic about the Lord as Bill was."

For Bill, Vonette's decision was the highlight of a conference week that was a turning point for many. Hundreds of hearts were moved, hundreds of lives redirected. Bill's own heart was further emboldened for an adventure of faith, and the relationship between Dr. Mears, Bill, and Vonette became welded for eternity.

The following spring Bill preached at South Hollywood Presbyterian Church. In his first message to be broadcast over radio, he spoke of "two things that have challenged my heart since those glorious days when the Lord spoke to us at Forest Home." He continued:

> First, that the pagan condition of our country and our
> University and college campuses in particular is not the result of
> skepticism and doubt necessarily, but rather, a result of a lack of

intelligent information concerning the claims of Christ and the new life of victory that we find in Him.

Secondly, in the eyes of the non-Christian today, there is little in our lives to challenge them to want what we have. Those rivers of living waters flowing from the innermost beings of the Apostles of old and great saints of God down through the ages, irrigating and feeding the parched and starving souls of men, have in our lives for the most part become mere streams or have dried up. And we have little or nothing to offer.

He invited the congregation to turn from their indifference or casual attitudes about Christianity and begin to practice what the Bible teaches about Christian conduct. Hundreds responded.

Once more Bill's faith was buoyed. By God's grace, his messages were connecting with groups of all sizes and all walks of life.

CHAPTER 7

"The Only Reasonable Explanation"

Bill Bright now seemed to be living in two thriving worlds: a spiritual world that was producing peace in his life and a business world that unexpectedly threatened him like a firestorm.

The specialty-foods firm that Bill had come back to from Princeton was still prospering. But it was rattled with change as the result both of the investment by the businessman Bill knew from Hollywood Presbyterian and of Bill's decision to hire the businessman's son to handle the company's daily responsibilities. Bill soon discovered that three members of the investor's family had straws in the malt, drawing on the father's investment and Bill's. Then the family became disgruntled with the partnership and suggested that Bill had been deceptive in not living up to his financial commitment to them.

"It was devastating to me," Bill would recall. "I had grown up with honesty drilled into me; integrity was paramount; to lie was unthinkable.... Yet here I was accused of dishonesty." The family's membership at Hollywood Presbyterian made the situation even worse. Bill was serving in ever-widening circles of responsibility and influence at the church, but whenever he gave a report or his testimony there, or taught or preached, he imagined some of his listeners viewing him as a phony. His sense of self-worth was challenged as never before. "God allowed me to believe that everybody thought I was a crook."

Bill was convinced he owed the family nothing; he also felt that he should not defend himself in the dispute but should leave that up to God.

After many months, the matter reached the desk of Hollywood Presbyterian's pastor, Dr. Louis Evans, who got the parties together with the church elders. Both sides had their say, but Bill made no counteraccusations against the family. Bill was cleared of any wrongdoing. But in order to remove any basis for even the appearance of disrepute, he voluntarily decided on a financial arrangement for ending the partnership.

To save money to pay for the buyout of his partner, Bill moved out of his apartment in Hollywood and into his company's plant, where he reflected on what God was doing in his life. He had perceived intellectually that no one ever accomplishes anything significant for God who doesn't go through a time of tremendous testing. He had read about the struggles of others. Now he was getting his test.

"Every night I was there alone with God in that plant," he would remember. "Sometimes, I would weep into the night. Yet strangely I had great peace. I knew that God was with me and that I was right. He was so real. But at the same time I knew there were those who questioned my integrity, and it hurt." The pressure for Bill on this issue would continue for years, climaxing with another painful encounter with the family.

Meanwhile, clinging to the certainty that he could trust the Lord through it all, Bill was able to compartmentalize his many activities and to focus on the task at hand. He stayed too busy to spend time in self-pity, and he attributed his ability to keep going to the Lord entirely. His mornings were devoted to Fuller Seminary, his afternoons to the business, his evenings to church work—especially the "deputation" ministry of visiting church contacts—and his late nights to study, prayer, and thoughts of Vonette. Their wedding was planned for late December 1948.

At Fuller, Bill's mind was set ablaze like coal in a furnace. A particular boost to his intellectual and spiritual fervor at this time was the widely reported news that the renowned atheist-philosopher Cyril E. M. Joad had declared his renunciation of rationalism and heralded his acceptance of Christ. Joad, head of the philosophy department at the University of

London, had aggressively sought to destroy the faith of student believers. Brilliant and articulate, he had been known as a socialist, pacifist, atheist, and advocate of free love. But in his new book, *My Return to Faith,* he wrote:

> I see now that evil is endemic in man and that the Christian doctrine of original sin expresses a deep and essential insight into human nature. Reject it and you fall victim, as so many of us whose minds developed in an atmosphere of left-wing politics and rationalist philosophy have fallen victims, to shallow optimism in regard to human nature.

Joad confessed how "Christianity seemed to offer...consolation, strengthening and assistance," while the rationalist philosophy "which I had hitherto done my best to maintain, came to seem intolerably trivial and superficial....

> I abandoned it. Once I had come as far as this, there was nothing to be lost and everything to be gained by going the whole way. What better hope was offered than by the Christian doctrine that God sent His Son into the world to save sinners?

All this was a bolstering injection to Bill Bright's faith. Joad's decision "had a profound impact on me," he would say, especially since "he was so brilliant, and I wasn't." Bill spoke of Christianity as "the only reasonable explanation for life itself," but he had feared the possibility of someday encountering someone whose anti-Christian arguments would appear to be a valid undermining of the logic of the gospel, leaving Bill hanging on a limb. "Joad's decision took away any intellectual anxiety. From that point on, I knew I could witness to anyone who was rational."

Another stimulus to Bill's faith and intellectual vitality was his association at Fuller with Dr. Wilbur M. Smith. After long service as a Presbyterian minister and nine years as a Bible professor at Moody Bible Institute, Smith had decided to come to Fuller Seminary and help build it to greatness. Here was a man who had spent his lifetime digging into the Scriptures and the person of Jesus, a man devoting himself to young people, a man who was a New Testament scholar (with a personal library of more than thirty thousand volumes), a writer, and a leader.

Smith's cogent, empirical, apologetical approach to the life of Christ intrigued and captivated Bill's mind. He found many of Smith's arguments etched in his thinking as he continued his own ministry of visitation, teaching, and preaching to individuals and groups ranging from up-and-coming collegians and young professionals at Hollywood Presbyterian to the castoffs on skid row or in the Los Angeles prisons.

Like a dry sponge tossed into a pail of water, Bill absorbed Smith's approach to Christ. "Who can this Man be," Smith asked,

> who, though He never wrote a single word Himself to be read by succeeding generations, yet has by His spoken words and unparalleled deeds, created a greater literature, led to more profound thinking about and brought more light upon life's greatest problems, than any other person who has ever walked among men? Indeed, the very words under which thousands of books about Jesus are classified are not used of any other historical person of any century, no matter how great they may have been—such as Incarnation, Virgin Birth, Sinlessness, Deity, Resurrection, Ascension, Second Advent, Prince of Peace, and Head of the Church.

Bill was freshly inspired by the hard facts of the life of Jesus as the bold questioning of Wilbur Smith brought them into focus. Smith made you think:

> What sort of man is this, who over and over again, gave numerous details about His death, months before it occurred, and added to each such utterance that on the third day after His decease He would rise again from the dead—and DID RISE, as even the city of Jerusalem soon came to believe? No other founder

of a great world religion (or a small one) ever made such statements, or ever came forth from the dead.

Bill would often linger after classes to talk with Dr. Smith and soon adopted the professor as a mentor and counselor, just as he would open himself to the profound influence of many on the Fuller faculty, including seminary president Dr. Harold Ockenga, Dr. Carl F. H. Henry, Dr. Harold Lindsell, Dr. Everett Harrison, and Dr. Gleason Archer.

Inspired by Smith's approach, Bill went to work creating his own presentation of "The Uniqueness of Jesus" with polished logic and pressing questions. He sought to write crisply, making sure each reader or listener actually understood his message enough to take action based upon its convincing truths. Simplicity of expression became his goal, especially after he learned of a study reporting that only fifty English words had been used to communicate 60 percent of all English literature.

"It occurred to me in a very definite, dramatic way that one of the reasons the Christian message was not better understood by every Christian, and the reason the Christian church was making such little impact upon a worldly society, was that many theologians—and consequently their students, pastors and missionaries—had complicated the good news of God's love and forgiveness.... Jesus, the greatest teacher of all, taught in such a way that the masses, largely illiterate and unlearned, heard Him gladly.... I made a concerted effort all through my ministry to try to communicate clearly by eliminating big words and philosophical and theological jargon, the kind of 'Christianese' that does not communicate except to those who are familiar with the usage." So it became something of a hallmark of Bill's writing that he would never enunciate the geopolitical and socioeconomic implications of a Christocentric theological orientation when he simply could tell you what Jesus meant to him!

A typical example of the Bright approach is found in one of his early treatises:

The life Jesus led, the miracles He performed, the words He spoke, His death on the cross, His resurrection, His ascent to heaven, all point to the fact that He was not mere man, but more than man.... It is important to consider that Jesus Christ claimed to be God. He claimed to be the author of a new way of life....

Either Jesus of Nazareth was who He claimed to be, the Son of God, the Savior of mankind, or He was the greatest impostor the world has ever known. If His claims were false, more good has resulted from a lie than has ever been accomplished by the truth.... Historically, we know that wherever His message has gone, new life, new hope, and new purpose for living have resulted....

Does it not make sense that this person (whom most people, knowing the facts, consider the greatest teacher, the greatest example, the greatest leader the world has ever known) would be, as He Himself claimed to be, and as the Bible tells us that He is, the one person who could bridge the chasm between a holy God and sinful man?

Every time Bill saw the lives of men and women change as a result of the words of Christ, he became even more enthused. His own life had been transformed; now he was seeing the lives of others realigned with the Almighty. This was sweeter by far than anything developing from his business, but he kept Bright's California Confections going, since it provided for his financial needs and paid for his seminary studies. As for a lasting and meaningful career, however, devoting oneself to others in the name of Christ was making the most sense to Bill. To see human spirits transformed was an exciting enterprise.

During the seminary's Christmas break in 1948, Bill returned home to Coweta to marry Vonette. As he drove eastward from California in a new Mercury convertible, he pondered how uncertain were the days that served as a backdrop for his marriage. The Cold War had erupted as the Soviet Union blockaded Berlin. Civil war seemed to be nearing a climax in China, with communist troops under Mao Tse-tung marching to victory while killing millions. Mohandas "Mahatma" Gandhi was assassinated after a lifetime of service to freedom in India. And in America, inflation plagued the postwar recovery. Bill took account of these things and wondered what difference he could make in such a world.

As he drew nearer Coweta, Bill was thinking about buying gifts for those in his wedding party. He stopped in Okmulgee, Oklahoma, which had been Grandfather Bright's hometown, to shop at a jewelry store. He entered the store only to realize he was out of cash. So he asked the man assisting him, whom he later learned was the owner, if out-of-state checks were accepted.

"No," the owner said, "it's against our policy."

Bill began to walk out, but the owner called him back.

"What did you say your name was?"

"Bill Bright."

"Do you know anyone in this city?"

"My grandfather used to live here, but he's been dead for several years."

"What was his name?"

"Sam Bright."

The owner smiled. "Sam Bright was the most honorable man I have ever known; if you're anything like your grandfather, I'll sell you anything in the store and I'll take your check!"

Reminded again of his family heritage, Bill was reinforced in the confidence and mettle that was to carry him so far beyond Coweta.

Bill and Vonette were married on December 30 in a ceremony that was front-page news in the *Times-Star*. A few days later they drove westward toward Vonette's new California home, but they weren't even out of Oklahoma before an eerily dark curtain descended in front of them. They had barely crossed the border into Texas when a violent storm hit, packed with wind and snow. Bill's convertible disclosed more outdoor access points than he could imagine. Vonette huddled next to him.

Suddenly the car made a coughing sound and the engine died. Bill guided it to a stop on the shoulder of the highway. They hadn't seen another car for miles. What a start for a honeymoon!

As Bill stepped out of the car and into the snowstorm, their urgent prayers were answered as a passing car appeared, then stopped. The newlyweds were taken to a small Texas town where they spent the night in a hotel. The storm proved to be a memorable one—the next cover of *Life* magazine showed pictures of cattle standing frozen in the Texas and Oklahoma panhandles. But Bill and Vonette were safe, ready to face other storms that God would bring their way.

CHAPTER 8

The Contract

After setting up house in Hollywood, Vonette accepted a teaching position in the Los Angeles school system. Bill's income was adequate, but Vonette wanted to apply what she had learned in college, and he supported her in that decision.

The Bright newlyweds soon found themselves sharing busy and eventful lives. Once or twice a week, in addition to regular meetings at church, Bill led "deputation groups" of more than 120 dedicated young men and women who wanted to become disciples of the Lord Jesus Christ. Going forth in teams to as many as thirty locations in a month, they visited local jails and hospitals, skid row missions, and "wherever we felt invited or needed.

"I soon discovered," Bill would recall, "that we had to wait our turn to go to jail services and skid row missions because many other churches were covering this area of service as well. One day it occurred to me that there were no waiting lines to reach college students or the top executives of the city. Here were the neglected leaders of our world, both today's and tomorrow's." The seeds were continuing to be sown in his heart and mind for a new and distinctive ministry calling.

Those seeds were watered in a conversation that took place between Bill and Billy Graham at Forest Home about this time. When Bill spoke of his search for what do with his life, Graham asked him, "What are you interested in?"

"Students," Bill replied.

"If that's your burden," Graham told him, "why don't you give yourself to students." For Graham to take the time to hear his heart at that particular period in his life meant much to Bill.

One night in the spring of 1950, Bill and Vonette were attending a Wednesday evening business session at Hollywood Presbyterian. As usual, they sat in the back. Suddenly Bill looked up as he heard his name announced on the nominating committee's candidate list for new deacons. He had no idea this was coming.

But the blessing of the moment quickly evaporated, as Bill saw a man rise to his feet and address the church body. It was one of his former business partners, a member of the family with whom Bill had endured the financial dispute. The man declared that he could not support the selection of Bill Bright as a deacon because Bright was dishonest. Another family member also stood to speak: "We know him, and he's not worthy of such a responsible trust."

The congregation that evening, numbering about a thousand, sat in stunned silence. Bill's heart plunged into humiliation. Wincing from the pride-smashing pain, he turned to look at Vonette.

With his imposing size and booming voice commanding attention, Louis Evans, the pastor, responded to the two protesting church members by announcing that the business session would be in recess while the nominating committee reconsidered its recommendation.

As the committee members adjourned to another room, Bill fairly flew out the back of the church, leaving Vonette to sit alone. He raced outside and around the building to a side door, where he entered and followed a hallway toward the committee's meeting room. When he arrived in the doorway, the committee was seated and Dr. Evans was standing.

"Please withdraw my name," Bill insisted. "I don't want to do anything that would hurt the church. I didn't know this was coming—"

Evans interrupted him. "Wait," he said to Bill, then turned to the committee. "I know all the issues in this situation; I have studied them carefully, and the accusations against this man are not true. I insist that you leave this man's name on this list." It was as if a cool mountain wind had blown into Bill's heart. He had never experienced such unhesitating, authoritative affirmation.

Just then a woman appeared in the hallway and said through the open door, "Look, I don't know what the issues are, but I know this: I wouldn't be a Christian today if it weren't for Bill Bright."

Bill left the group to continue their discussion and returned, by his outside route, to sit with Vonette. He was teary-eyed and speechless, uncertain what to think or what would happen next.

After Evans and the committee reentered the sanctuary, the committee spokesman addressed the congregation. He reported that they had considered the accusations against Bill Bright and in their judgment the recommended list of nominees for deacon "should stand as originally presented."

At that moment, the congregation erupted in applause and began rising to its feet. The hot, healing sounds of approval streamed into Bill's ears and heart. It was as spellbindingly beautiful as the accusations had been disturbingly ugly.

"In that moment," he recalled, "I was set free, free from years of feeling that no one trusted me. All those lonely nights in the plant, all the weeping; in a moment it was gone."

In hindsight, Bill could view all the pressure he had known from his partners' accusations of dishonesty as the thumb of God on his neck during these years, making sure that no Bill Bright pridefulness would run unchecked into the ministry. "He guarded my heart, but He let the pressure stay on me.... What God was doing was making sure that everything necessary would be done to obliterate my ego....

"Had it not been for that crushing, ego-smashing experience, I'm sure I would not have been able to make the later commitment to become a slave of Jesus, nor would God have given me the vision for Campus Crusade for Christ to help fulfill the Great Commission."

As far as Bill was concerned, God had cleared him and restored his good name. But like the Old Testament experience of Joseph, Bill's public favor was coming only after an unjust ordeal that built within him a deep reservoir of trust in God. He was to draw on that reservoir for the rest of his life.

Meanwhile God's molding of that life continued through Bill's marriage, the seminary, his business, and the church. One of his visitations as a new deacon became an occasion that would forever convince him of the connection between happiness and obeying God. Bill was visiting an elderly couple, and the wife was dying of cancer. The husband had spent most of what had been a considerable fortune seeking to save her life. They had "moved down" from a mansion into a trailer to do their best to afford her care.

Bill was unsure of what to say or do to comfort them, but it mattered little; they comforted him. "When I stepped into their humble little trailer home, it was as though I were entering a corner of heaven. There, sitting beside his dying wife, was this godly man holding her hand. Both of them had radiant countenances. The joy of the Lord filled the place.... They had learned to trust and obey God and seek His will, even in the midst of tragedy."

From this and other encounters with ordinary people displaying extra-ordinary faith, Bill developed a law of happiness: There are no unhappy obedient Christians, and there are no happy disobedient Christians. He came to see happiness as a contentment and inner peace about circumstances as well as an exuberance about God. This condition, Bill decided, comes from knowing one's sins are forgiven and from knowing the faithful Forgiver who holds tomorrow in His hand. The joy of knowing he was forgiven by such an amazing God made him want to bask in that condition, literally, all the time. He found his sinful acts were terrible interruptions of this joy, and he wanted to get back into the joy as fast as possible.

Another life-marking experience in his service as a deacon came when he was serving communion for the first time. In the earlier days before his commitment to Christ, the Christian focus on the blood of Jesus had seemed pagan and unseemly to him. Later, as he read the Scriptures, God had spoken to him through Hebrews 9:22—"Without shedding of blood is no remission [of sin]." Bill had been overwhelmed. "In a moment of revelation, I became aware of my sin and of the reason for Christ's death for me. I sobbed with deep gratitude. What had appeared in my agnosticism as so gruesome and unappealing now became the most important part of my relationship with the Lord."

A renewed realization of this truth made him weep again on that Sunday when he first served "the body and the blood of Jesus" at Hollywood Presbyterian. His appreciation for the cross and the blood of Christ would remain as a motivating force in his spiritual life and ministry. "'What can wash away my sin? Nothing but the blood of Jesus!'"

During this period, Bill began to assess, on the one hand, an impotent American church and, on the other, an omnipotent God. What was wrong with that picture? The disobedience of Christians, it seemed to Bill. "If we can just demonstrate to God our total allegiance by obeying and following Him, the world would be changed overnight."

Bill's own commitment to obeying God shone through in a strained encounter with one of the most powerful religious leaders in America in those days, Eugene Carson Blake. Dr. Blake was senior pastor of a Presbyterian church in Pasadena and the most influential Presbyterian in the Los Angeles area and later in the nation. In the coming decades he would hold the top leadership posts in both the National Council of Churches and the World Council of Churches, organizations whose beliefs conflicted with those taught at Fuller Seminary.

Bill had first met opposition from Blake when the youth director at Blake's church invited Bill to speak to their youth group. Bill had agreed, but as a matter of policy, he asked for the invitation to be cleared with the church's pastor as well. Afterward the youth leader telephoned Bill to say apologetically that the invitation must be withdrawn. He let Dr. Blake explain the reason: He didn't want Bill's brand of Christianity in their church, and he didn't appreciate Hollywood Presbyterian's teachings, which Blake characterized as "the theology of a Baptist church."

Bill replied that he understood, adding that if he were a pastor, he also would want anyone teaching in his church to hold beliefs compatible with his own.

Later came a more serious disagreement. Through the sanction of Hollywood Presbyterian Church, Bill's seminary training was under the oversight of the Los Angeles Presbytery. First as a Princeton enrollee and later as a student at Fuller, Bill met regularly with a small group of Presbyterian ministers in Los Angeles to discuss his educational progress. But he was under increasing pressure from this group to leave Fuller and to finish his education either at the University of Southern California's religion department or at a nearby Presbyterian seminary whose teachings Bill regarded as too liberal. Bill continually resisted their suggestions and stayed at Fuller.

The matter came to a head in one of these conferences when Blake stormed into the room, as Bill recalled, and told Bill his behavior could not be tolerated. "When you took the vow to be under the care of the presbytery," he told Bill, "that means you do what we say!"

"Sir," Bill replied, "God called me to serve Him, not you," and he requested to be released immediately from their oversight. That ended Bill's formal relationship with the Los Angeles Presbytery, although he maintained membership in Presbyterian churches throughout his career while worshiping occasionally in several other denominations as well.

But perhaps the most life-changing personal encounter in those days was not with a religious leader, but with the person who loved him most—Vonette. It was a situation Bill would frequently point to later as an example of how insensitive he was as a young husband.

One Sunday in the spring of 1951, the Brights drove as usual to Hollywood Presbyterian for another day of worship and service, beginning with the Sunday school hour. Soon after they arrived, Bill was taken aside and told about an urgent counseling situation involving the daughter of a prominent evangelist. A member of the college and career class, she was now an unwed mother-to-be. Bill, already an experienced counselor, joined two others in a counseling session with the woman. Vonette, however, did not know where he had gone.

The counseling session lasted through the Sunday school hour and beyond the morning worship service, which Vonette attended alone. She had experienced periods of waiting for Bill before, but nothing like this. Usually he would send someone with a message for her. Not this time. Now the church service was over and everyone had left. Where was he?

She proceeded to the parking lot to wait in their car. Another hour went by. Then two hours. It was well into the third hour when Bill finally appeared.

The ensuing conversation was intense. Vonette argued mainly from the Golden Rule: What if the roles were reversed? What would *you* expect of me?

The heated dialogue continued on the ride home and through Sunday dinner and beyond. "She expressed her displeasure very strongly, and she had every right to be impatient, even angry with me.... That afternoon as we talked and prayed together, I asked her to forgive me because I had not been sensitive, and not on that occasion only. I had brought her into an overly busy life of business, church, seminary, and deputation meetings. She wasn't really getting the attention she deserved as my wife."

Over the dining room table, where so many of the issues of their lives were to be resolved, they began to focus on the expectations each had for their marriage. After considerable discussion, Bill proposed that they each take a sheet of paper, go to a different room, and write down their expectations before God. Then they were to ask Him what He wanted them to do.

They approached it differently. Vonette, always the practical complement to Bill, wrote of fundamental goals for their marriage: children, a suitable home nice enough to minister to people from all walks of life, a suitable car, and God's blessing. Bill, on the other hand, took the wide-angle perspective: What did he want out of life? He wrote that he renounced every single thing in his life to the control of the Lord Jesus Christ. He placed life and wife and family and home and car and business—all that they owned or ever would own, past and future—entirely under the Lord's ownership. He thought of Paul's New Testament description of himself as a slave of Jesus Christ. So Bill declared in writing that before God he assumed the position of a bondslave, a role exemplified in the obedient life of the Lord Jesus Christ. Whatever the Master said to do, Bill would do, with God's help.

Vonette and Bill came back together in the living room and compared their papers. Bill didn't attempt to draft a single document reconciling their two approaches. Each acknowledged the validity of the other's goals before God, and agreed in an act of faith to sign the papers as an expression of the surrender of their lives to God.

Bill proposed that the documents represent their "Contract with God." Vonette agreed, and they prayed, telling God that their lives were surrendered totally and irrevocably to Him; He could do anything He wanted to do in them and through them for His glory. Wherever He wanted them to go, whatever He wanted them to do, whatever it cost, they wanted to be His bondslaves.

There was peace now in their hearts and in their home, and the future seemed brighter than ever.

Throughout their lives they would look back on that Sunday afternoon

Contract with God as a turning point. "Apart from my salvation," Bill would say, "this was to be the most important decision of my life. That day I became a slave of our Lord Jesus Christ, and for the first time in my life I was actually free."

What Christ called His followers to—denial of self and daily taking up one's cross and following Him—became a reality for Bill and Vonette. "We chose that day to put aside our own dreams, our own aspirations, and our own little puny plans, and embrace His magnificent plans. That day was the beginning of a whole new era, a whole new lifestyle."

Some might say that Bill made a big deal that Sunday out of a relatively small matter. But this became a pattern for Bill: When hard things and hard times arose, he would look for the higher principles of how God could be working in the matter and how He would be glorified. Then he would take specific action, expressing it in written form whenever possible, to transform the immediate crisis into a God monument in his life.

Bill Bright wanted no small things, no small events, no trivial matters— only opportunities for a great God to do great things. Difficult times would come, and the way in which he and Vonette responded to them would determine everything. Trials were not merely to be endured but welcomed as a launch pad to a new dimension of grace and spiritual development in their lives, and not only for themselves, but for all who would listen to the testimony of God at work in their world.

In time, Bill became increasingly persuaded that God would not have given him the vision for what became Campus Crusade for Christ "had I not first surrendered my life totally, completely, and irrevocably to the lordship of Christ. I was no longer my own; I had been bought with a price—the blood of my beloved Savior."

Years later, the papers that first held the terms of the Contract were given by the Brights to Campus Crusade's publications department, along with the letters of their courtship. When the department's building burned in a fire in 1980, the papers and letters were destroyed. Vonette regretted the loss, but Bill chose to see in it a providential protection against any worship of documents that might detract from devotion to the Lord.

CHAPTER 9

The Vision

O ne night during the week that followed the Brights' signing of the Contract, Bill had an experience with God that would finalize his life's change in course from business executive to leader of a worldwide ministry to help fulfill the Great Commission.

It was late, about midnight, and he was studying for a Hebrew exam with a friend from Fuller Seminary. Suddenly, "God in an unusual way opened my mind, touched my heart.... I can't translate into English or any other language what happened, but God met with me....

"My experience that midnight hour was so rich, so meaningful, and yet so indescribable. People have asked me what happened. There is no way I can describe it. Without apology all I can say is I met with God. I didn't see a physical form, I didn't hear an audible voice, but I have never been the same since that unforgettable encounter."

It was a vision to help reach the world for Christ and fulfill the Great Commission in his lifetime. (The one specific thing Bill sensed he could "see" was a great spiritual movement emanating from Australia and spreading out across the globe.) He was to start by reaching the leaders on the college campuses of the United States and later the world. The slogan would be: "Reach the campus for Christ today—reach the world for Christ tomorrow."

But the Vision was more than that; it was first of all an intimate relationship with God, a warm envelopment of Bill as a person ready for partnership with the Holy, of being persuaded fully of God's presence in his life and the utterly astounding significance of that. It also was a revelation of his own total inadequacy as a human being and the absolute adequacy of God in all things, and it left the clear impression that God and he could partner in an enterprise greater than anything Bill had ever known.

What was especially astonishing to Bill in that moment was his sense that this partnership, this venture, this helping to reach the whole world with the message of God's love and forgiveness through Christ, could actually be accomplished. It was achievable! How would he see it all fulfilled? He didn't know. But in unbroken communication with God, it was as feasible as planting a spring garden, cultivating it all summer long, and harvesting it in the fall.

Decades later he would say, "I'm often asked if I'm surprised at the remarkable growth and size of Campus Crusade for Christ. My answer: No, I am not surprised, for the vision God gave that midnight hour in the spring of 1951 was of such great magnitude—far greater than anything we have yet experienced. The best is yet before us."

The Vision lasted perhaps only a few minutes, although Bill really had no awareness of time, feeling transported from the earth.

The experience left him ecstatic and a bit dazed. He could think of nothing else. He turned to his classmate, who had no awareness of what was happening to Bill. "I was so filled with energy, I suggested to him that we go running, right then, at midnight. He looked at me a bit strangely." But his friend agreed.

Bill hardly slept that night. Early the next morning, when Vonette awoke, he shared with her what he had experienced, and she rejoiced with him.

Later that same morning he fairly floated through his classes. Then he rushed to Dr. Wilbur Smith's office on Orange Grove Avenue. As Bill shared his vision with his mentor, Smith got out of his chair and began to pace back and forth, declaring as he went: "This is of God. This is of God. This is of God!"

Smith was to Bill as Ananias was to Saul of Tarsus, lifting the scales from the eyes of a man who had received a heavenly vision, confirming, encouraging, nurturing. The professor's enthusiasm, coming from a man of such letters and intellect, further accelerated Bill's exuberance.

"Let me think on this," he told Bill. The next morning Bill was called out of class to see Smith. The professor told him, "I believe God has given me the name for your vision." He showed Bill a small piece of paper with "CCC" written on it; underneath were the words, "Campus Crusade for Christ." They prayed, and Bill went home with more stirring news to share with Vonette.

The more they prayed about it, the more excited Vonette became. She had a husband who was heaven-bent on telling the story of God's love, and she loved him for it.

How to start? That was literally their first question. The answer was easy: Pray. Bill and Vonette and their friends at seminary and from Hollywood Presbyterian set up a twenty-four-hour prayer chain divided into fifteen-minute blocks. Someone would be praying for this new ministry around the clock. They didn't have a strategy meeting with anyone; they only strategized how to get an answer from God to their compelling desire, and they believed that answer would come through prayer.

Having received the vision for his life's work, Bill and Vonette decided it was time to launch immediately into full-time ministry. Somewhat like Jesus on the road to Jerusalem, Bill steadfastly set his face to pursue his calling—no turning back. He did not investigate theories on how to start ministries. He simply began, and he began simply.

Despite initial misgivings from Vonette, Bill believed it was time for him to leave seminary, although he had nearly completed the requirements for a degree. The Vision was a consuming fire, and he couldn't imagine spending another minute in seminary while the Vision was waiting to be implemented. No seminary degree was going to change what he knew he had to do for his lifetime. Later it became clear to Bill that the absence of a seminary degree declared him a layman, not a clergyman, a distinction that seemed to open far more doors for him than seminary degrees would have opened. Over the years, however, he would counsel many to pursue study in theological seminaries unless God had clearly shown them otherwise. And in recognition of his own academic efforts and worldwide ministry, Bill Bright would later receive honorary doctorates from six academic institutions.

Bill was continually sharing the Vision with other mentors, friends, and authority figures. All reacted positively and affirmed him. He also began to form a board to guide the ministry. The first person he asked to serve on the board was Wilbur Smith. The second was Henrietta Mears. The third was Billy Graham, the increasingly prominent evangelist who in 1949 had led an evangelistic crusade in Los Angeles (a watershed event in his ministry) and was holding another in Hollywood in 1951. Graham had attended the third annual Briefing Conference at Forest Home in 1949, where he had times of prayer and private discussion with Henrietta Mears, and where he made a life-changing commitment to the authority, trustworthiness, and inspiration of the Scriptures.

The fourth person Bill asked to join his board was a comrade from Forest Home experiences, Richard Halverson, whose long and fruitful ministry as a pastor would be capped by many years of service as chaplain of the U.S. Senate. Then came Cyrus Nelson, director at Forest Home; Bob Stover, a successful businessman; Ralph Byron, a surgeon and cancer specialist; Bill's seminary classmates Dan Fuller and William Savage; and Edwin Orr of the Fuller faculty, who had earned his Ph.D. at Oxford University in England.

In the Vision, Bill had seen the campus as the place to begin actually ministering. Bill had sensed the importance of reaching student leaders who would be the future's decision-makers, and who had the social skills and intelligence needed to influence others to seek to know God personally. Now he and Vonette gathered a team of students to make presentations of a Christian perspective of life on campus, beginning in the Kappa Alpha Theta sorority house at UCLA. It was their first meeting, the beginning of the outward manifestation of Campus Crusade for Christ.

Bill had shared his faith publicly in other campus meetings, but he had never witnessed a public profession of faith after any of his meetings. Prior to speaking that day at Kappa Alpha Theta, he prayed, "O Lord, please let there be at least one who will respond, to confirm the vision You gave me."

His message that day was on the subject of Jesus—who He is and how we can know Him personally. After he concluded his remarks, he invited anyone who wanted to receive Christ as Savior and Lord to come and tell him personally.

He looked up and saw a line forming. Of the sixty women present, more than half expressed an interest in knowing how they could receive Christ. The response strengthened Bill's faith; God had answered his prayer, abundantly above his expectations.

Another meeting was announced for the following night at the Brights' home near the campus, and he challenged the women to bring their friends. Among those in attendance that second evening were the editor of the student newspaper plus several top student athletes and musicians.

More meetings followed over the next few months in fraternities, sororities, and dormitories. More than 250 UCLA students—including the student body president, the student newspaper editor, and a number of top athletes—committed their lives to Jesus Christ. So great was their influence on the entire campus that the chimes began playing Christian hymns daily during the noon hours.

The Vision's fulfillment had begun.

CHAPTER 10

Inspiration
with Perspiration

News of God's blessing on the ministry launched at UCLA prompted pastors and interested laymen to encourage Bill to start ministries on other campuses. He realized that he needed additional workers to expand.

Bill and Vonette set standards for the kind of workers they wanted to recruit. They were looking for Spirit-filled seminary graduates, intellectually sharp believers who had made a life commitment to God and were already fruitful in their witness for Christ.

Bill hit the road and visited the seminaries of America. But the harder he pursued this recruitment approach, the less fruitful it became. Most seminarians he came across were studying to become pastors. Few had ever considered a ministry to students.

After much prayer, he and Vonette changed course. They began to ask God whom they should recruit from whatever source or situation. They knew that the ministry must be carried out by men of the Spirit, afire with a personal relationship with a living God, whose lives were an open book, who would say yes to God without reservation, and who wanted to change the world—right now! A seminary degree, the Brights determined, would not be a requirement; they decided a college degree was needed, however, since these workers would be ministering to college students.

The first recruit was a young collegian named Gordon Klenck, whom Bill met at Bob Jones University. Klenck was so fresh-faced he could have passed for a high-school student. When Bill brought him by their home, Vonette asked Bill, "You don't think you're going to change the world with people like that, do you?" They would later laugh about that quick judgment as they increasingly saw how God looks first for availability in His servants, then provides them with the necessary ability for accomplishing His purpose.

The second recruit was Roe Brooks, who interrupted his second year at Eastern Baptist Theological Seminary to join Bill and Vonette. (Both Klenck and Brooks would still be on Crusade staff at the end of the century.) By the beginning of Campus Crusade's second year, there were six recruits at work on three local campuses.

Bill and Vonette's home now become a training center. The kitchen table was the most active spot in their home, a place for research and for writing, editing, copying, formatting, and designing training manuals.

To further her teaching career, Vonette had begun work on her master's degree at the University of Southern California, where she took a course in curriculum writing under the direction of Dr. C. C. Crawford (who happened to be a distant relative). Crawford had perfected a system of information gathering that focused on the pooling of research by various individuals involved in a project. Through this procedure, under Vonette's direction, the members of the growing Campus Crusade for Christ staff pooled their information and experiences. Over time, the result was a comprehensive manual about four inches thick, addressing virtually every problem and challenge that one could encounter in introducing students, professors, laymen, international students, and others to Christ and in building them in the faith to the point where they, too, could reach others and build them as disciples.

Discipling, training, nurturing, and coaching in ministry concepts and details became the focus of Bill and Vonette's activities. They were determined to provide the necessary practical help for making the difference in ministry between mere desire and true effectiveness. As Bill put it, "Inspiration without perspiration leads to frustration and ultimately to stagnation."

He later wrote:

> I have been inspired to the heavens by eloquent addresses and
> sermons. However, more often than not, I have soon forgotten

what it was that inspired me. Statistics on memory retention prove that I am not the exception, but rather that I am quite typical....

Time and again I have heard testimony given at various Christian conferences in about these words: "A year ago at this same conference I dedicated my life to Christ and I vowed that I would live for Him whatever it cost. I went away aflame for Christ, determined to capture my campus for the Lord (or to win my community to Christ)."

But a year later the same individual would be back at the next conference saying, "I fell flat on my face after the first week (or the second week, or the first month) and I could hardly wait to get back up here so that I could get my spiritual gas tank filled and go back out to serve the Lord."

Bill believed that effectively training men and women to build them up as disciples of God could stop this frustrating cycle, so he determined that the organization they were leading would major in perspiration rather than inspiration. The training would be practical, comprehensive, and repetitive, with a strong emphasis on the basics, which were to be reviewed again and again without apology. Bill was convinced that repetition aids learning.

From Campus Crusade's inception, three major thrusts were identified, providing the ministry with a simple and unified mission: First, initiating evangelism; second, training men and women; third, building disciples and sending them forth to witness for Christ.

The pattern was set that would continue decade after decade. In meetings and conferences, almost all the teaching messages would be designed to build Christians in the faith and challenge them to become disciples. "We train carnal Christians to become spiritual Christians, teaching them the difference between walking in the flesh and walking in the Spirit, and showing them how to share their faith in Christ more effectively with others."

The same approach would be carried out even in a gathering in which a large minority of non-Christians was present. "The end result is that within a matter of a few hours after the carnal Christians have become spiritual Christians and have learned how to communicate their faith, they begin to share

Christ with the nonbelievers.... Thus, more people come to Christ through the awakened Christians than we could ever hope to reach for Christ through directing all of our messages toward non-Christians. Of course, the Christians are also greatly benefited through their experience of introducing others to Christ."

Crusade's continual focus on training sprang not only from the strategic need for greater ministry effectiveness, but also from Bill's own love of learning. An inveterate reader, Bill's developed the habit of underlining key portions in whatever he was reading. He devoured books, testing their propositions with his understanding of the Bible and his own experience. He read theology, history, and science and began focusing especially on leadership. George Washington became his favorite historical figure outside the Bible, and his library in time would include several Washington biographies, including one from the early 1800s.

He also read the newsmagazines and newspapers of the day, as well as Presbyterian periodicals and conservative political writers. He began keeping files of clippings organized by topic for his future reflection and as research for his writing and speaking. His most frequented topics included the lordship of Christ, evangelism, the Holy Spirit, crime, love, the veracity of Scripture, and science.

Bill had frequent visits with Dawson Trotman, founder of the Navigators, and leadership was a common topic of their discussion. Bill's notes during this period included these words: "When an organization is created it is largely made up of explorers and artists; after several years it will be made up largely of judges and warriors"—meaning *judges* in the sense of "critics" and *warriors* in the sense of "infighters." Bill gleaned from this a warning that Christian leaders must keep ministries productive and mission-driven and not get bogged down in paralyzing self-analysis and tactical feuds.

Meanwhile, the primary underpinnings of his personal ministry were set in his own daily Bible reading, both morning and night. From this time with God would flow a pattern of emphasis that would continue throughout his ministry—an emphasis on personal revival, fasting and prayer, dependence upon the Holy Spirit, and the need for a strong church to take the initiative to reach the world with the good news of Christ.

CHAPTER 11

God Loves You

A t the Brights' kitchen table in those early days, Bill drafted a brief summary of the gospel to be used for training Campus Crusade staff in evangelism. He called it simply "God's Plan," and as the months and years went by and the ministry grew, he continued to ponder how to refine this gospel presentation, consistent with his deepening conviction that how-to instruction in practical Christianity must remain a foundation stone in his ministry.

The longer he worked in ministry, he later observed, "the more I realized the necessity of developing simple how-tos for the Christian life." What value, really, was a profound theological proposition if the masses could not understand it? What kind of a God would make Himself known in a way that only the brilliant could comprehend? Bill was driven by the challenge of how to make the great truths of God understandable to everyday human beings, and in such a way that they, too, would be able to communicate it to others.

A turning point in his thinking about God's Plan came in the summer of 1956 at a ministry staff conference near the UCLA campus. Bill had invited a noted sales consultant to speak to the assembled staff from his experience about the significance of having a clearly stated message—a pitch.

Inside the new chapel, the sales professional was at the rostrum contending that every successful salesperson needed a message that was plainly and often stated. The more basic that message and the more clearly stated, the more it communicated and the more likely people would buy. He noted that a common danger in sales is "presentation fatigue," when the salesperson simply wearies of saying the same thing and starts changing the message. Yielding to this temptation, the consultant said, leads directly to ineffectiveness.

Bill was taking this in when the speaker began to compare the "pitch" to Christian witness. He stated that several prominent and successful Christian leaders each had a distinctive "spiritual pitch" in what they communicated, saying fundamentally the same thing over and over, thereby boosting their effectiveness.

Then he struck closer to home. "Bill Bright," he said, "who works with students and professors and outstanding business executives, as well as with men on skid row, thinks he has a special message for each of them. But the fact of the matter is, although I have never heard him speak or counsel, I would be willing to wager that he has only one pitch. Basically, he tells them all the same thing."

Bill bristled. "The very thought that I needed to resort to what I considered Madison Avenue techniques to do the spiritual work of God was repugnant and offensive to me. I resented anyone suggesting that I or anyone else who truly loved and desired to serve the Lord had to depend on gimmicks or that we were not led of the Spirit in such a way that the Holy Spirit was able to be original through us to the various individuals with whom we worked, according to their various needs. Further, I resented his using me as an example before the rest of the staff.

"So when it was all over and I was licking my wounds—the most serious of which was a lacerated ego—I began to reflect on exactly what I shared with the various ones with whom I worked: students, executives, prisoners, and people on skid row."

Bill sat down that afternoon and wrote down what he commonly did say in witnessing. To his amazement, the salesman was right. "I had been sharing basically the same thing with everyone without realizing it." Therefore that message deserved to be as clear and essential as possible.

With fresh motivation, Bill further polished his essential God's Plan statement into what he now called "God's Plan for Your Life." It was a positively stated synthesis of the truths of the gospel, which Crusade staff were to memorize and, at the slightest opportunity, begin to share in a witnessing experience with seeming spontaneity.

The content focused on the person of Jesus and His claims: who He is, why He came, and how to know Him personally. It reflected the distilled and validated truths that Bill had seen work; it was a road-tested compilation of what he had studied in two seminaries and what had actually been effective in his personal witnessing.

With the content of God's Plan memorized, each Crusade staff member would carry with him a printed copy of "the Van Dusen letter," originally a lengthy letter from Bill addressed to a prominent, nonbelieving businessman. Bill had adapted the letter as a conversation-starting device for the staff as they talked one-on-one with individuals on college campuses. With the door thus opened, the staff member could "spontaneously" write on the back of the letter the various points and illustrations of God's Plan.

Refinement of God's Plan continued, as Bill and Vonette were constantly reminded of the challenge to be relevant in how they presented God's truth to questioning minds. With the Russian launch of the Sputnik satellite and the advent of the technology age, Bill searched for words that would bridge the current interest in science with the ageless truths of Scripture. Looking to science for an analogy, he found one. Scientists, especially in physics, were forever referring to some "law" of aerodynamics or thermodynamics or whatever. That was it—he would focus people's attention on the spiritual "laws" of God. "Just as there are physical laws governing the physical universe," Bill wrote, "so there are spiritual laws governing your relationship with God."

The most revolutionary development in the wording of God's Plan came about in the spring of 1958. The Brights at the time were staying in the beautiful Bel Air home of Henrietta Mears, paying rent and helping to maintain the lawn and facilities. The spacious house served as a place for both work and ministry, and could accommodate about three hundred students for gatherings.

About two o'clock one morning, Vonette and several other women were in a downstairs room retyping manuscript drafts of God's Plan for a presentation deadline later that day. Suddenly Bill called down the stairs that the first law had to be rewritten.

Until then, all the versions of God's Plan had begun with an emphasis on human evil, consistent with the prevailing approach to evangelism in those days in conservative American church culture. But now, reevaluating their message in those dark night hours, Bill had written down the simple words "God loves you" as a new first law, instead of beginning with an indication that man's sin was God's prime concern. This was a chance to proclaim more effectively the truth that "God so loved the world, that he gave his only begotten Son," and to live out the apostle Paul's declaration: "The love of God constrains me."

Bill reasoned that this new focus was more consistent not only with his theological studies, but also with his own testimony. Love, forgiveness, acceptance, provision, peace, delight—these were the attributes of God that had drawn him. He had lived long enough to recognize special personal acts of God's love—the many answered prayers of his mother for him, his release from guilt and his amazing infusion of confidence in God that happened when he became a Christian, and God's timing in leading him and Vonette along life's journey—all this spoke to him not of a God who indicted first but of One who lovingly invited you into His living room.

What was the ministry God had given him really about, anyway? He had been captivated by the vastness of God's love and compelled to share that great love with all who would listen. Bill wanted everyone to be as thrilled as he was about the great adventure of walking with a wonderfully loving Lord.

There seemed no reason not to start where God starts—with His love. Besides, why begin with a negative note that people can easily see for themselves?

Bill bounded with enthusiasm down the stairs of the Mears house and presented the change to Vonette and the others. Their reaction was mixed.

Some were simply flabbergasted. This was so different. Had Bill departed the faith? Ever since the days of Jonathan Edwards, it seemed, every evangelistic tract began with something like, "Man is a sinner, depraved, separated from God, in rebellion against the Creator and the Redeemer...." Where did Bill come off with this emphasis on God *loving* us as the preeminent spiritual law of the universe? To begin by attaching such importance to love might even seem to place Campus Crusade on the wrong side of the modernist-fundamentalist conflict that had raged within Christianity throughout the twentieth century. It mattered a great deal not only *what* you believed, but also what you emphasized about your beliefs.

Some of the women in the room were weeping. Bill respected their tears and listened to their concerns. He prayed with them and shared his heart with them as he considered again his reasons for the change. He knew that in his own inner core, in that place Blaise Pascal referred to as "a God-shaped vacuum in the heart of every man," he had been and still was overwhelmed by God's love. In the quiet place at night where peace either is or isn't, Bill had experienced the revolutionizing effects of the love of God. It had turned him from a money-hungry, status-conscious, Hollywood-enthralled "happy pagan" into a God-conscious, Christ-centered, self-giving, world-burdened missionary evangelist.

He had also done his share of Bible study and theological research, on his own, in his church, and for five years at Fuller and Princeton seminaries. He had dug into the incredibly sweeping statement of Paul: "Neither death, nor life, nor angels, nor principalities, nor powers, nor things present, nor things to come, nor height, nor depth, nor any other creature, shall be able to separate us from *the love of God,* which is in Christ Jesus our Lord" (Romans 8:38-39). Bill had studied the incredible Old Testament portrait of God as the loving husband of promiscuous Israel, and he had seen the prophet Hosea's depiction of God buying back at a slave auction the wife who had deserted Him and gone awhoring. Bill had been struck by David's exclamation to God, "How priceless is Your unfailing love!"—and even more by the historical fact-scene of the divine Jesus of Nazareth hanging on a Roman cross, mocked, jeered, and spat upon, praying for His executioners, "Father, *forgive them.…*"

For Bill, it could be no other way. Beginning a presentation of the spiritual laws of the universe with *man's* condition simply wouldn't work for him. In fact, it rubbed like sandpaper on the soul to a man for whom being loved by God had meant a total change of life. The First Spiritual Law of the Universe had to be "God *loves* you! *God* loves you! God loves *you!*" It was the only way Bill Bright could speak of God's view of man and be true to himself and to what he knew.

Furthermore, by adding this new first law, Bill would not be departing from the reality of man's depravity. That, in fact, would be the second law, following immediately after the first about God's love.

And there was more he wanted to add. In his annual read-through of the Bible, in his understanding of Holy Scriptures, and in what he had learned from those "spiritual giants" who had affected his own journey, Bill caught the perspective that Christianity was not a drudgery of self-deprivation; it was a wonderful adventure to be viewed each day on tiptoe, radiantly discovering God's Word and His ways. It was choosing to see a sovereign hand guiding, coaxing, pausing, blessing you to the fulfillment of His purposes in your life. Bill remembered the exhilarating promise of Jesus: "I am come that they might have life, and that they might have it more abundantly" (John 10:10).

So the first law became, "God loves you and offers a wonderful plan for your life"—its phrasing not the result of some promotional afterthought, but of Bill's steady digging and heartfelt conviction. And although plainly stated, it was profound, touching on deep theological issues by assuming God's intimate interest in the details, destinations, and destiny of every person on planet earth.

Love *and* a plan! What a God! It was the greatest news Bill Bright had ever articulated. In years to come this declaration would have appeal on every continent, in scores of languages and countless cultures. "God loves you and offers a wonderful plan for your life" may be the most frequently heard single expression of the gospel of all time.

This newest version of God's Plan would continue for nearly a decade to exist primarily as training material that the Campus Crusade staff would memorize in order to write it out on the back of copies of the Van Dusen letter or elsewhere. Not until 1965 were the Four Spiritual Laws produced in printed form as a standalone booklet.

Imitations of Bill's gospel presentation popped up almost overnight as many other ministries and churches created their own adaptations. Billy Graham's team consulted with Bill before creating its *Peace with God* tract. In Chicago, there was even an adaptation for Jews entitled "The Six Spiritual Laws," conveying Christ as the Messiah presaged in the Jewish feasts and the prophecies of Isaiah. Although Bill appreciated being asked for permission, he never minded those who borrowed and adapted his themes into their own forms. He was always seeking to improve his own tools anyway. Besides, if someone else's version helped advance the Great Commission, this was to be celebrated. "Give it away" became a commonly heard expression as Bill modeled his leadership style before Crusade staff and as he interacted with other Christian leaders.

As the Crusade staff evaluated the effectiveness of the Four Spiritual Laws as a gospel presentation, their studies showed that most people easily grasped the first three laws:

1. God loves you and offers a wonderful plan for your life.
2. Man is sinful and separated from God; thus he cannot know and experience God's love and plan for his life.
3. Jesus Christ is God's only provision for man's sin. Through Him you can know and experience God's love and plan for your life.

But for the fourth law—"We must individually receive Jesus Christ as Savior and Lord; then we can know and experience God's love and plan for our lives"—the ministry's surveys showed that people commonly did not understand the need for a personal relationship with God through Christ or how to begin such a relationship.

This was where Bill's persistent pursuit of how-to instruction shed new light. He devised simple diagrams to clarify the truth. A circle represented the total person; a chair inside it represented "the throne" or control center of the person's life. Contrasting circles showed how a person could either keep his own ego "on the throne" or place Jesus Christ there (represented by a cross drawn on the chair). To bring Christ onto the throne, giving Him authority over your life, you had to make a conscious choice to invite Him into your life. Otherwise, Christ remained outside—represented in the diagram by a cross drawn outside the circle. (See Appendix F for the complete text and diagrams.)

The presentation made it crystal clear: Jesus Christ waits to be invited into your life and promises to enter if invited. A transaction must take place; you must invite Him in. The critical question in the presentation was this: *Which circle best represents your life?*

Then the Crusade staff member would offer more specific instruction:

One must pray. Prayer is talking with God. A sample prayer would be presented, along with the question, "Does this reflect the desire of your heart?" It was not merely intellectual assent, but submission of the will.

The truth represented in these circles would also become, both in the Crusade ministry and in Bill's life and home, a way to gauge one's obedience to the command of Ephesians 5:18, where believers are taught to be continually filled—directed and empowered—by the Holy Spirit moment by moment. A practical way to apply this concept was to give yourself a "throne check": In the current situation, am I allowing Jesus to reign? Am I walking by faith in the control of the Holy Spirit? Or am I trying to put myself back on the throne?

To the Four Laws presentation, Bill also added a train illustration to show faith in action. It depicted the engine named Fact in the lead, then a fuel car labeled Faith, and finally the caboose, labeled Feelings. The explanation made it clear: The train could not run by the power of a caboose (feelings). It could run only as the Fuel (faith) was placed in the Fact (God's Word). Then the feelings would follow.

In time, this simple depiction from Bill's mind would bring these profound concepts into proper clarity for millions of Christians. Once again, Bill was accomplishing a major goal of his life: making the deep truths of God understandable by ordinary people.

As the Four Spiritual Laws become more widely presented, there were critics of all kinds. The approach was criticized by some as providing a basis for "easy believism" in which a person could say a few words to make a "decision," yet not experience a true conversion and change of life. The criticism was sometimes stinging for Bill, but it merely made him stronger as he further evaluated the Four Laws. To respond affirmatively to all the plain statements and direct questions presented in the Four Laws presentation, it seemed clear that an individual must shift his or her dependence from self to the Savior in a way that involved the entire person, not just emotion or intellect. Bill became even more confident that this approach had been inspired by God. He saw that ordinary people did not easily understand many other gospel presentations because they bypassed common language and concepts and relied instead on Christian jargon.

Another Crusade evangelism tool was a booklet containing Bill's further developed thinking on "The Uniqueness of Jesus." It featured six "infallible proofs" for the bodily resurrection of Jesus:

1. Jesus predicted His resurrection; therefore He either told the truth or was mentally disturbed.

2. The resurrection is the only reasonable explanation for the empty tomb.

3. The resurrection is the only reasonable explanation for how the early disciples changed from cowering and fearful folk into bold proclaimers of a living Lord.

4. The resurrection is the only reasonable explanation for the growth of the church in the face of persecution.

5. The resurrection is the only reasonable explanation for the hundreds of persons (1 Corinthians 15:6) who said they had witnessed a resurrected Christ.

6. The resurrection is the only reasonable explanation for the total transformation of Saul of Tarsus from a zealous Pharisee engaged in the systematic persecution of Christians to Paul the apostle, the most prolific advocate of Christ as the resurrected Savior and living Lord.

By 1959 Bill had received plenty of feedback suggesting that the churches of America would profit from Campus Crusade's proven approach to evangelism. Bill believed that his ministry was always to be a supportive partner of the church, and his commitment to gain disciples in the churches of America was central to his vision of helping to reach the whole world for Christ. So he started an intense new program of cooperation with local churches, which he called LIFE—the Lay Institute for Evangelism.

These institutes enlivened local churches, giving them communication tools as well as clear Scripture teaching emphasizing the lordship of Christ and the Great Commission. Bill also strove to lessen the inappropriate pressure for achieving "results" in personal sharing of one's faith. "Successful witnessing," he said, "is simply taking the initiative to share the claims of Christ in the power of the Holy Spirit and leaving the results to God."

With the popularity of these institutes, Bill was soon in such demand as a speaker that his Lay Institute teachings were recorded on sixteen-millimeter motion picture film, the best available technology of the day. Of the thousands of people who would eventually join the Crusade team, many of the more mature leaders were those who caught the vision in a Lay Institute for Evangelism.

Bill's heart for evangelism and his understanding of God's love for the lost would always continue as a hallmark of his life and ministry. One staff member's recognition of this will serve as an example of the observations of many.

Ney Bailey had started her ministry with Campus Crusade at the University of Arizona, and one summer at Campus Crusade headquarters her job was to supervise a team in tabulating results of a survey taken by the staff on scores of campuses. The survey asked questions about church attendance and about one's opinion of people such as Mohammed, Buddha, and Jesus Christ. It also asked, "In your opinion, how does one become a Christian?"

After weeks of tabulating, Ney's team found that an astounding 97 percent of the students said they did *not* know how to become a Christian.

Ney took the findings to Bill. She later recalled: "As he looked at survey after survey, he said, 'They don't know how. They don't know how.' And he put his head down and just sobbed for a long time.... All my life, as I thought about Bill, I thought, *That is the heart of that man.*"

CHAPTER 12

Home Front

———————————

I n Campus Crusade's earliest days, Bill used the proceeds from his business interests to pay staff recruits $100 a month with room and board.
But as the ministry quickly grew and his business resources were out-
stripped, Bill saw that he would soon be spending most of his time fund-
raising if he were to pay everyone.

"Lord, what am I going to do?" he prayed. God's apparent answer, he
would recall, "was immediate, direct, and simple: Require each staff member
to raise his or her own support." He consulted Vonette, she agreed, and a
major policy shift ensued.

This turned out to be a key to the rapid growth of the ministry's staff.
Each recruit, after all, had access to his or her own base of resources, resources they might not have considered.

Bill and Vonette began countless hours putting together the training to
help Crusaders raise their own support. It was extremely detailed—the chief
characteristic of all Crusade training—right down to instructions about
being sure one had a breath freshener, proper dress, and the right opening
and closing words to give individuals or groups.

As time went on, several unforeseen benefits emerged from the policy of
requiring each staff member to raise financial support:

- It gave each of them autonomy, as opposed to any cultlike dependence on Bill or any other leader except the Lord. Each staff member
  became, in effect, the "president" of his or her own "subministry." He
  or she had a sense of ownership of the ministry and could say, "This

81

is *my* ministry, not Bill Bright's." One staff member would describe the approach as "highly relational, highly individualized; you must find your own people, in your own way, talk to them, stay in touch with them. It's not a program." Meanwhile, any tendency toward unhealthy independence among the staff was countered by common commitment to Bill's vision to "fulfill the Great Commission in our lifetime" and the voluntary submission to the ministry's operating standards. (A further unifying factor: In decades to come, staff members would be contributing a 5-percent share of their individual financial support to Crusade's international efforts, plus another 7 percent to the ministry's administrative overhead.)

- The common experience of having to raise financial support gave all the staff members a further bond with one another. They knew they weren't alone in whatever difficulties they encountered in raising support. And virtually every staff member was on another staff member's financial support team.

- Raising financial support was something the staff also had in common with their ministry leaders, including Bill Bright himself. They could view themselves before God as being every bit as disciplined and credible in the ministry as he was.

- They also experienced the encouragement of being the focus of a team of supporters who not only provided money, but also offered their calls, letters, and prayers.

Despite the strength of this approach, Bill was slow to let go of pursuing ways in which he could personally develop more revenue streams to help fund the ministry. He was still in the mode of exploring what he could do for God when, as he would later explain, God wanted to demonstrate what He could do in and through Bill.

Bill once purchased a couple of well-drilling rigs and, following the example of his successful grandfather, launched Bright's Oil Company. Perhaps the Lord would bless this endeavor in such a way that the ministry could be endowed from his oil investments. "I envisioned making millions of dollars which we could invest in the cause of Christ."

He and his partners drilled several wells in Oklahoma, which slowly began to pay off. One day word came of a particularly big oil discovery. But when Bill went to Oklahoma, he learned that one of his partners had illegally drilled an offset well on adjoining land.

"You're not in this deal," his partner told Bill.

Bill simply turned on his heel, got in the car, and drove back to California. "When you're a slave of Jesus," he would later observe, "it saves you a lot of heartache. This was the Lord's problem, not mine, because everything I now owned had been given to Him. This fellow was stealing the Lord's property, not mine." The right response, he knew, was to "take your losses and move on."

Later the partner's offset well was flooded with water and ruined.

Meanwhile Bill and Vonette learned over time that the probability of their bearing children was remote. Their hearts ached, and questions burst on their minds: Why? What about our dreams for having many children? What is God trying to tell us? Is one of us being punished? What can we do now? Is there medical research we should know about, something experimental? Does this mean we should plan to adopt? Or should we channel all our parenting energies into the ministry?

They shed tears. But having signed the Contract, they soon came to a point of being able to say amid this crisis, "Thank You, God. And although we don't understand it all, we accept Your leading this way in our lives."

Acceptance of circumstances, Bill would explain years later, is the role of a slave. Whatever needs the Master permits in the life of the slave are the Master's responsibility to meet. It is not for the slave to rush out and fix the situation for the Master or, even worse, to rise up and rebel. The slave is to present the need to the Master and rest in the Master's handling of it. This requires total trust in the Master's honor, justice, and goodness. The slave awaits the Master's move and the Master's provision.

In this particular arena for Bill and Vonette, the Master did in time make provision for what might have become a void in their lives. In 1954 they were able to adopt a baby boy whom they named Zachary. Four years later they adopted another son, naming him Brad.

Bill and Vonette quickly began to enjoy the uniquenesses of children and the distinct challenges of parenthood. Through the years it seemed uncanny how much the boys behaved as if they were conceptions of Bill and Vonette. Zac took after Bill in many ways—quieter, creative, often reflective, thoughtful, and caring. Brad was his Mom's child—more extroverted, assertive, and confident. Both sons reflected their parents' intelligence. No one on the outside had any reason to think they were not the Brights' biological children.

As the boys asked questions, Bill and Vonette communicated honestly about their adoptions, though volunteering only as much information as they knew their sons could understand. There was a theme to Bill and Vonette's responses: What difference does it make? Some children are naturally born to a family, some are adopted; neither way of arriving makes a child more superior in a family.

Bill and Vonette decided not to publicize the fact of the boys' adoption. Although they gave Zac and Brad freedom to share this information with others if they wished, they also fostered the approach that this was essentially "family business," and the boys understood and agreed.

During these child-rearing years, Vonette felt the tug of being all things to all people. She was immersed both in mothering and in ministry to the extent of being overloaded. This finally prompted Bill and Vonette's decision to have her back off from her ministry duties as a director of staff training, a writer of the policy manual, an editor for Crusade publications, and leader of Crusade's women's involvement. Bill told her how much he needed her first as a wife, then as the mother to their sons, and only third as a staff member. Now she could redirect her drive from the ministry to concentrate on developing their sons—going to PTA meetings, getting involved in Boy Scouts, and pursuing other activities purely for the boys' sakes.

She would also support her husband in his leadership of Campus Crusade for Christ, and lead the boys in such a way that they wouldn't feel slighted by their father's ministry. This meant pulling out maps and tracking their father's travels around the world, discussing the cultures of the countries he traveled, praying together for him and for the fulfillment of the Great Commission, and sharing Bible passages with the boys. Vonette made it a mission.

She reasoned that Bill had received a call upon his life, having been given a vision of helping to reach the entire world with the gospel. He had accepted the Great Commission as personally binding upon him as one member of a great army of God. A primary obligation of the soldier is to go to the battle. Therefore he would have to be on the go most of the time. He was compelled to travel the world, since spiritual troops had to be recruited, trained, and inspired worldwide. Vonette accepted her partnership in that vision.

She made no big deal of this choice; it was merely something God had assured her was His will for her life. But in later years Bill would weep upon reflection of Vonette's commitment to being a complementary partner in his life, always fitting in and flexing according to the family's needs at the moment. He was convinced she was not "throwing her life away," as militant feminists would later suggest about homemakers; she was, in fact, making the wisest investment of her life in the high calling of wife and mother.

Meanwhile Bill promised that wherever he was in the world he would return at any time Vonette or their sons needed him. He also promised that when he was at home, they were always his priority and they could interrupt him at any time.

As Bill traveled in those child-rearing years, he and Vonette and the boys talked regularly on the telephone. Bill called almost every evening he traveled, sent postcards every other day or so, and brought home gifts, which Zac and Brad looked forward to, they later confessed, about as much as their father's return.

When the Brights moved to Campus Crusade's new headquarters at Arrowhead Springs in the San Bernardino Mountains of Southern California, Zac was seven years old and Brad was three. Besides playing ball, their favorite activities with Dad now included hiking in the hills or, Bill's favorite, riding a borrowed dune buggy. He would also nurture their sense of the family's destiny by pulling his sons into various meetings with famous people. Zac and Brad got to see firsthand the revolutionaries who were committed to helping fulfill the Great Commission.

There were, however, all too few father-son activities for these growing boys; it was in fact a sacrifice for them to do without Dad. By God's grace they came through with balanced lives. Their mother's example was especially helpful. Both Brad and Zac would later say they could recall no occasion when their mother bemoaned Bill's absence. Eventually they concluded that if she could handle his absence patiently and quietly in dependence on the Lord, so could they.

As with almost everything, Bill and Vonette shared with the other Crusade staff their thinking about how to pursue their family life. This was done first in small groups, then larger ones. The way they chose to handle their parenting roles became a model for the entire Crusade movement, not by dictate but by the staff's own decisions to incorporate Bill and Vonette's principles into their own family lives.

The Brights' example also influenced staff policies and procedures. Credibility in the homes of staff members became an institutional priority. Marriage between staff members was encouraged; wives and husbands were seen as full partners in the ministry. For the Brights and for others on Campus Crusade's staff, everything at home had something to do with the higher purposes of the God who so loved the world.

CHAPTER 13

The World

Go ye into all the world…." At first the *go* of the Great Commission had been foremost in Bill's thinking. Further into the 1950s, he began increasingly to concentrate on *the world* in that command, with Asia as the first focus.

Jesus had said, "For unto whomsoever much is given, of him shall be much required" (Luke 12:48). Bill looked at America's wealth, far more than enough to reach the world with the gospel within a single generation. How could the potential of America's wealth be unlocked? It probably depended on the average American Christian, Bill thought. And that was a problem. How could Bill be serious about reaching the world for Christ if the average American Christian's priorities were so out of kilter?

Reaching the world, Bill concluded, would take both a revival in America as well as the dedication of committed "nationals" serving in their own lands. So he began to pray for these nationals even while focusing his work on Americans. He continued to find inspiration in the Scriptures. "One is overwhelmed with the magnitude of this task," he wrote, "but the problems that faced the first-century Christians were infinitely greater."

More and more, Bill traveled the globe recruiting campus-based ministry leaders. His goal was for nationals to take immediate ownership of their own nationally controlled ministries; Americans would help with literature, training, and some funds, but responsibility and authority for doing the work would belong to nationals themselves.

At the time, most American mission groups had policies that essentially made Americans in charge of the mission in a foreign land. Bill, on the other hand, was totally open to training a foreign national to lead the ministry in his or her country. Looking back, he would say, "I didn't know any better but to think of the Great Commission as would a businessman: A national already knows the language and the culture of his nation, so all he needs is training, tools, techniques, and materials."

Much of this national-oriented policy developed as Bill shared his thinking with Dr. Joon Gon Kim, a lean and thoughtful Korean who had come to study at Fuller Theological Seminary. He and Bill met frequently to discuss the possibility of his launching Campus Crusade for Christ in South Korea.

Bill was awed by the story of Kim's survival of a communist attack on his home village in Korea. On a rainy spring day, communist guerrillas invaded the village, intent upon killing everyone in their path. Kim's wife and father were murdered, and Kim himself was beaten and left for dead. In the cool rain of the night he revived and fled to safety in the mountains with his young daughter. They were the sole survivors.

As a man of God, Kim had learned from Scripture that he was to love his enemies and pray for those who persecuted him. What was to be his attitude concerning those who had killed his beloved wife and honored father? The Spirit of God impressed upon him that he was to seek out the communist chief who led the guerrilla attack, tell him that he loved and forgave him, and tell him of God's love in Christ and his need for the Savior.

This he did, and God honored his obedience. The communist chief knelt in prayer with Kim and committed his life to Christ. Within a short time a number of other communists were converted to Christ as well, and Kim helped them build a church for themselves and other communist converts before he came to America to further his education.

After completing his work at Fuller Seminary, Kim on one occasion was a houseguest with Bill and Vonette before his return to South Korea. He and Bill had late-night discussions about Kim's calling from God and the future of Campus Crusade in Korea. The next morning, at the breakfast table, Vonette noticed that Kim seemed hesitant to take food. He seemed troubled.

"Please, eat!" Vonette urged him.

Finally he explained that, although he was very thankful for the food, he simply could not take it—he had vowed not to eat until he had successfully launched Campus Crusade for Christ in Korea!

That was but a glimpse of the devotion, discipline, and character of the man who was both the first Campus Crusade national committed to return to his homeland to help change the world for Christ and Crusade's first national director outside the United States. Kim's faith and his program for advancing the Great Commission quickly took root in South Korea, which was mostly Buddhist at the time.

While Kim envisioned large undertakings, he also persistently practiced one-on-one evangelism with persons from all walks of life, including national leaders. Among those he personally discipled were the daughter and son-in-law of South Korea's president.

The Campus Crusade ministry thrived under Kim's direction. By 1964 he and his staff of fifteen had won thousands of students to Christ.

As Bill and Kim continued working together—sharing the Bible, evangelism and discipleship methods, and the vision of fulfilling the Great Commission through Campus Crusade for Christ in partnership with churches and mission bodies worldwide—Bill became increasingly convinced that he was being yoked with an anointed man of God.

Another of Bill's key national recruits was Kundan Massey, a Pakistani intellectual and devoted believer who, like Kim, was someone Bill met at Fuller Seminary. After Kundan returned to his homeland, he launched Campus Crusade for Christ in Pakistan, the second outpost for the ministry outside the United States. Within five years, despite intense political, religious, and social oppression of Christians, hundreds of students had been reached and were receiving regular training and discipling from Kundan and his staff of four.

Bill's pattern continued to be partnering with peoples of other lands and trusting them to reach their own. He traveled the world recruiting leaders and coaching them into bold undertakings.

The result was several more beachheads for the Campus Crusade movement elsewhere in Asia and throughout the world: in the Middle East in

1959, in Latin America in 1962, in Canada and Europe in 1967, and in Africa in 1968. Bill's recruitment of international leaders exploded.

Meanwhile Campus Crusade became a literature partner with scores of missionary organizations, and the Four Spiritual Laws were taught on every continent. Whatever the language or culture, the simple diagrams effectively communicated the love of God and the tragic condition of sinful human beings separated from a holy God and the amazing news of what God did in Jesus Christ to bring them back to Himself—the good news that still blazed in Bill Bright's heart.

CHAPTER 14

Spiritual Breathing

Bill Bright knew that God's Word commanded him to be filled with and controlled by the Holy Spirit (Ephesians 5:18, TLB). And Bill truly wanted to soar—all the time.

But he wasn't perfect—"far from it," he would say, often describing himself as a "depraved termite." Sometimes he snapped at people. He gave orders when he could nurture people instead. He demanded when he could coach. He wrestled with selfishness, a desire for power, and weariness in the face of duty and demands, both in the ministry and in his family. He sometimes found himself frustrated—defeated, powerless, and disobedient.

He struggled for the key to this dilemma. He reasoned that his intellect, his emotions, and his will all needed to converge in obedience to God, but this was something that simply did not "happen" very often. Yet he also knew God was not devious; He wouldn't give us commands that we have no hope of ever obeying.

Bill kept searching for the rational relationship between God's commands and God's power versus man's sinfulness and human frailty. Bill had tumbled these issues through his mind for years. He wrestled with them, identifying completely with the apostle Paul's words in Romans 7:15-17,19-20:

> I don't understand myself at all, for I really want to do what is right, but I can't. I do what I don't want to—what I hate. I know perfectly well that what I am doing is wrong, and my bad conscience proves that I agree with these laws I am breaking. But I

can't help myself because I'm no longer doing it. It is sin inside me that is stronger than I am that makes me do these evil things....

When I want to do good, I don't; and when I try not to do wrong, I do it anyway.... It is plain where the trouble is: sin still has me in its evil grasp. (TLB)

Whatever the solution, Bill knew it would require faith—trusting God in the face of circumstances to operate according to His promises, and expectantly depending on God to provide the strength to succeed in that obedience.

Bill recognized that God had promised to forgive our acts of sin as we confess them (1 John 1:9), thereby indicating that we have the same mind as He does about our sin—hating it, sensing it as a stench to be fled.

Bill also considered carefully the relationship between two critical statements in Paul's epistles. The first was the command, "In every thing give thanks: for this is the will of God in Christ Jesus concerning you" (1 Thessalonians 5:18). In everything? Including the awareness of one's bent toward sinning? Yes, because "it is God which worketh in you both to will and to *do* of his good pleasure" (Philippians 2:13).

There it was! Bill saw that the solution was to roll the problem of human weakness right back onto the Creator and claim the promise of God (1) to forgive our act of sin and (2) to enable within us the very obedience He requires, an enabling that comes by His Spirit through our faith-filled response to His promises.

One night when Bill was in Portland, Oregon, for a Lay Institute for Evangelism, these truths came together for him in another manifestation of loving logic from God. Bill coined a term for his discovery: Spiritual Breathing.

Jesus had said the Spirit of God was like the blowing wind. Spirit. Wind. Oxygen. Inhale it! Sin, meanwhile, was a pollutant. Exhale it!

So it was up to the human will to decide whether to keep choking on the pollution of sinful acts, with no faith at work, or to take God up on His promises to control and empower the follower who asked for the control of the Spirit.

Once again Bill Bright was taking profound biblical truths and bringing them down to a practical level where people could see, taste, and touch them.

Spiritual breathing, Bill later wrote, "has enriched my life as has no other truth." He described it as "a process of exhaling the impure and inhaling the pure, an exercise in faith that enables you to experience God's love and forgiveness and to walk in the Spirit as a way of life.

"As you walk in the Spirit by faith, practicing Spiritual Breathing, you need never again live in spiritual defeat." He meant that a person need never remain in spiritual defeat for very long; the failures of the flesh need not govern us. We're to deal with them promptly. Once our conscience makes us aware of a sin, we're to confront and confess it and immediately ask God to resume control, to take the driver's seat. And we're to *believe* all this will happen, because God hears the prayer of earnest people asking Him to deliver on His promises.

Do all this the very moment you become aware of sin, Bill taught. Seek not only the Father's forgiveness but also the Spirit's empowerment not to go to the point or place of failure again.

"You can relax. You can say 'Thank You' when the whole world is crumbling around you because your God is sovereign and omnipotent. He holds the world in His hands, and you can trust Him. He loves you, and He promises to fight for you.

"Before I made this discovery I used to lose my patience when things went contrary to my wishes. If closed doors did not open before me, I tried to break them down if necessary. I was often tense inside and impatient with others. Then I discovered what a fool I was. Tragically, we injure our brothers with our impatience, our criticism, our thoughtlessness."

Bill was reminded that Jesus not only gave us the Great Commission but also promised that by faith we would do even greater things than He had done. Bill now saw how this promise could be fulfilled even in light of our human sinfulness. God's plan for dealing with that sinfulness was for us to decide by faith that God had forgiven those sins through the death of His Son as the only acceptable sacrifice and payment for them. We are then, by faith, to agree with God about the wrongness of those acts, to turn away from the self-control that was the source of them, and to call in Spirit control. By faith we can then find in His promises the strength to do those "greater" things in life's adventure.

His developing thoughts on the Holy Spirit came into further focus on another occasion. After an extended time of travel and work, Bill and Vonette had gone to a friend's cottage on the California coast for a two-day break. Bill fell exhausted into bed that night but found he couldn't sleep.

He had been asking himself, What if the average Christian were Spirit-filled, yielded to God, and able to communicate the Good News? What if the church were really on fire? If only…

He was inspired and had to write. God was saying something important that would dramatically accelerate the vision of helping to fulfill the Great Commission in his lifetime. He had no paper handy, but he did find a few pieces of cardboard that came with laundered shirts.

On the cardboard he first wrote down the opening words of Christ's promise in Acts 1—"You shall receive power." Then he explained our need for supernatural strength in personal sharing of our faith and asked the question, "Have you made the wonderful discovery of the Spirit-filled life?"

Bill incorporated his thoughts that night into a booklet on the Holy Spirit that would become widely used in Crusade ministry, with an estimated fifty million copies printed. It spelled out what to do about the sin problem *after* a person had become a Christian, concisely conveying the problem of self-centered living versus Christ-centered living and explaining how to be filled with the Holy Spirit to receive power for holy living and a fruitful witness for Christ. It explained with clarity the relationship between inner peace and outer stress and the issue of why believers who focused on self rather than the Savior tended to lead lives that were so similar to the lives of nonbelievers.

The booklet's message was centered on an illustration showing three circles representing three lives—a life without Christ, filled with inner turmoil; a life with Christ present but strained by inner turmoil because it is still self-directed; and a life with inner peace because Christ as Lord is directing it.

Many both inside and outside the Campus Crusade movement would later say that of all Bill's writings, this booklet on the Holy Spirit was the most essential to their own lives and to those they ministered to. Bill later developed the booklet's teachings more extensively in his book *The Key to Supernatural Living*. From that night in the borrowed beach cottage and the scribbled cardboard came a profound package of personal power that was essential for fulfilling the calling God had given to Bill Bright and so many others.

CHAPTER 15

The Arrowhead Story

L ate in 1956, a five-acre retreat center in Mound, Minnesota—on Lake Minnetonka just west of Minneapolis—had been donated to Campus Crusade, which now had more than sixty staff members serving on two dozen campuses in ten states. The following spring, staff members had descended on the site and, in the fashion of an old-fashioned barn raising, built a chapel with a seating capacity of 150 to enhance the Mound facility's usefulness as a training center. But the Minnesota center had been outgrown almost from day one.

By 1961 the Crusade staff had grown to more than a hundred people serving Christ on forty campuses in fifteen states. Ministries were established in Korea and Pakistan, and Bill was speaking on a weekly Crusade radio broadcast carried by a handful of California stations. Bill and the team knew they must find larger facilities somewhere to accommodate effective training for the growing staff of an expanding ministry.

It was then that word came from a longtime friend, Los Angeles businessman George Rowan, that the Arrowhead Springs Hotel and Spa in the San Bernardino Mountains was for sale at "a greatly reduced price." This fabulous 1,800-acre property featured a 136-room executive hotel owned at one time by Conrad Hilton. There were also 10 private bungalows, dormitory facilities for several hundred, an auditorium that could accommodate 700 people, a recreation house, 4 tennis courts, a stable, and 2 big swimming pools.

The site, noted for its mineral hot springs, had been a place of healing for various Indian tribes long before the first hotel and spa were built there in 1854. The current hotel had been built in 1939 with financing from a group of film stars. Present for the gala opening had been some of the biggest names in Hollywood and the business world. Rudy Vallee, Al Jolson, and Judy Garland entertained on that first night, and Esther Williams performed in the swimming pool.

Bill sent Gordon Klenck, who was then serving as his personal associate, to investigate the property and evaluate its suitability for conversion into a Campus Crusade training headquarters. The normally conservative Gordon came back saying, "This facility would revolutionize our ministry and increase our outreach a hundredfold."

As Bill went himself to view the property, driving up the mountain with George Rowan reminded him of his many trips to nearby Forest Home with Teacher Mears and others. Here in the same mountain range was a facility that had the potential to immediately propel the Campus Crusade ministry to wider effectiveness.

"The remoteness and beauty of the property immediately enchanted me," Bill noted from that first visit to Arrowhead. "The grounds were beautiful and quiet. In a way, an ethereal quality permeated the place, and more than once I found myself almost whispering to Mr. Rowan as we walked among the many buildings." The facility had been vacant for a few years, so Bill expected to find it somewhat deteriorated. But it was in good condition. The beds were even made; spare linens were in the closets; and china, silverware, and cooking utensils were ready and waiting for guests.

All they had to do was buy it and move in…*if* they could find $2 million. That was the seller's firm asking price, George Rowan told Bill. It was a good value, only a fraction of the property's appraised worth of $6.7 million.

Bill excused himself from Rowan to go back inside the hotel alone to pray. "I moved past the unattended reception desk, through the empty lobby, out into the entrance of the glass-enclosed Wahni Room, the click of my shoes echoing as I walked. There was a shiny bar, empty of customers. Behind it, glasses were neatly stacked, awaiting business. The shelves, where a good supply of bottles once stood, were now empty. Tables and chairs were grouped in intimate clusters so holiday visitors could look out on the city, which I could imagine would be a starry wonder at night. But it was broad daylight at that moment, and I had not come there for a drink or to see the panoramic view, but to share with the Lord the dream that was working overtime in my head."

Bill knelt and prayed. Suddenly, "I heard the Lord say, 'I've been saving this for you.'" The voice wasn't audible, but it was as real to Bill as if the words had been shouted over a loudspeaker.

Tears filled his eyes. Immediately, he claimed Arrowhead Springs as God's property, then prayed, "But how, Lord? How?"

Buying the property seemed impossibly beyond the reach of an organization which, in Bill's words, had "never had an extra dollar in its ten years of existence." He couldn't conceive of any scenario in which they could raise such a large amount of money.

Bill knew that to become involved in fund-raising for such a big project could potentially sabotage Crusade's spiritual ministry. He felt certain the Lord did not want him to write letters inviting people to invest, believing instead that God had a plan already working.

For fourteen months, Bill, Vonette, and other members of the Campus Crusade staff asked God to provide the funds in some supernatural or unusual way if He wanted them to have the property. Meanwhile the staff completed a feasibility study of the property and a cost analysis of what would be involved in operating and maintaining the facility.

The situation also prompted Bill and Vonette to pray "that everything God would do through Campus Crusade for Christ and through our own personal lives would be characterized by the supernatural and the miraculous." They wanted God to do things in such an unusual and wonderful way that onlookers would realize He was responsible, bringing glory to God instead of to man.

Bill began telling a few friends and key Crusade supporters about the property. He was told by some of them that purchasing Arrowhead might be foolhardy and poor stewardship of the Lord's money. Others believed differently and supported their convictions with offers to help make the down payment.

After prayerful consideration of the advice and financial backing he'd received, Bill made an offer for Crusade to purchase the property with an initial $15,000 deposit plus a $130,000 down payment due within thirty days after signing the contract. The rest of the purchase price would come later in monthly payments. Amazingly, the offer was accepted. "With an empty bankbook we were buying a $2 million property! It was the greatest act of faith I'd ever had a part in."

Bill had to borrow the $15,000 for the deposit. Nor did Crusade have the remaining $130,000 for the down payment, but at the last minute the money was donated by interested friends. On December 1, 1962, Campus Crusade for Christ International moved into its new headquarters and training center at Arrowhead Springs.

The monthly payment schedule was a stiff one, and there followed more financial cliff-hanging experiences that forced the Brights and the Campus Crusade staff to depend wholly upon the Lord. For years, every financial move by the organization was a precarious one. But God used the faith, work, and prayers of a dedicated staff and faithful financial partners to make possible the Arrowhead dream.

Hundreds of young men and women were now coming for training to Arrowhead. Bill would later say, "The decision to acquire Arrowhead Springs as our international headquarters and institute for evangelism for the worldwide ministry was to be one of the most significant ones that we had ever made."

A dedication service was scheduled for May 17, 1963. Meanwhile, George Rowan, the businessman who had first connected Bill with Arrowhead Springs, had started drilling for a steam well on the property, with its abundance of hot springs. Steam has great value for generating electricity and, if discovered on the site, would be very valuable for the Arrowhead operations.

On the night before the dedication service, the crew was rushing to drill as deeply as possible and reached a depth of five hundred feet. They had not yet struck any sign of steam or any large vein of thermal water, and it looked doubtful that anything would come of their work. On the following day, out of respect for the scheduled dedication program, they held off from their noisy drilling.

Meanwhile several hundred people gathered for the dedication service. U.S. Congressman Walter Judd of Minnesota delivered the main address. Also participating in the program were Dr. Bob Pierce, president of World Vision; Dr. Dick Hillis, president of Overseas Crusade; Armin Gesswein, director of Pastors' Revival Fellowship Association; Dr. Carlton Booth, professor of evangelism at Fuller Theological Seminary; Dr. Roger Voskyle, president of Westmont College; and evangelist, pastor, and radio preacher Dr. John MacArthur.

Bill closed the dedication program with a prayer, asking God "that there might flow rivers of living water from this center of training, that a great spiritual blessing would engulf the world through the tens of thousands of men and women trained here in the ministry of evangelism, proclaiming near and far the good news of God's love and forgiveness in Christ."

He didn't realize that at the same moment, on a mountainside a few hundred yards above the ceremony, the water pressure broke through the porous granite at the drilling site and began to flow in a stream of hundreds of gallons of hot water per minute.

Only moments after the benediction, George Rowan came running back from the well, out of breath. "We hit an ocean of hot water!" he told Bill.

"When?" Bill asked.

"About five minutes ago." Bill realized it was the exact time he had been praying for rivers of living water to flow from Arrowhead Springs to the world. "We interpreted this as being symbolic of what God was going to do spiritually," Bill recalled. "Just as this great artesian well was thrust forth, so was God to send forth His blessing from Arrowhead Springs to the far reaches of the world."

Among those present for the dedication ceremony was Guy Atkinson, one of the world's leading construction experts. He had been in on the biggest of projects—Grand Coulee Dam, the Hanford atomic works, military installations in Alaska, railways and highways in Greece and Okinawa, and what was then the world's largest hydroelectric project, the Mangla Dam in Pakistan. Sharp, alert, and astute, this was a man whose eighty-five years had been spent thinking big. He was a perfect match for Bill.

Atkinson was keenly interested in future plans for the property. Bill recalls fielding more questions from Atkinson about the ministry of Campus Crusade for Christ than he had ever been asked before.

Atkinson expressed interest in helping pay for the property, but first he sent his attorney to review the ministry's financial records, corporate structure, and bylaws. Finally in 1964 he announced that he would provide $300,000 of the balance due on the purchase if Campus Crusade raised the rest—a total of more than $1.5 million—in exactly one year. Bill agreed. "We set forth with enthusiasm and determination to raise a sum so great that I could hardly comprehend the amount. It might as well have been a billion dollars, yet we were confident that God would help us."

As the months went by and the goal seemed increasingly impossible, a plan came together for selling off 400 acres of the property for $1 million, representing the major part of Crusade's required amount. A group of twenty businessmen agreed to purchase the 400-acre portion, using a loan from an insurance company. Nevertheless, as the deadline of June 30, 1965, approached, the total raised was still short of the funding needed.

A week before the deadline, Dr. V. Raymond Edman, president of Wheaton College, was at Arrowhead Springs to speak at an educators' conference, and he shared with Vonette and Bill a verse that God had given him that morning while he was praying for their needs: "He that putteth his trust in me shall possess the land, and shall inherit my holy mountain" (Isaiah 57:13). He later sent a $5,000 check for the mountain property purchase. Bill never forgot that encouragement.

In the last two hours before the midnight deadline on June 30, five different miraculous donations produced the final $33,000, including the last $5,000 at 11:58 P.M. An immediate and unforgettable praise gathering erupted in the auditorium at Arrowhead. "It was a beautiful experience," Bill remembered. "One of the highlights of my spiritual life. Never have I heard the doxology sung with such vigor. Never did the lyrics, 'Praise God from whom all blessings flow,' hold so much meaning." Bill immediately sent a letter to Crusade supporters announcing the miracle.

But then came heartbreaking news regarding the $1 million that was supposed to result from selling off part of the Arrowhead property. To achieve that amount, an appraiser reported that the portion of land required for the sale would have to be 520 acres rather than 400.

Guy Atkinson was disturbed by these developments and immediately asked for a meeting with Bill. He firmly opposed the sale of the property at the lower price-per-acre required by the appraiser's report. "You would be foolish to sell at this price," Atkinson told Bill. "Whatever you do, don't sell it." Otherwise, he said, he would withdraw his contribution.

Bill realized that Atkinson, because of his warm friendship and interest in Campus Crusade, was seeking to prevent the ministry from making an unwise move. Nevertheless, this was a crushing blow. After escorting Atkinson back to his car, Bill returned to his office, closed the door behind him, fell on his knees, and wept.

"All our hopes and dreams had suddenly crumbled.... We were in an impossible position financially. Not only could we not write off the debt, but we would actually lose the property unless God intervened immediately, which seemed rather remote in those bleak moments of discouragement. Furthermore, I would have to write the thousands of friends who had just read only a few days before that God had worked a miracle and tell them there had been no miracle at all. There was personal humiliation involved, of course. But worse than that, the cause of Christ would suffer, and many Christians would be confused."

What was he to do? Bill got out his Bible and looked for help and assurance. He was admonished and assured that "all things work together for good to them that love God, to them who are the called according to his purpose" (Romans 8:28). He read that "without faith it is impossible to please him" and that "the just shall live by faith" (Hebrews 11:6; 10:38). He also read a command from God that on several previous occasions had proved very meaningful: "In everything give thanks: for this is the will of God in Christ Jesus concerning you."

Bill quickly processed a faith logic. He knew of no better way to demonstrate faith than to tell God, "Thank you." So he got back down on his knees and, through his tears, thanked God for what had happened. "I thanked

Him that in His wisdom and love, He knew better than I what should be done, and that out of this chaos and uncertainty I knew would come a far greater miracle. There on my knees, while I was giving thanks for this great disappointment, God began to give me the genuine assurance that this greater miracle was really going to happen."

Even so, the next day Bill drafted the dreaded letter to inform friends that "the miracle" had been only a mirage. He held back, though, from mailing the letter.

Ten days later, Atkinson called and offered a plan that involved borrowing the required additional money from the same insurance company that was loaning money to the twenty businessmen for purchasing the land; the twenty men were to sign the notes as guarantors. If all parties approved of the deal, Atkinson said, he would still give the amount he had originally pledged.

When everyone agreed to this arrangement, Bill viewed this second miracle as even greater than the first. He tore up his letter of apology and instead sent another explaining all that God had done:

> To God be the glory, great things He has done! I wanted to take this opportunity to explain this change in plans so that our friends who have been so faithful to pray for and invest in this project would be acquainted with God's miraculous provision.... Join with us in giving thanks and praise to Him.

CHAPTER 16

More Miracles, More Trust

O
n so many occasions Bill found himself leading a ministry that seemed to exist from surprise to surprise and miracle to miracle, in large ways and small, in immediate answer to prayer as well as after long periods of waiting.

One Saturday morning, Bill was alone on his knees in the office, praying for an urgent need the ministry had for $485. He heard a knock at the door; it was the mailman, carrying a registered letter.

"It's a good thing you were here," the mailman said, "or I wouldn't have been able to leave this letter."

Bill signed for it and went back into his office where, "while I was praying, God suggested I open the letter." Inside he discovered a bank note for $500 sent by a couple in Zurich, Switzerland, whose entire family had become Christians through Bill's ministry when they were in California. They wrote that they simply wanted to express their appreciation for what God was doing in and through their lives as a result of Bill's ministry. The $485 need was met.

Years later, Bill received a call one evening in his hotel room from Crusade's office manager, who reported an urgent need for $10,000. "Do you know where we can get it?" she asked.

Bill didn't. "The only thing and the best thing I knew to do was simply to ask the Lord." He suggested they pray over the phone. Together they asked God to supply the money. "We reminded the Lord that this is His work and that to the best of our ability we were seeking to do His will. We claimed His promise that if we ask anything according to His will, He hears and answers us."

An hour later Bill received another call. It was a friend, Wes Ney, a new Christian in Louisville, Kentucky. Wes said that Bill had been on his heart and he wondered if the Lord was trying to tell him to help out with any particular need the Crusade ministry might have.

Bill told him what he had just been praying about. "You don't know anybody who has a surplus ten thousand dollars floating around, do you?" he chuckled.

That was a sizable amount of money, Wes replied, but he promised to see what he could do and call back within an hour.

An hour later Wes called to say that he was sending the money. "Call it a loan without interest," he added. "I'd like to make a gift later, but I'm short on cash and I'm not sure I can swing it at this time."

A year later Wes asked Bill to consider the ten thousand as a gift, not a loan—his business had profited greatly, and he wanted Campus Crusade to have the money.

On another occasion the ministry's desperate need was for forty-eight thousand dollars to meet a scheduled payment on the Arrowhead Springs loan. Bill and the staff had already prayed much and worked hard to raise the money, but to no avail.

The deadline was only days away when a lawyer friend who knew of the need introduced Bill to someone who agreed to loan the needed amount for sixty days. Bill was in the lawyer's office ready to sign the papers when someone from the Crusade office called; ministry supporter Dean Griffith in Chicago wanted Bill to contact him right away. Within minutes Bill reached him at his Chicago office. "I've been praying about your need for forty-eight thousand dollars," Dean said, "and my father and I would like to send you a check for that amount today."

From these and other testings, Bill concluded: "Faith is like a muscle; it grows with exercise, and the more we know of the trustworthiness and faithfulness of God—His grace, love, power, and wisdom—the more we can trust Him."

The purchase of Arrowhead Springs had involved the ministry's biggest leap of faith, but by 1967, with Crusade's full-time staff now numbering more than eight hundred people, the facilities on the property were already taxed to capacity for staff training. Bill called together a group of businessmen, planners, and builders for counsel. A detailed proposal was soon in place for a major addition to be known as Arrowhead Springs Village. The emergency fund-raising campaign, called Operation Explosion, was quickly embraced by an anonymous group of five men who agreed to cover the $450,000 cost. A plaque on the site of the finished project honored their motives: "Arrowhead Springs Village, Donated by Five Businessmen Who Want to Give God All the Glory."

Later a new dining and auditorium facility was constructed at a cost of almost $300,000, underwritten again by anonymous friends of the ministry. Campus Crusade's mission was being multiplied by godly men and women who understood how to "lay up treasures in heaven."

In these excellent facilities at Arrowhead Springs, providentially and sacrificially supplied, an estimated 1.5 million people would receive training in the basics of Christianity and effective evangelism over the next three decades.

It was training not only in what and how to communicate spiritual truth, but also in how to rely on God's power, as evidenced especially by prayer. At Arrowhead Springs and elsewhere, many would observe Campus Crusade's emphasis on praying. Dr. Earl Radmacher, president of Western Baptist Theological Seminary in Portland, Oregon, was once invited to join a group of Crusade leaders in conducting a session for students. He later reported, "We met together for prayer before we left. We prayed on the way to the meeting in the car. We prayed when we got to the assignment before we got out of the car. All of us continued in a spirit of prayer before the meeting, and on the way home we prayed, thanking the Lord for what He had done, asking Him to continue to work in the hearts of the students. Never before had I seen such a great volume of prayer surrounding any other Christian activity. I concluded that these people associated with Campus Crusade for Christ must be truly dependent upon the Lord, or they wouldn't pray so much."

To Bill, the need for prayer was obvious: "We are engaged in a spiritual ministry, a ministry of changing people's lives, a supernatural ministry.... We must depend upon the supernatural resources to accomplish supernatural objectives."

This dependence on God came through also in Crusade's focus on knowing God's will. Bill's teaching on this topic became an important part of the ministry's recruitment message for young people who were asking, "How can I know what God wants me to do?"

Bill believed the safest approach in determining God's will is to follow what he called the Sound Mind Principle of Scripture. It is based on Paul's statement, "For God hath not given us the spirit of fear, but of power, and of love, and of a sound mind" (2 Timothy 1:7). This soundness of mind comes from conforming one's thinking to biblical teaching. "Since the Christian is to live by faith, and faith comes through an understanding of the Word of God," Bill taught, "it is impossible to overemphasize the importance of daily searching the Scriptures."

Bill developed a basic framework for discerning God's will that involved asking three questions: "Why did Jesus come?" "What is the greatest experience in my life?" "What is the greatest thing that I can do to help others?"

Each question demanded faith-filled responses. Is coming to know Jesus Christ as my personal Savior *really* the greatest experience of my life? To say no was to somehow reduce the importance of one's conversion; to say yes honestly required deep faith in the Lord and His Word and also called for an appropriate answer for the third question: Do I value God's gift of salvation enough to want to help others to receive it as well?

"We must allow Christ to so control our lives and minds," Bill urged, "that we will do those things which ultimately result in the largest number of people receiving Christ...that the fulfillment of the Great Commission might be accelerated."

He pointed out that "just as turning the steering wheel does not alter the direction of the automobile unless it is moving, so God cannot direct our lives unless we are moving for Him." And "moving for Him" could be achieved by fulfilling these basic requirements in knowing God's will:

1. There must be no unconfessed sin in your life, a requirement met by following 1 John 1:9.

2. Your life must be fully dedicated to Christ and controlled by the Holy Spirit, as taught in Ephesians 5:18 and Colossians 2:6.

3. You must walk in the Spirit, abiding in Christ moment by moment (John 15:5).

A further exercise for gaining a "sound mind" was to take spiritual inventory regularly by asking these questions:

- Is my time being invested in such a way as to introduce the greatest number of people to Christ?
- Are my talents, or spiritual gifts, being invested to introduce the greatest number of people to Christ?
- Is my money, my treasure, being invested to introduce the greatest number of people to Christ?

This last need for devotion of one's money and possessions to the cause of Christ was especially important for someone like Bill, who had been such an unabashed materialist before he became a Christian. It was an issue that also produced tension. Bill was recruiting winsome, professional people to attract others in their level of society to the cause of Christ; he had no ambition to raise up an army of impoverished monks. On the other hand, he didn't want to see any materialistic competition among "the troops" over cars, clothes, or other possessions.

As for himself, Bill had joined Vonette in renouncing materialism by signing the Contract, but they still had to relate to people of all walks of life. They seemed to be forever walking the tightrope of maintaining a professional standard of appearance without practicing materialism.

In the kind of car they drove, for example, Bill looked for the balance of being neither dowdy nor dudish. The issue came to the forefront when he was offered a free Oldsmobile by Guy Martin, a Christian car dealer in Los Angeles who years earlier had asked Bill to come and prayerfully dedicate his first automobile franchise. Bill declined the notion of personally owning the car, but he allowed it to be given to the ministry—it was his *Father's* Oldsmobile.

In the matter of clothing, Bill at one point declared he needed only one suit of clothes, since that's all he could wear at one time. Quite often on his travels, where he was spending most of his life, he did in fact carry only one suit of clothes. Meanwhile he learned the virtue of consignment shopping, especially in larger cities, where the next-to-new stores were filled with what had been expensive items when bought off the rack at Macy's, but which now sold for ten cents on the dollar. He counseled Campus Crusade staff members in such methods for saving money while still dressing impressively.

Meanwhile, as Bill traveled the nation and the world, Vonette continued holding their home together while also working on Crusade training materials and leading women's groups. She talked and prayed with Zac and Brad about developments in the ministry, helping them understand how God was leading their father in building a worldwide ministry and how their support of him counted in God's eyes.

Once, while Bill was in Rio de Janeiro on a recruitment and training trip, he received a call from Vonette with a doctor's report. She had a large growth that might be malignant. Bill was ready to drop everything and catch the next plane home, but Vonette insisted he first complete his work in Brazil.

Her surgery was set for a date immediately upon Bill's scheduled return. Meanwhile they both focused on praising and thanking God—they were His slaves, and He was their Master responsible for their welfare.

Three weeks later, after Bill returned from South America, they went to a hospital in Loma Linda for Vonette's surgery. Bill waited and prayed in the chapel. The operation was a success, and there was no malignancy.

They continued in thanksgiving, but Bill wondered aloud: "Why did God allow us to go through this experience?" He finally settled on an answer: "In order that we would be reminded of His faithfulness and learn to love, trust, and obey Him *more*."

CHAPTER 17

New Partners and a Blitz

A n array of young, talented leaders was continuing to enter the ranks of Campus Crusade for Christ. Among the new faces in 1966 was an assertive young man from the upper Midwest named Paul Eshleman, who years later would head the *Jesus* film project.

Joining that same year was a football player from Oklahoma, Dave Hannah, who approached Bill with the idea of establishing a ministry of athletes. That idea would become Athletes in Action, turning college sports venues into chapels and imparting spiritual truths in the language of athletics.

Also established in the midsixties was Crusade's high-school ministry, Student Venture, led by Carl Wilson.

It was at this time as well that Bailey Marks joined the Crusade staff as Bill's personal assistant. A businessman from Alabama, Bailey and his wife, Elizabeth, had attended a Lay Institute for Evangelism a few years earlier in Birmingham. On sixteen-millimeter, black-and-white film, they had watched a dark-haired, raspy-voiced man named Bill Bright as he taught clear, compelling concepts about Jesus Christ—how to know Him, how to communicate to others about Him, and how to "breathe spiritually" in His presence. It made sense to them, compellingly so.

As a layman, Bailey started presenting the same message to various churches in the area, taking along a sixteen-millimeter projector, Bright's message on film, some literature, and most important, his own enthusiasm. As a result, there was soon a group of businessmen in Birmingham eager to help push forward Crusade's presence in Alabama and especially to start the ministry on the state's college campuses. They planned a banquet and invited Bill; it would be an "international banquet" in which they would "adopt" a foreign country by raising five thousand dollars designated for that nation's Crusade ministry.

When Bill met them for the event he asked, "How many countries are you praying for tonight?"

Bailey replied, "Well, Dr. Bright, we were praying for Venezuela."

"Gentlemen," Bill responded, "I didn't come all the way from California to believe in God for just one country tonight." He told them they should trust God for their ability to support at least five countries.

They did raise enough money that night to adopt three countries, and within two years the same group had adopted ten more. "I didn't know a lot about faith or anything else," Bailey later observed, "but Bill caused us to open our faith to new boundaries."

The bond between Bill and Bailey would continue to deepen over the years, in the sharing of struggles and dreams and efforts, as well as in lighter moments. On one occasion they were together in Nigeria, where Bill was taking questions after speaking to a group. Although Bailey was younger than Bill, his hair had become totally white, but Bill's was jet black—partly by nature and partly by dye. During the period for questions, a woman related the confusion she felt about the two men's ages. According to their native culture, she explained, Nigerians were to give the most veneration to the oldest figure—and that would appear to be the white-headed Bailey.

"But Dr. Bright," she said, "you are older than Bailey Marks, yet your hair is black; can you explain this?"

Quick as a flash and without batting an eye, Bill responded: "That's in the providence of man.... Next question."

Bailey rollicked in laughter and never forgot it.

Bill later explained his hair-color philosophy: "When I look in the mirror, I want to see the image of a man like I feel! And so far, I feel much younger than the color of my hair would indicate. The day may come when I feel much older, and then it'll be silver."

In 1968, Bill experienced a great personal loss in the death of Guy Atkinson. After playing such a key role in the purchase and development of Arrowhead Springs, Atkinson had become one of Bill's best friends and advisors, giving time, wisdom, and financial support to the ministry.

At the same time, Art DeMoss, president of a large national insurance company, agreed to serve on Crusade's board of directors. While not replacing Atkinson, he did succeed him as a spiritual and financial giant in the life of the ministry.

Bill first met DeMoss in 1955, when Bill was between airplanes one day and found himself on a commercial bus somewhere in Tennessee. He struck up a conversation with the fellow next to him, a young man in his thirties named Arthur DeMoss. Bill discovered he was involved with a new concept in audio recording, one that used spooled wire rather than magnetic tape. Always curious about science and gadgets, Bill soon struck a friendship with DeMoss and resolved to stay in touch with this quick-witted Christian businessman.

Now, years later, DeMoss became a primary agent of vision, love, faithfulness, financial blessing, and guidance to Bill and to Campus Crusade. He and his wife, Nancy, became intimates of the Brights and forged an unending friendship.

Bill encouraged Art and Nancy to expand their personal ministry of using dinner parties for business executives in various regions around the country. The DeMosses knew from experience that this method worked for connecting with high-powered, fast-track leaders in a less formal, low-key way. These events became a part of Campus Crusade, most of them sponsored by Art himself.

In those years, Campus Crusade's list of "officers and advisory board" was a long and notable one, reflecting Bill's desire to seek the advice and involvement of trustworthy people who were well known in a variety of circles. In addition to those still serving from the beginning years—Wilbur Smith, Henrietta Mears, Billy Graham, Richard Halverson, Bob Stover, Ralph Byron, Dan Fuller, William Savage, and Edwin Orr—the list now included Wheaton College president V. Raymond Edman, Armin Gesswein of Pastors' Revival Fellowship Association, Fuller Seminary president Harold John Ockenga, Dallas Theological Seminary president John F. Walvoord, and Whitworth College president Frank Warren.

Also listed were several pastors, including Robert Munger of Seattle; Oswald J. Smith of Toronto; Harold L. Fickett of Van Nuys, California; and Martin Luther Long of Burbank.

Bill included professionals such as Tim Spencer of Hollywood Christian Group, Los Angeles publisher W. C. Jones, retired Army Lt. Gen. William K. Harrison, and business executive Harold Moore of Bakersfield, California, plus political leaders such as Governor Mark Hatfield of Oregon and Congressman Walter Judd of Minnesota.

And there were other parachurch ministry leaders such as Bob Pierce of World Vision, Lorne Sanny of the Navigators, and Abraham Vereide of International Christian Leadership.

Public support from such a distinguished group was helpful when a complicated and unsuccessful business involvement brought some negative press for the ministry in 1967.

Bill had continued to be open to business opportunities that could support Crusade, and one such plan involved the 233-unit Birkley Apartment Hotel in Fort Worth, an eleven-story, block-long building owned by the Federal Housing Administration (FHA). A Campus Crusade holding company, Campus Associates, was handling the $727,000 purchase of the building in the form of a loan from the FHA. The sale, late in 1965, was "regular in every way," FHA commissioner Philip Brownstein would conclude in a report two years later.

The concept was to lease the units to college students. With reasonable occupancy rates, there would be adequate cash flow to pay the mortgage and also provide an income stream that could be donated to Crusade itself. Campus Associates had successfully handled two similar projects in Phoenix.

But the Birkley deal didn't work out. The Texas partners whom Bill was counting on to manage the apartment complex didn't manage it successfully. The income stream for paying the loan wasn't there. The only money Campus Associates ever paid on the deal was a $22,500 payment when the apartments were first acquired.

In January 1967 the FHA decided to foreclose on the property. Three months later, the *Fort Worth Press* ran an article on the matter, with the headline "Crusade Richer, but U.S. Holds Bag" and a subhead saying, "Birkley Apts. Loan Goes Unpaid." The story quoted IRS records showing Campus Crusade with a net worth of $2.9 million as of June 1966. The implication was, Why isn't a financially healthy Christian organization paying its bills?

The pastor of a major Fort Worth church wrote Bill to say that his board of elders was concerned about the ministry's "financial policies and Christian testimony" and to ask for "any word you care to send us which may help clear up the matter."

Finally, after two years of red tape, the FHA sold the building for $675,000 to its parent agency, the U.S. Department of Housing and Urban Development, and Campus Associates got out of the Fort Worth apartment business.

Fortunately there was much better and far more significant news for the ministry in 1967, and it came from the unlikeliest of places: the Berkeley campus of the University of California, which had become synonymous worldwide with student riots, demonstrations, and radical movements of all kinds. Many of its professors were Marxists who promoted confrontation with authority as the outward expression of commitment to Marx. Communism was the preferred political ideology, and the idea was promoted that the God of the Bible and of Creation was dead.

So Bill and Campus Crusade decided to attack Berkeley with the message of Jesus Christ. Their battle plan for reaching the twenty-seven thousand students began with giving each of the six hundred participating Crusaders a list of student names and the responsibility for sharing Christ with each person on their list during the weeklong campaign. A battery of fifty telephones was set up in houses leased for the occasion. When the calls began, thousands of students made appointments for interviews, and hundreds of these would make commitments to Christ.

The Berkeley Blitz began on a Sunday afternoon with a banquet for the university's athletes, and some four hundred of them came to hear recognized sports figures give testimonies to Christ. Bill presented the plan of salvation and invited them to receive Him as their Savior. Scores of athletes prayed to receive Christ.

The following morning 125 student leaders attended a "student leadership breakfast" and heard Christian testimonies from an Arizona state senator and the student body president from Florida State University. Once again Bill followed with a message explaining who Christ is, why He came, and how the students could know Him personally. Some 40 of the leaders made decisions for Christ.

During the course of the week, another 28 special events were held for international students.

As the blitz kicked into high gear, the Crusaders issued their own syndicated news release to provide a clear description for the news media of their intent:

> A new kind of revolution talk was heard today on the steps of Sproul Hall on the campus of the University of California at Berkeley. This site has been the scene of student protests and demonstrations and unrest for several years, but today about 3,000 students gathered to hear about a different kind of revolutionary leader—Jesus Christ.
>
> The occasion was a rally put on by the Berkeley chapter of Campus Crusade for Christ, an organization that is having its national convention this week in the Berkeley Student Union building.
>
> While other students passed out handbills for and against the firing of the University of California President Clark Kerr, and others distributed buttons reading, "Impeach Reagan" [then governor of California], a folk singing group sang gospel songs with a contemporary sound and the Campus Crusade leader proclaimed a new kind of revolution.
>
> The students were asked to trust Christ as the one who has the answers to all the problems of the day and the one who can bring spiritual revolution and change to the world. They claimed that the Christian message is revolutionary because it has changed history, creating vast social reforms through reshaping the lives and attitudes of individuals.

DATES · PRUNES · APRICOTS · FIGS

BRIGHT'S

ORANGE JUICE · BRANDIES · WINES

RAISINS · PECANS · WALNUTS · HONEY

Top: Bill Bright, the young entre-
preneur of Bright's California
Confections (1946). *Inset:*
The California Confections plant.

Bill's bride on the day
she became Vonette
Zachary Bright,
December 30, 1948.

Billy Graham and Bill Bright at Forest Home Conference Center in California (1949).

Bill's discipleship mentor, Dr. Henrietta Mears, addresses a 1955 gathering of Campus Crusade supporters in her home. Bill and Vonette are at far right.

Bill in 1952 with three UCLA athletes whom he personally led to Christ. *Left to right:* football quarterback Bob Davenport, Olympic decathlon gold medalist Rafer Johnson, and football all-American Don Shinnick.

The Mears home (which she shared with Bill and Vonette for many years) was near the UCLA Campus. Bill speaks here to a Crusade gathering in the home, circa 1955.

Bill in 1958 with recruit
Dr. Joon Gon Kim,
who pioneered
Crusade's first overseas
ministry in Korea.

Dale Bright with son
Bill in 1955.

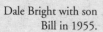

Bill and Vonette
with their two sons:
Zac, the oldest, and
Brad (1958).

Mary Lee and Dale
Bright in 1962,
on their fiftieth
wedding anniversary.

On the march in the 1960s:
Bill and Vonette with Campus Crusaders at Arrowhead Springs.

Bill joins Billy Graham
and Joon Gon Kim at
Graham's 1973 Crusade
in Seoul, South Korea.

Campus Crusade's Explo '74 in Seoul, the largest Christian
gathering in history at that time.

The tent city at Seoul's Explo '74, where more than 320,000 were trained in discipleship and evangelism during one week.

At Explo '74: Gordon Klenck, one of Bill's first recruits to Campus Crusade for Christ in 1951, with Vonette and Bill.

Left and below: Bill in the Soviet Union in 1978, more than a decade before the communist government's collapse.

Bill with sons Zac (left) and Brad in 1978.

The Brights with Dale Evans and Roy Rogers on a television special
for the 1970s Here's Life, America campaign.

In Germany, Bill draws the three circles that show how everyone
on earth is in one of three spiritual conditions.

Bill and Vonette join other Christian evangelists for the
1980 March for Jesus rally in Washington, D.C.

Bill with Pat Boone (left) and Charles Colson in 1976.

In 1983, President Ronald Reagan signs the "Year of the Bible" proclamation. Behind him, Bill Bright is flanked by U.S. Senator Bill Armstrong (left) and Congressman Carlos J. Moorhead.

In 1983, then–Vice President George Bush greets the Brights.

Bill is awarded a medal by U.S. Senator James M. Inhofe, signifying his induction into the Oklahoma Hall of Fame in 1996.

Bill receives the Templeton Prize for Progress in Religion, flanked by Prince Philip (left), Sir John Templeton, and Vonette (1996).

Bill's acceptance speech for the 1996 Templeton Prize was given in the historic Church of Santa Maria in Trastevere, Rome.

Bill meets with Pope John Paul II in Rome (1996).

The Brights in December 1998. Brad stands at left with his son, Keller;
Brad's wife, Katherine (seated next to Vonette), holds their daughter, Noel.
Behind Bill are Zac and his wife, Terry, flanked by their children,
Rebecca and Christopher.

Bill had asked Billy Graham to join the outreach on Friday, the campaign's last day. Following an evangelistic faculty breakfast that morning, an outdoor rally was scheduled at the campus amphitheater at noon. But the morning dawned with a downpour and threatened to rain out the event. Bill called the team to prayer. The clouds parted, and the sun shone through.

Approximately eight thousand students and faculty heard Graham's clear-cut presentation of the gospel as he invited the students to commit their lives to Christ. Late into that final night, the six hundred Crusaders were counseling and praying with those who had remained behind to learn how they could become Christians.

"For the first time since I've been here," recalled a thirty-year faculty veteran at Berkeley, "the topic of conversation at this university has changed from Karl Marx to Jesus Christ."

Looking back, one Crusade staff member present at the blitz said, "We exhibited some of the same boldness we saw in the early Christians in the book of Acts," although he acknowledged that over time "we found nowhere near the long-term staying power in those we reached." Nevertheless, most of the visiting Crusade staff gained such confidence from the Berkeley invasion that similar campuswide blitzes were later carried out on dozens of campuses across the nation.

The following year, Bill would include the Berkeley story, along with a summary of the Crusade world strategy, in a book he wrote and published entitled *Revolution Now!* At the same time, an event unforeseen in that strategy would bring Bill a disturbing and unforgettable jolt.

CHAPTER 18

Showdown

One night in October 1967, Bill and Bailey Marks were together on a road trip when Bill decided to talk by phone with one of Crusade's regional directors. He asked Bailey to place the call. Bailey did so and was told that the staff leader was away for a short time in Lawrence, Kansas—a location that wasn't in his area.

Bill then asked Bailey to try calling a certain leader in another region. Bailey phoned and was told that this person, too, was in Lawrence.

Their attempt to reach a third leader brought the same result—he was in Lawrence as well.

"Do you want me to call Lawrence?" Bailey finally asked.

"No," Bill answered. "We'll find out what they're doing there sooner or later."

Bill wasn't sure what might be going on in Lawrence with his leaders or what might result from it, but he had earlier picked up rumblings of discontent among the staff.

Bill and Bailey went about their business and in a few more days returned to Arrowhead. At about three o'clock in the morning following their return late the night before, Bailey received a call from one of the disaffected leaders.

"Bailey," he said, "I'd appreciate if you'd call Bill," adding that he and some other staff leaders wanted to meet with him immediately.

"You've lost your mind," Bailey responded, reminding him of the hour and of the fact that he and Bill had just come off the road.

The caller persisted. Then Bailey told him that he and Bill knew about the staff leaders getting together in Lawrence earlier that week.

There was a long silence on the other end.

"You can come in at nine in the morning," Bailey told him, "and I'll have Bill there. Don't come before then."

The following morning at nine, about twenty staff members were packed into Bill's relatively small office, including some who hadn't been involved in the designs of the leaders who had met in Lawrence.

These leaders were men whom Bill had trained to share his vision. They were gifted, articulate, able, and popular, and each had constituencies of people whom they had recruited and trained. Bill had given the men financial autonomy and had trusted them to manage reliably their areas of responsibility.

They began by reading from a typed list of concerns. The issues included Bill's leadership style and philosophy. One after another cited his failings as a leader—saying, for example, that he was dictatorial and didn't consult them.

Others assaulted Bill's ministry tactics on campus in those years when the nation's colleges seemed to be dominated by antiwar riots, moral revolution, and anything but Christianity. As one of them expressed later, "As much as we loathed to admit it, while we were busy winning the campus, the world was getting worse. We get the decisions, we get the commitments to Christ, we're building the organization and recruiting the staff, but we aren't effecting a change. We're a failure in the midst of our own success." It seemed that Bill's own bold vision and great faith had inspired great expectations that were not being met.

Concerns were also expressed about Bill's abilities. After all, virtually every leader there could claim superiority to Bill in teaching, preaching, or some other ministry skill.

Theological differences were also raised, especially with Bill's emphasis on repentance. But no charges were made against Bill's integrity or character. No one accused him of doing anything illegal, immoral, unethical, or financially imprudent.

There were six staff leaders who were the core of the dissatisfied faction along with another half-dozen or so who also seemed to believe Bill had "lost it" as a leader. But even among the others present who were not a part of the faction, little was said in Bill's defense.

The leaders were not merely presenting discussion points. They had already drawn conclusions, and the foremost was that Bill had to go. The ministry couldn't go on with him at the helm. They felt they could do a better job of leading the ministry than could its founder. They told Bill they wanted him to resign—with the inference that if he didn't, they would walk away and take with them the numerous staff they believed would follow them. They would take control of the movement.

Bill had stayed calmly seated, listening quietly and praying, looking his critics straight in the eye. He would later say, "I loved these men; I did then and I do now. I had poured myself into them. I trusted them. This was shocking, but it was as though God wrapped a protective shield around me. I didn't feel as if I had to react."

Finally, he sat back in his chair. "Let's talk about this," he said. "I've got blind spots just like anybody else, and I'm very sorry I've disappointed you." He added, however, that he didn't think he was "that blind."

He continued: "Gentlemen, there's one thing you need to know: Vonette and I started this movement by ourselves with the Lord. By the end of the day there may be only the two of us left, but we started Campus Crusade for Christ and we will continue to direct it. God gave me this vision, and I'm going to be faithful to that vision." He was loving but firm.

After two hours, the meeting ended. There was nothing more to say. The staff members left Bill's office. It remained to be seen whether they could dismantle the organization and take its people with them.

Bill closed the door and, with Bailey, went to his knees. There were tears. These young men were like sons and brothers to Bill. He had appointed them to each of their positions of responsibility. The sense of betrayal hurt deeply.

But his praying wasn't lengthy. "He just took it to the Father and left it there," Bailey recalled. "That amazed me. I would have been paralyzed for weeks. But by noon he wanted to talk about the tasks of the day. He had other things to do."

Bill had, in fact, left the matter with the Father. He had known before the hurt, embarrassment, and disappointment caused by trusted friends. The Father had been faithful then; He would be faithful now.

Bill made a call to Dr. Henry Brandt, well-known Christian psychologist and leader. He wanted the perspective of a senior figure in Christian ministry. It helped to ventilate with a mentor, however briefly. They prayed over the telephone.

Bill determined to stay focused on what was best for the movement in trying to fulfill the Great Commission. Unity was crucial. Love was paramount. Was his reservoir of trust in God up to such a draining situation? He decided he could count on God to work things out.

Vonette was unwavering in her support. Almost dutifully, Bill had told her at once the bad news. She wasn't surprised; she had heard the rumblings.

"We may have to start all over," he told her.

"We can do that," Vonette promptly replied. "If that's what it takes to have loyalty in the movement, we can do that." They prayed, hugged, and kissed. He knew he had God's promises and Vonette's assurance; that would be enough.

When Bill talked later with Roe Brooks—one of the first two staff recruits from Crusade's earliest days—Roe recalled his leader asking, "Have these men any valid objection? Have I in any way been indifferent to their feelings?"

"Well, Bill," Roe answered, "there have been some minor things that could give them grounds to say that."

Bill sat down and, through tears, asked for forgiveness.

To Bailey Marks, meanwhile, the staff members' charges amounted to blatant betrayal. He felt like going back into the business world or starting his own ministry. "Really, I would have walked away," he observed, "if it hadn't been for Bill's response."

Thinking about Bill's reaction stabilized Bailey for the moment and later began to inspire him. How could Bill have accepted their sweeping criticism so calmly? He saw in Bill a living portrait of love falsely on trial. He came to see that there really is a Christian dynamic, a Holy Spirit's control, an ability to turn the other cheek and not retaliate, an option of committing yourself to Him who judges fairly.

It emboldened Bailey, making him willing to tackle the entire world when he was later asked to oversee Crusade's Asian ministries. If Bill could conduct himself so patiently—with such "gracious goodness," as Bailey described it—then this Birmingham businessman could stay in the harness and try to see the world come to the Christ he saw in Bill Bright. But he would look back at what the staff directors had done with bewilderment and aversion, and on the rare occasions in later years when a staff member seemed to evidence a rebellious spirit, he would ask wryly, "Is this another mutiny?"

Following the confrontation, Bill did not seek to punish any of the critical leaders. He did not ask for resignations or circulate a loyalty oath or convene a meeting for a vote of confidence. He prayed, stayed in the Bible, and listened to God and to men of God.

When Bill shared what had happened with the ministry's board of directors and allowed the board to hear some of the concerns, he mentioned the possibility of mass resignations and a drop in revenues for the ministry. The board declared its total affirmation of Bill's leadership. From their standpoint, there was no issue. Bill's character had not been questioned. Bill and Vonette's marriage was loving and lasting. Virtually all of his organizational decisions were open to public scrutiny. No bylaw had been violated. The organization had certainly had its days when money didn't flow smoothly, but no financial mishandling was even considered as a context for criticism. There was nothing deceitful anywhere.

In the weeks following the showdown, Bill was inspired to write the book *How to Love by Faith*. It was simply and profoundly what he had practiced in the face of the most stinging criticism of his ministry. There seemed to be a God-given logic to what he had done, without his doing so consciously or by formula. He was under holy orders to love his enemies, even more his brothers. His obedience to those orders was not to be based upon feelings. By choosing in an act of the will to love them, he was in fact following the model of the Lord Jesus as pointed out by the apostle Peter: "Who did no sin, neither was guile found in his mouth: who, when he was reviled, reviled not again; when he suffered, he threatened not; but committed himself to him that judgeth righteously" (1 Peter 2:22-23).

The creative impetus of writing *How to Love by Faith* led later to a full array of practical how-to manuals. Bill had prayed, "Lord, what does every person need to know to be a vibrant, dynamic, fruitful witness for You?" He then wrote down what came to be called the Transferable Concepts, his effort to capture "the distilled essence of the Christian life." Bill would observe, "Our experience has proved that we can teach these transferable concepts with life-changing results in a very short period of time to any sincere Christian who wishes to know them so they can teach others also."

These concepts would include:

1. How to be sure of your salvation.
2. How to experience God's love and forgiveness.
3. How to be filled with the Holy Spirit.
4. How to walk in the control and power of the Holy Spirit.
5. How to witness for Christ effectively in the power of the Holy Spirit.
6. How to love by faith.
7. How to pray.
8. How to study the Bible.
9. How to grow in faith.
10. How to worship God.
11. How to know God's will for your life.
12. How to prepare a personal strategy to help fulfill the Great Commission in this generation.
13. How to train Christians to train others to learn these transferable concepts.

In time, the six dissatisfied regional directors left the organization—some in January 1968, some in the spring or later. But that summer, the largest gathering of new staff to date arrived at Arrowhead for training—more than six hundred persons from all over the world. Bill seized the turnout as a sign from God—the finest kind of vindication, the blessing of fruit for the labor of the faithful.

Over the years, most of the disaffected leaders came back at one time or another and apologized to Bill, with their chief spokesman acknowledging two years later that Bill had been the greatest spiritual influence in his life. Each of these men has continued in ministry in some way. Bill has continued to express his love for them and his sense of peace in his relationship with each one.

In the meantime, Bill began on multiple occasions publicly to invite "constructive criticism." He taught staff members about the role of criticism in leadership—how it can be either harmful or helpful. He did not stop being president, nor did he shift to purely consensus-based decision-making. But he avoided pressured control and insisted on submission to Christ as the head of the movement. He also found himself more sympathetic to other leaders in business, in churches, and in mission organizations who were frequently hounded by criticism.

In public, Bill did not describe the confrontation with his staff leaders, but he did speak of there having been a clash of values and of the pain he experienced and the love he chose to continue to give, even as God had given him.

Meanwhile the theological difference raised by the dissenting staff members had troubled Bill deeply. He thought the majority of them were tending toward the extremism of "easy grace," allowing one to sin with little compunction and with God's almost automatic forgiveness. Bill taught, however, that Christians have been given freedom *from* sin, not freedom *to* sin. He sensed that deep, heartfelt repentance and commitment to cease from sin were missing from the theology of some of these leaders at that time.

Their differences spawned a theological struggle that rippled through the Crusade movement. It was the issue of Christian grace—Christian liberty versus legalism. At the time, Bill listed the ways in which a Christian could move from grace to legalism:

1. Not relying upon the Holy Spirit—not being filled; trying instead of trusting.
2. Having the wrong motivation: Obeying to please men or performing in hope of receiving something from God in return.
3. Following human standards of conduct and action that are not taught in the Word of God.

CHAPTER 19

Big Ideas

Out on the road again in 1968, Bill was scheduled to address the student body at a high school in Hong Kong where the principal and others had been praying for years for revival. The principal believed it was Bill whom God would use to trigger that revival.

But early on the morning he was to speak, Bill was sick and hardly able to get out of bed. Believing God would use him in spite of his illness, he claimed His supernatural power and made it to the school. There he discovered that the interpreter for his message, a Chinese evangelist, had for several years been ill with a mysterious disease that medical specialists were unable to diagnose. He, too, had gotten up that morning out of his sickbed.

"Here we were, two very sick men delivering a message on revival," Bill recalled. "However, I had hardly spoken more than a sentence or two when I felt the supernatural healing touch of God upon me. The power was reflected in the message, and God did send revival—not only to the students and faculty, but also to this speaker."

Bill later joined the principal and others who gathered around the chronically ill evangelist and claimed the man's healing by faith. Then Bill went on his way. He learned later that within days the man was restored to fullness of health and within weeks he was on his first evangelistic speaking tour in several years. Bill came away convinced anew that prayer for healing is "a privilege and power available to believers that we can claim for the glory of our risen Savior by faith."

The same year Bill, out of curiosity, allowed a graphoanalyst to evaluate his handwriting. The analyst reached these conclusions:

> You are an extremely busy person with so many irons in the fire that you hardly know which one to pull out next. You do like people, and will always take time to stop and chat with others no matter how rushed you may be. You have a broad margin of interests: from the arts to the sciences, philosophy to psychology, sports to a good book.
>
> You seem to be happiest when creating and organizing new projects. You work well with others and expect their cooperation. Sometimes others cannot keep up with you, although you never ask them to do more than you yourself are doing. You do drive yourself a little too relentlessly at times, with some resulting problems, which I cannot begin to cover in a short analysis. Slow down a little.
>
> You are a man of many moods. Because of your changeable nature, you may sometimes be misunderstood. You may often wonder why other people react as they do and what they are really thinking.
>
> Because your feelings are so deep and long lasting, it is difficult for you to take things lightly. There are many things that happen that bother you a great deal more than you would care to admit.
>
> It is hard for you to resist good food. In fact, you are prone to overeat. And the richer the food, the better you like it.
>
> You are a fluent speaker with a real flair for showmanship.

Bill thought that pegged him pretty well. As for his fondness for rich food—well, after all, tasty foods had been his business! Bill had to admit a particular weakness for ice cream, especially peach flavor, which sparked childhood memories of those wonderful ice cream treats made with fresh peaches from his Uncle Ed's orchard. Wherever he traveled, Bill would often ask for directions to the nearest ice cream shop.

Might there be a relationship between his ice cream consumption and the extra weight he was beginning to carry? As the years sped by and his metabolism slowed down, he began to feel quite bad about his weight. Crusade had a policy on the desirable weight of its staff, and Bill tested those limits.

The policy said if one were overweight, one should be engaged in "professional efforts" to reduce. So Bill tried "every diet ever invented and then some"—as many as fifty, by Vonette's count—but none was successful long-term. After significant weight loss following months of extreme discipline, Bill found that he soon regained all he had lost—and more.

Frustrated, he referred to his appearance as "like a sack of potatoes." It bothered him, but it did give him insight into the weaknesses of the human condition.

In that larger scheme, Bill certainly had moments when "ego was on the throne," but he consciously tried to trap those sinful impulses in a net of Scriptural statements—including "I am crucified with Christ" and Jesus' command to every follower to "deny himself." His family and closest associates would testify that Bill regularly chose to follow the Way of the Book as closely as his yielded intellect and will would permit.

His weaknesses were there, and they occasionally brought criticism, but that seemed only a small part of the critical comments he and Crusade received. Bill was definitely learning that one of the perils of leading such a diverse movement as Campus Crusade for Christ was having to live with disparagement and negative feedback. There always seemed to be someone sniping at them.

In London, Bill had once taken note in Westminster Abbey of an inscription on the burial monument for a certain Lord Lawrence. It was inscribed with his name, the date of his death, and these words: "He feared man so little because he feared God so much."

Bill applied this thought several times when his back was against the wall: He did not dare to disobey what God had showed him in the Vision. Adapting the apostle Paul's statement, on rare occasions he explained his actions to critics by saying, "I couldn't be disobedient to the heavenly vision." It sounded melodramatic, but to Bill it was a simple decision: If he were going to err, it would be on the side of his intention to keep faith with God rather than mollify men.

In prayer he would leave the critics to the Lord. As for whatever additional response was needed, he would rely on promptings from his study of the Bible as well as from his inner circle of associates—his "multitude of counselors," who would testify that Bill held no grudges. He seemed to put them in a trunk somewhere and give God the key. "I don't count my critics, I weigh them," Bill once said.

Sometimes help came from other friends and supporters. In 1968 a Christian lawyer in Fort Worth wrote to Dr. John Walvoord, president of Dallas Theological Seminary. The lawyer was worried about Crusade being "liberal" (as evidenced by Bill's consorting with such "liberals" as Billy Graham!) and about the appropriateness of his own church's financial support of Campus Crusade. He wondered if Bill Bright was pushing people toward the National and World Councils of Churches (which, of course, were far removed from the evangelism and discipleship mind-set of Campus Crusade). The attorney was throwing around heavy charges, but he had the good sense to seek out Walvoord for understanding.

Walvoord replied:

> While it is entirely possible that some representatives of Campus Crusade, who often are young and only shortly out of college, may say and do things which open them to criticism, I would say that the main thrust of Campus Crusade is definitely in support of the Bible as the inerrant Word of God, the deity of Christ, the substitutionary atonement, and His personal bodily return to the earth....
>
> I do not believe it would be fair or accurate to say that Campus Crusade is guilty of "embracing of the National Council and World Council."... The main thrust of Campus Crusade is evangelistic, and their primary purpose is to reach the lost rather than to combat apostasy in the churches.... Their conviction is that the great need is to get the Gospel to those who have never heard it and present the claims of Christ in such a way that individuals will be led to put their trust in Jesus Christ as Savior. I

would say from personal observation that they are very effective in this and literally thousands are being led to Christ every year through the ministry of Campus Crusade....

As far as financial support of Campus Crusade is concerned, each church has to think through its own problem. I personally believe it is well worthy of our support and that there is no other organization which is doing what Campus Crusade is doing. An investment in them is, accordingly, an investment in winning college students for Christ. Their workers operate on very nominal salaries, and they are accomplishing a great deal for the amount of money that is being spent. A dollar goes a long way with Campus Crusade.

Some of the criticism Bill and the movement received was simply the innate reaction of small minds and hearts to big ideas. As the ministry's goals and activities kept expanding, Bill often was asked the underlying why and how questions: Why think so big? How do you know these things are of God?

For Bill, it was a matter of focus. Who or what is at the center of your concentration and your ideals? When one focuses on the God of the Bible, Bill would say, such a God releases power to the individual to accomplish activities that are in harmony with His own thinking.

"How much power?" Bill asked. "Far more than we would ever dare to ask or even dream of!

"Let your mind race," he would say, "let your prayers be without limit; and yet whatever you believe, whatever you think, whatever you pray for— God's power is infinitely beyond it all."

This God who was so powerful had proven His personal concern for human beings. "Think of it: The omnipresent Creator God, who created the heavens and the earth and the vastness of billions of galaxies, has come to die on the cross for our sins and to take up residence within us!"

These premises, in Bill's logic, led to an inevitable conclusion: "There is nothing too big for us to attempt for the glory of God. *If our hearts and motives are pure,* if what we do is according to the Word of God, He hears and is able to do more than we ask or even think!"

For Bill, this requirement for purity of heart and motive—so easily overlooked—had many implications. He saw that it means our having no unconfessed sin. The Holy Spirit is in the driver's seat of our life; we aren't giving Him the directions, but merely going wherever He takes us. Hidden pride is gone. Self is not being served. The motives of the life are honest. Our motives are in pure consonance with the expressed will of God, in a perfectly paced rhythm.

Bill further applied this reasoning to the supreme task at hand. He would ask, "Is it God's will that the Great Commission be fulfilled?" How could anyone say no to that?

Then Bill would take his listeners farther down the road: "Let your mind soar over the vastness of the earth, where there is a continuing population explosion, and each generation is faced with another billion or more souls to pray for; I challenge you to believe God for the entire world to be blanketed with His love and forgiveness."

As Bill himself believed God for this, his mind raced with ideas and action plans: "I am praying for a billion souls to come to Christ before the end of A.D. 2000."

With such arguments, well-honed and persistently delivered, Bill challenged the Crusade troops. As a result, armies of faith were recruited. Millions were moved into action. Mountains of doubt disappeared. Monuments of faith were established.

He found ready partners who had the distinctives that set "evangelical believers" apart: They claimed complete unity on obedience to the Great Commission. They quoted Peter's second letter: God is "not willing that *any* should perish, but that all should come to repentance" (3:9). They quoted John: "For God so loved *the world,* that he gave his only begotten Son, that whosoever believeth in him should not perish, but have everlasting life" (3:16). And they were on their way.

Of course other priorities in the Christian life are arguably just as important. But Bill and his comrades had a lock-grip logic that worked like this: Obey in what we know to do—evangelism—and trust God for the rest. That approach was supported by surveys showing that the groups performing the most humanitarian and socially constructive programs were Christians dedicated to "reaching" individuals whom they could "win" to Christ, "build" in their faith, and then "send" to the world to do the very same thing with others. For them, social action was an entrée or a by-product of their commitment to obey Christ's Great Commission.

"Therefore *go....*" Jesus says. "God is with you...and so am I." So are the saints and pioneers of faith down through the ages. And they're all saying— shouting—*You can do it, in Jesus' mighty name! Go for it! Think big! Dream without boundaries! Be limited only by what He limits. Change the world!*

And even as Bill was leading Crusade into uncharted worldwide expansion, he sat down to clarify for all exactly what he and the movement stood for. The ministry's fundamental beliefs had been stated before, but new issues arose, and with a new team assembling and a broader application of the Vision being mapped out, a Magna Carta of doctrine was needed for clear citation and to facilitate potential partnerships with other mission groups, churches, and individuals.

In 1971 Bill drafted a seventeen-point statement of faith, the culmination of several years of discussion within the movement's ranks. It was adopted by the ministry's board of directors. Each Crusade staff member and each board member was asked to sign the statement "without mental reservation" and to "pledge...anew to help fulfill the Great Commission in our generation, depending upon the Holy Spirit to guide and empower."

The introductory paragraphs of the statement of faith affirmed Crusade's belief in "the Bible as God's infallible Word, uniquely inspired, the Spirit's supreme and final authority for man in all matters of faith and conduct, His sustenance for every believer." Bill himself tackled the issue of the Bible's divine inspiration from the standpoint of a layperson. His simple and powerful case was that the Bible is to be believed because "the signature of Jesus Christ" is found throughout its pages.

He reasoned this way: Jesus of Nazareth, the historical figure for whose statements and life there is more than adequate empirical evidence, quoted the books of Moses as authoritative. Likewise, Christ quoted the Psalms, Isaiah, and Jeremiah and specifically cited the record of Jonah as "the only sign" He would give His own generation—resurrection from the earth "just as" Jonah was disgorged from the "great fish." In addition, Bill cited the more than three hundred Old Testament prophecies fulfilled in the life of Christ—from His birthplace to the gambling for His cloak at His crucifixion. All that was more than enough evidence to support the Old Testament's inspiration.

As for the New Testament, Bill noted that Jesus' life and teachings permeate the Gospels, He appeared in the book of Acts, and He foretold that there would be "many more things" about Himself to be written, which would include the epistles. And Jesus personally gave the content of Revelation to John.

So Bill would take the person first to Christ, then having shown Him to be credible, he let Jesus validate the Bible.

Campus Crusade's doctrinal statement was solid enough, but Bill's bold approaches to living it out disturbed those who were comfortable in American Christendom. He irritated many with his notion that individual Christians had a personal obligation to be confrontational with the gospel. Who was he to tell Christians they needed such an aggressive aspect to their personal walk? Who was he to say they needed to be regularly doing something assertive that reflected obedience to the Great Commission? His ideas prompted confrontation, consternation, and controversy.

By the middle of 1971, Bill was on the verge of asking more from God and from man than he ever had. He therefore knew that the "troops" would need confident assurance in what they were doing. If seeds of negativity were left untended, he would only have to face them later as full-grown thistles.

Ever a maker of lists, Bill wrote down "some of the lessons I have learned about evangelism and follow-up through the years." With this list he wanted both to instill confidence in Crusade staff as well as to chill the arguments of his critics. To those who found fault with his mission and methods, the thirty candidly written points gave plenty to think about:

1. Jesus came to seek and save the lost (Luke 19:10).
2. The greatest thing that has ever happened to any Christian is coming to know Christ; therefore the greatest thing we can do for another person is to tell him how he or she can know Christ.

3. The one thing dearest to the heart of our Lord, assuming that you are living under the control of the Holy Spirit, is that you tell others about Him. Although not everyone has the gift of evangelism, every believer is chosen and ordained to "go and bring forth fruit" (John 15:16). In other words, every Christian is to witness for Christ as a way of life.

4. There is no way you can become and remain a truly vital and vibrant Christian without sharing your faith continually as a way of life.

5. If you do share your faith regularly, as a way of life, in the power of the Holy Spirit, you will inevitably be a fruitful Christian.

6. You can be an authority on the content of the Word of God and still be spiritually impotent and defeated if you do not share your faith.

7. Success in witnessing is simply taking the initiative to share Christ in the power of the Holy Spirit and leaving the results to God. It is God who produces the fruit. He only requires that we be faithful in the sharing.

8. Jesus said, "Follow me and I will make you fishers of men" (Matthew 4:19). It is our responsibility to follow Jesus; it is His responsibility to make us fishers of men.

9. According to John 15:8, we prove that we are following Jesus when we bear much fruit, when we are actively involved in introducing others to Him. Thus, according to Jesus, we do not prove that we are following Him just because we live a good life, read the Bible, pray, and are active in the church (though all of these are important).

10. The more people to whom you talk about Christ, the more there will be who receive Him. (The more you sow, the more you reap.)

11. The more people who receive Christ, the more there will be who will become disciples.

12. Jesus said, "No man can come to me, except the Father which hath sent me draw him"(John 6:44). Men are born into the kingdom of

God through the work of the Holy Spirit, not as a result of gimmicks, arguments, or high-pressure techniques. At the same time, experience has demonstrated in thousands of lives, during almost a quarter of a century, that to be a truly fruitful Christian, you must first be sure you are filled (controlled and empowered) by the Holy Spirit, and second, be trained to communicate the gospel simply and clearly. Keep the presentation of the gospel simple as per the Four Spiritual Laws. In a spirit of love, and being sensitive to the leading of the Holy Spirit, always seek to bring men to a personal commitment to Christ. Encourage them to pray with you whenever possible. If they are unwilling, encourage them to pray privately and to inform you of their decision. (Exercise care to avoid arguments or high-pressure situations that might result in a premature decision.)

13. God has promised He will honor His Word; there is no truth to the idea that we should not talk to men whom we cannot follow up lest, by hearing the gospel and responding and later falling away because of a lack of follow-up, they will build up a spiritual immunity.

14. The parable of the sower is not based upon the extent to which men are followed up; the fact that some will turn away while others will grow at varying rates is evidenced among those who have extensive follow-up, as well as among those who have no follow-up by another person.

15. Essentially, our responsibility in follow-up would seem to be summarized in 2 Timothy 2:2: "And the things that you have heard from me among many witnesses, commit these to faithful men who will be able to teach others also" (NKJV). The question then is: How do you find those who are faithful among the many who indicate an initial response to the gospel?

16. It is good to ask all new converts to study the parable of the sower and tell you with which kind of soil they wish to identify.

17. Those who want to be true disciples and fruitful followers of Christ can be followed up through prayer, institutes, personal contacts, lit-

erature, taking them witnessing with you, College Life, the ministry of the local church, Lay Institutes for Evangelism, Bible studies and tapes, action groups, Ten Basic Steps toward Christian Maturity, the Institute of Biblical Studies, and the Bible correspondence course from Arrowhead Springs.

(Through all of the above means and many more, Campus Crusade for Christ has one of the most extensive follow-up programs with which I am familiar.)

18. Try two areas of follow-up—primary and secondary, which incorporate the above means and other methods. Primary follow-up is building men in a person-to-person situation, as in small groups. Secondary follow-up employs one or more other methods, including most of those listed in point 17. The secondary method should be applied to everyone. The primary method should be applied to those who are eager to proceed and who respond to the secondary.

19. The cream will rise to the top. Spend time with "the movers," as they are most likely to become disciples and multipliers.

20. We should not be satisfied with spiritual addition; our ultimate objective should be spiritual multiplication. Ask yourself, "How many spiritual great-grandchildren can I name?"

21. The key to building many disciples is a strong emphasis on evangelism. Few, if any, groups have as many converts involved in full-time Christian service as Billy Graham and Campus Crusade for Christ—and both groups have a strong evangelistic thrust. The president of one of our leading theological seminaries stated that 40 percent of its student body was introduced to or influenced for Christ by Campus Crusade for Christ. Hundreds of other young people with whom Campus Crusade has worked are studying for Christian service in other Christian schools or seminaries.

22. Keep emphasizing the church in follow-up. There are those who say the traditional church has lost its relevancy and "real meaning and fellowship is experienced only in small group fellowship in the home." There is nothing new about that. Thousands of vital

churches have small Bible studies, action groups, fellowship, and similar meetings and have had these for years as they seek to minister to the total spiritual need of man: worship, Bible study, fellowship, Christian service opportunities, etc. I was introduced to this concept twenty-five years ago when I became a Christian at the First Presbyterian Church of Hollywood. Don't be deceived by new names for old practices.

23. Prayer is one of the most important factors in successful evangelism and successful follow-up. The Scripture gives our basis for prayer: We have not because we ask not (James 4:2). God is "not willing that any should perish" (2 Peter 3:9). God wants all of His children to be more and more like Christ in every way. Therefore, according to 1 John 5:14-15, we know God will hear and answer if we pray for multitudes to become Christians and for many to become disciples, because we know that we pray according to God's will.

24. We should not fear repetition in follow-up. New Christians need most to understand how they can experience an abundant life in the power of the Holy Spirit and share their faith effectively. Repetition aids learning. The Holy Spirit keeps old truths fresh and meaningful through repetitions if our hearts are right.

25. We should not be deceived by critics who say Campus Crusade for Christ is shallow and superficial so we need to spend more time in deep Bible truths. First, what are these so-called deep truths? Second, are these "truths" producing holy, Spirit-controlled Christians who have a vital, fruitful witness for Christ? Many years of good Bible and theological training in the best Bible schools and seminaries do not ensure victorious and fruitful lives for Christ; whereas emphasis on the ministry of the Holy Spirit and sharing one's faith will. What "deeper truth" is more important?

26. Most Christian leaders whom I know have never been followed up personally in the traditional sense. Some years ago I was participating in a seminar devoted to follow-up. Many Christian leaders were present. All of us were concerned with the need for better follow-up

of new converts. Suddenly, it occurred to me to ask each of these leaders, "Who followed you up?" Not one of these men, including myself, had been followed up personally. Most had been followed up in the fellowship of various church meetings, Sunday school, Bible studies, etc.

27. Philippians 1:6 is a reminder that the Holy Spirit, who produces the new life in the believer, will continue to help the believer grow.

28. The heart of the matter is whether we can believe that the Holy Spirit is able to finish what He has begun according to Romans 8:28-29, which tells us: "And we know that all that happens to us is working for our good if we love God and are fitting into his plans. For from the very beginning God decided that those who came to him—and all along he knew who would—should become like his Son, so that his Son would be the First, with many brothers" (TLB).

29. Never forget the necessity of the Holy Spirit's power. After years of discipling, most of the disciples deserted Jesus at the cross and one betrayed Him. It was Pentecost that made the ultimate difference!

30. The Holy Spirit is the only one who can adequately follow up and help the new convert to grow and mature in his faith. Encourage the new convert to depend upon the Holy Spirit and not on your clever ideas or on excellent follow-up material.

This list served as a manifesto on evangelism and discipleship—and as a call to action only months before Crusade would burst upon the world stage with global strategies and huge events unlike anything Bill had ever before undertaken.

CHAPTER 20

Bill Bright, CEO

Another new face on the Crusade leadership team—and one who would provide fresh insight in organizational development at this crucial period—was that of Steve Douglass, a graduate of the Harvard Business School and the Massachusetts Institute of Technology.

Douglass promptly demonstrated such skills that Art DeMoss asked Bill for permission to recruit him as president of a DeMoss company. But Steve decided the challenge wasn't big enough; he had caught the vision of seeking to create worldwide change through the Crusade movement. He would more than prove his value to Bill, who as CEO of what was now a burgeoning enterprise had to keep his eyes on the law, taxes, and financial management as well as on ministry goals.

On the way to becoming Bill's right-hand man, Steve was learning what it was like to relate to a visionary who also happened to be a perfectionist. One day at Arrowhead Springs they were discussing strategies to reach the world. They happened to be standing next to a window overlooking the beautifully landscaped grounds. Suddenly Bill said, "See that brown spot out there. You need to get that green right away."

"Uh, yes sir, sure. *What* brown spot?"

Sure enough, more than a hundred yards away, Bill had spied a patch of only a few square feet where the sprinklers missed the grass.

Such was Bill's way, and it became part of the Crusade culture: Everyone cares about the little things as well as the big things. Attention to detail pays off.

At Harvard, Douglass and his colleagues had studied hundreds of companies undergoing growth and had identified the patterns and stages of development they went through. Steve and three associates chose to analyze the organization of Campus Crusade and make recommendations. The request reflected one of Bill's strengths—and weaknesses: He often invited new thinking from the best and brightest and the latest person to drop by. It contributed to his own intellectual vitality but occasionally drove his staff and leadership team daffy. For Bill, other people offered a valuable source of ideas, manifesting his own faith that the Holy Spirit of God could, day by day, lead him into new ways of witnessing to the Truth.

So Douglass and his team analyzed Crusade. After nearly twenty years of existence, Crusade had student ministries in about forty countries and on three hundred campuses in the United States. Other unique ministries were focused on laypersons, the military, high-school students, and athletes. The ministry staff had been growing approximately 30 percent each year.

In their report, Steve's team noted that the ministry was growing much more rapidly than most secular organizations, and they identified growing pains associated with such expansion. They targeted three areas for possible change: more decentralization of functions, more coordination of these functions on a geographical basis, and more management talent at a lower level. In the decades to come, decentralization would especially become a major focus for Crusade, especially in terms of ministry funding. It would allow each subunit of Campus Crusade to be a funding champion for its own projects and outreaches, enabling the ministry to embark on hundreds of teaching and training thrusts that would have been otherwise impossible.

Meanwhile Bill used the Douglass team's report as the context for a wider discussion about organizational development. He called for feedback from ministry leaders on the front lines and pushed for a "dialogue atmosphere," making it "safe" for Crusaders to express their frustrations without fear.

One staff leader responded, "Many of the frustrations that staff members have experienced in the past few years have not been the result of too much organization but too little. The frustration has come because of the fantastic blessing that God has given.... Crusade has expanded in a phenomenal way.

In some ways, we have not been able to keep pace with the rate of expansion. So today we are like tangled fishing line."

Through debate and discussion, Crusade strengths were identified and reinforced. The staff recognized, for example, the distinctiveness of the Crusade approach. One of the movement's chief characteristics was its emphasis on taking "the religious into the secular." Crusaders had a "best foot forward" style, dressing to the situation and watching their language. They knew to adjust in order to be relevant.

Although they kept their basic message unchanged—Jesus Christ as Savior and Lord—they didn't talk about being "saved" or "born again." They believed in those biblical phrases, but they saw them as incomprehensible to most people. They didn't talk about church before leading a person to Christ; they talked about having a personal relationship with God through faith in Jesus Christ. And to get to that subject, they knew how to use whatever people liked to talk about.

This emphasis on stark relevancy—always at the heart of Bill and Vonette—had taken root in the movement. And the Crusaders were intensely personal in the way they went forward. That's what Bill and Vonette taught: Make it personal.

Another Crusade distinctive was an openness to new techniques and tools. Over the years, with Bill's encouragement, Crusade would apply every manner and means for communicating the claims of Christ, from banquets and bumper stickers to seminars, movies, satellites, and Web sites. Bill's personal example of creativity sparked others to be equally creative, although this philosophy often encountered what someone called the "seven last words" of Christendom: "We've never done it that way before."

As new ideas surfaced, they were challenged. The ministry of illusionist Andre Kole was a notable example. A magician sharing the gospel? It was opposed by all the staff leaders except Bill and one other. Bill insisted that Kole come aboard anyway. Kole's ministry skyrocketed and became a powerful rallying point for other Crusade ministries as well.

A pattern emerged: Bill would propose or endorse a new idea or method and receive initial opposition from the staff, especially campus leaders. He would pray and exercise patience as he sensed that the new methods and means were consistent with the Vision. There would be additional meetings, then growing support. More prayer. More meetings. Finally the latest idea would take root with enough leaders so that Bill felt it could go forward without damaging the movement.

Bill learned to react to resistance with patient persuasion. He'd sit on a table and listen to every objection, rebut some, overcome some, and dismiss others. "This is my heart," he'd begin. "All we need to do is—" and the staff would wince at the logistics they foresaw. He could tip off that a big project was coming by saying, "This may take a little faith...." Another persuasive phrase Bill frequently employed was, "You know, an idea is worth a million dollars."

When the staff responded by protesting that they were overloaded already, he would reply, "God has his leaders out there...."

Even when he found his idea utterly clobbered, he'd still claim, "There's a kernel of God's leading in this...."

Most of the time Bill's initiatives prevailed, although they were typically made better by input from others. The conversations would race throughout the entire organization: "Dr. Bright believes God wants us to...." Then more meetings, with debate, dialogue, sharpening, adjustment of focus.

One twenty-five-year staff member observed, "It's not always comfortable for Bill in such meetings. He can squirm when people challenge him. You can almost hear the wheels turning inside of him, wishing an objection had not arisen because now it will take more time from concept to reality. Still, he's willing to take the heat if something does not go well."

But Bill never wanted to hear the capitulating response, "Well, you're the boss." The ministry indeed had a chain of command, and Bill expected it to work, but the movement was far from military.

There was always, of course, an inner circle influencing Bill, although he insisted that all of them had better be trusting God with their recommendations. One of the most profoundly influential words of counsel would come with a sigh from Vonette: "Oh, Bill..." That sigh was the "Vonette Check," sometimes corresponding to a "Throne Check" or even causing one.

In addition to Vonette, from the seventies through the end of the century the inner circle usually included Steve Douglass, Bailey Marks, Marvin

Kehler, Paul Eshleman, and Dave Hannah. For discussions of particular issues the group would also include the top leader of the specific ministry involved, perhaps the board attorney, and usually, it seemed, the visitor-of-the-hour, whose brain Bill would pick.

Even so, in this movement the buck stopped with Bill Bright. He invited counsel from the best minds available, accepted feedback, and was patient with most discussion, but he didn't seek votes or polls. He led the movement by being decisive and by taking responsibility when things didn't always work out.

There were times, of course, when staff members failed. In routine management matters involving administrative or procedural foul-ups or even inept leadership, he was nonconfrontational and would let appropriate deputies handle the problems as needed. But with a major moral failure—adultery, financial misdeeds, or expropriation of Crusade's good name or corporate status in a foreign nation—look out! Bill would pounce. He would be on a plane going straight to the offender, and when it landed he expected answers. At times staff leaders had to be fired or have their support withdrawn.

Bill's high standards for financial integrity would be reflected in his helping found the Evangelical Council for Financial Accountability (ECFA) in 1979. He assisted in shaping the ECFA mission: "Helping Christ-centered organizations earn the public's trust through developing and maintaining standards of accountability that convey God-honoring ethical practices." Years later, when *Money* magazine in the 1990s began evaluating charities of all kinds, including religious organizations, Campus Crusade earned top ratings for efficient use of gifts for the purposes intended.

On the personal front, Bill would go beyond ECFA's requirements and include in the ministry's annual report a statement of his and Vonette's income as reported on their tax returns. He and Vonette accepted no honorariums for themselves and no royalties from any of Bill's more than fifty publications—these went to Crusade itself. They owned no houses, land, or cars. After moving to Orlando, Florida, in 1991, they lived in a condominium donated to the ministry, but they still paid monthly rent. They also paid rent to Crusade for return stays at Arrowhead Springs.

CHAPTER 21

"I Do What I Can"

S ometimes things don't come together as planned.

In the late 1960s, Bill conducted a Lay Institute for Evangelism for an enthusiastic group of Australians in the great Saint Andrew's Anglican Cathedral in Sydney. The sessions were videotaped for use later throughout Australia.

Bill and his team then traveled on to New Zealand, where they received a call from Sydney. The production company reported that never in all their history had anything like this happened, but all of the videos were ruined.

What to do? Bill decided to thank the Lord and fly back to Sydney to try recreating the situation and tape again.

So there stood Bill, in a lofty pulpit looking out over an empty cathedral, with no one there but the camera crews and one of his associates. As he began to re-deliver each of the talks, his colleague kept falling asleep on the front pew. "He was probably as dead tired as I felt," Bill recalled.

In raising a family, however, there's no going back to try it over when things don't go as planned. As Zac and Brad grew closer to adulthood, Bill and Vonette were as determined as ever to strongly influence their sons' lives.

A special treat for the Bright family came in 1971 with the ministry's twentieth anniversary. The Crusade staff gave them a trip to Europe. Bill and Vonette and the boys toured seventeen countries. As a special highlight for Zac, who as a high-schooler had become acutely philosophical, Bill arranged a side trip in Switzerland to L'Abri Fellowship and a meeting with Dr. Francis Schaeffer, the celebrated theologian and philosopher.

At home the family had heavy discussions and even debates on a number of philosophical, social, and theological issues. One of those issues was the growing charismatic movement, with its emphasis on "speaking in tongues"—to some a mindless babble, to others a glorious infusion of godly refreshing.

Bill struggled with several aspects of the issue. His main worry was that seekers of "experience" would be drawn away from the propositional truth about Jesus. On the other hand, he could relate to a contemporary observation by theologian and evangelist Vance Havner describing those "whose orthodoxy is straight as a gun barrel but whose doxology is just as cold!" Bill saw the apparent contradiction: The "most joyous news ever announced" was expressed in great hymns with profound poetry as lyrics, yet these same hymns were played and sung in funereal somberness—joyless, lifeless, boring. At the other extreme he saw those who "got happy" but whose basis for faith was entirely governed by an experience and untested by the Bible.

It was a confusing issue to many in the body of Christ, and some Crusade leaders felt the ministry should make a policy statement, especially since several campus ministries had been torn apart by overly zealous individuals who gave priority to speaking in tongues above obedience to the Great Commission. So a directive was passed down that one could neither practice speaking in tongues nor advocate it while a member of Crusade staff. Bill's life focus was missionary evangelism and follow-up training, and logic required that any religious practice by Crusade staff must not conflict with those overarching objectives.

But soon the Bright home became a reflection of the disruptions occurring over this issue. Zac had what he called a charismatic experience, and he was high on the encounter. He had attended some charismatic meetings and had witnessed the warmth of worship, the enjoyable music, the vibrancy, the openness, the apparent freedom.

He had opened himself to what was called "the baptism of the Holy Spirit." This decision and his persistent defense of it hurt Vonette and Bill; their teenage son was deliberately practicing a form of religion he knew was counter to their beliefs.

By this time Zac had started working in one of the ministry departments at Arrowhead Springs. This presented Bill and Vonette with an obvious problem: Their own son, now an employee of Crusade, was violating a ministry guideline.

One day, prodded by Vonette, Bill called Zac's supervisor and explained that Crusade had a policy standard that Zac was breaking. Zac's boss told him to go to Bill's office. The son found his father waiting for him. Bill opened the staff manual and asked him to read the statement on speaking in tongues. Then Bill presented his arguments against the practice. The implication was clear: Zac was supposed to change his mind.

This approach was unacceptable to Zac, and they argued. To Zac there seemed to be no middle ground. He could debate further, but he knew there was little prospect of changing Bill's mind. And his mother wanted obedience, not debate.

So Zac decided to move out. He found another family in San Bernardino to live with, and for several weeks he chose not to communicate with his parents.

Bill was trying to lead Crusade into new global dimensions of ministry, but the very pillars of his family were quaking. He thanked the Lord but wondered what was to be learned from this.

Finally, Zac telephoned. He agreed to meet with his parents on neutral ground.

Zac explained to them how he sensed in the charismatic movement a community with a strong awareness of the immediacy of God. At the same time, he came to believe that no single form or style of worship was proof of the Spirit's presence.

Little by little, over the next several months, Zac and his parents reconciled.

Eventually, many months later, Campus Crusade adjusted its official policy by allowing staff members privately to speak in tongues as long as it contributed to the ministry focus of evangelism, discipleship, and the fulfillment of the Great Commission. Over time, there came to be more and more Crusade staff members who were tolerant and even sympathetic to the charismatic movement but who did not themselves practice speaking in tongues.

After high school, Zac would go on to enroll in Life Bible College in San

Dimas, California, a school associated with the Foursquare denomination. Later, as something of a symbol of their reconciliation, Bill accepted an invitation to give the address at Zac's graduation ceremony. Zac felt that both he and his parents had moved a little toward the center.

While Zac stayed interested in theology, philosophy, music, and art, and saw himself as more pensive and intuitive, his younger brother, Brad, seemed more focused on administration, planning, and getting things done. Brad would go to Wheaton College after high school, with dreams of being a congressman. While Zac moved on to a career as a pastor, Brad finished at Wheaton and headed for Washington to serve on the staff of U.S. Senator William Armstrong and later on the staff of the National Republican Committee.

In Washington Brad would become deeply engaged in the battle to save unborn children. He was convinced that one could not claim a biblical heritage and accept a decision to abort a child, a belief that reflected his parents' absolute conviction that life began at conception. Wanting to be a positive voice on the subject, Brad began to champion the obvious alternative to abortion—adoption. On that score, his own background could be a plus. In a strategic leadership meeting in Washington, D.C., he shared the fact of his having been adopted, something that wasn't commonly known. He eloquently contended that his own life had been worth saving by adoption, and so were millions of others.

For Bill, meanwhile, political involvement would prove to be a tricky issue. He had not sought to be a national figure, but Campus Crusade's growing national presence in the 1970s would change that forever, bringing new opportunities for him to continue applying his principle of "moving with the movers and shakers" on the national landscape. It enlarged his contact and leadership base and eventually led to more recruits and greater support for the movement. But it also set him up for criticism. Some said he was straying from his mission; others complained that he was not political enough.

He was often asked, "Are you engaged in some kind of political movement?" To some extent he invited such questions with his public criticism of the drift of American politics, of a nation gone amok and running away from

God. He sounded like an Old Testament prophet bemoaning his nation's ills. He cited the Supreme Court decisions to ban organized prayer in the schools and to permit abortion. He spoke of the depravity of Hollywood, the corruption among elected officials, the perversions behind closed doors, and especially the abandonment of the Ten Commandments and the God who gave them. His heart was particularly broken by the proliferation of abortion, and he included an indictment of abortion as sin in almost every public remark.

The premise that his nation had left its founding God was firmly fixed in his mind. The United States had systematically turned its back on God.

He participated in rallies against these trends, including a Jesus Rally in Washington, D.C., in 1976 where he challenged Christians to stir the coals of evangelism and personal discipleship to help change America. He was also seen cooperating with high-profile Christian political activists such as Jerry Falwell, founder of the Moral Majority, and Pat Robertson, with whom he served as a co-host for the 1980 Washington for Jesus gathering, the first event in the nation's capital to draw more than a million people. Bill and Vonette also founded the Christian Embassy in Washington, D.C. For a time during the 1970s, the Brights spent an average of one week per month in Washington until the ministry there was fully launched.

Taking note of some of these developments, *Sojourner* magazine suggested that Bill Bright was operating from a political agenda. The magazine also cited Bill's endorsement of a political action book published by the archconservative Third Century Publishers. A staffer had recommended the book, but Bill hadn't inspected its origins.

Was Bill Bright just another conservative evangelist doing a political thing?

Bill said no. People had simply "added two and two and come up with a hundred. They have misinterpreted my motives. We have never spent a penny trying to elect a person or promote a party, and we have no plans to do so, even though I strongly believe every Christian should work at helping to elect honorable, godly officials from both parties, from the precinct level to the White House."

His formal comment on the topic during this period was a published booklet on the essential duties of a Christian citizen. It was bare-bones citizenship: Pray. Register to vote. Be informed. Pray about your vote. And encourage others to do all those things as well.

Bill's increasing visibility prompted some to criticize him for not being more militant in marshaling political forces to change the moral face of the nation. Didn't he have a duty to lead? Some even suggested that he consider running for president. His response wasn't surprising to those who knew him: "To be president of the United States would be a great privilege but actually a demotion compared to the higher calling God has given me." His priority was evangelism. He had his own political views, but the movement was dedicated to fulfilling the Great Commission, and he would not be distracted from that objective.

Nevertheless, Bill believed that in fulfilling the Great Commission, God would use a *cleansed* America—not the filthy one that was multiplying its rebellion and lust. Standing in the way of reaching the world with the love of God in Christ was the rottenness of his homeland.

And he was forced into political involvement by repeatedly having to defend the right to free speech for Crusaders on campuses and in high schools. He helped found one legal-aid organization and supported others so that the average person who wanted to speak freely of his or her faith would not be stopped by the well-funded and persistent American Civil Liberties Union (ACLU) program for secularizing America.

Meanwhile, Vonette's own ministry life took wing as, encouraged by Bill, she embraced prayer as her public mission. It began in 1972 as she organized seven thousand women for a prayer campaign in support of Crusade's Explo '72 event in Dallas.

As she observed how little effort seemed to be focused nationally and internationally on prayer, she urged more action. She established the Great Commission Prayer Crusade and served as a member of the original Lausanne Committee for World Evangelization. She chaired the Intercession Working Group from 1981 through 1990.

Later she helped to found the National Prayer Committee and served for years as chair of the National Day of Prayer Task Force. In that capacity, she found herself working with other Christian leaders and with members of

Congress from both parties. Their efforts paid off in 1988 with a unanimous act of Congress, signed by President Ronald Reagan, establishing the first Thursday of every May as a specific occasion for America to pray.

With Bill and Vonette's increased prominence, they often received praise for the health of their marriage. Bill would quickly reply, "Yes, but we have to work at it." He had always sought to include Vonette in all decision making, both in the family and in the ministry. He respected her strong views, and she felt freedom to share her opinions. These exchanges occurred in a prayer-laced partnership of mutual and regular submission to each other and to the God of the Contract. They each took the time independently to envision happy marriage moments and to schedule, buy, or create something special for the other. As in so many areas of their lives, sometimes this was done by faith and not by mere feelings.

They began writing a book about it: *Managing Stress in Marriage*. The project itself was stressful. They couldn't seem to get together long enough to weave a single-voiced manuscript, so it was produced with both voices commenting on issues from their respective viewpoints. Writing it took two years.

"I do what I can," Bill would say about his many pursuits, "and then try to relax."

CHAPTER 22

Explo

From the success of the Lay Institutes for Evangelism and the Berkeley Blitz, Bill had learned how to use a large rally to launch personal, one-on-one witnessing campaigns. It was time to take these strategies and apply them at another level.

He envisioned mass training in a huge football stadium that would spawn witnessing to an entire city. The Dallas–Fort Worth Metroplex was chosen as the target. The event would be called Explo '72.

Long-range planning, a Bright trademark, kicked in. He foresaw the synergy with local churches that could help move Dallas–Fort Worth and the nation toward spiritual thought and personal devotion.

He turned to Paul Eshleman, who now was directing the Crusade ministry at the University of Wisconsin, to devise the Explo '72 strategy. Paul moved adroitly, and the feasibility of the undertaking began to come alive.

The sheer vision and boldness of the plan to bring together such an unprecedented and large infusion of Christian young people was received warmly by Dallas and Fort Worth business leaders. They had seen and heard enough of riots and turmoil in urban America. They wanted to help.

But Paul encountered difficulties in obtaining enough temporary housing for the expected eighty thousand attendees. Bill stepped in to help; it was a bit like the supposed old pro moving to rescue the younger warrior. Bill offered one idea after another, none of them successful. "It was God reminding us, reminding me: 'Not by might, nor by power, but by my Spirit, says the Lord.'"

There were vacant portions of apartment complexes that might be assigned for Explo '72 participants, but a huge legal and financial issue accompanied that possibility. The deal turned on whether Crusade would be able to afford the liability insurance for use of the apartments. The premium was far beyond any Crusade funding.

Bill and Paul spoke with the heads of banks, insurance companies, and property management companies. No solution was found.

The situation had reached emergency status by the spring of 1972. There was earnest prayer for a miracle. It came, and not in any way Bill had imagined. A Fort Worth banker who was not a Crusade sympathizer reversed his earlier decision and decided to guarantee the insurance premium against the revenues projected from the participants' registration fees. Bill and Paul had faith that the participants would indeed come and enable them to meet the financial obligations.

And in June of that year they did come: Eighty-five thousand students and laymen from across the country and around the world gathered for a week of training in evangelism and discipleship at scores of sites around the city and at evening mass meetings in the Cotton Bowl. At that time it was the largest Christian training session in history.

"The city of Dallas was enveloped in the love of God," one journalist reported. One incident among thousands occurred at a busy intersection, where a white Dallas police officer was directing traffic. Suddenly an African-American woman got out of her car, ran up to him, gave him a big hug, then turned and ran back to her car. Bill's message was getting around: "God loves you and has a wonderful plan for your life."

Behind the scenes, local and national elected officials sent word that they would like to participate in platform ceremonies in the Cotton Bowl. But Bill drew the line: no politicians. He didn't want anything or anyone to distract from the main business of the event—lifting up Christ and training thousands to do the same. Bill did invite his good friend Billy Graham to join him in Dallas, as well as African-American pastor Dr. E. V. Hill of Los Angeles.

Bill was invigorated as he addressed the Cotton Bowl crowd: "If I could choose any time in all of human history to be alive, I'd choose right now."

His invitation seeking commitment each night was specific: "If you know that Christ has come tonight to dwell within you, whatever has happened before tonight, I'm going to ask you to stand right now as an expression of your faith. Right where you're seated, stand to your feet."

As thousands stood, he told them, "Jesus Christ has taken control of your lives and from tonight on you will be changed. 'For if any man be in Christ, he's a new creature. Old things are passed away and behold all things are become new.'"

Before the week was out, thirty-five thousand people indicated salvation decisions both among the participants and as a result of their personal witnessing in the city.

A further highlight of that week in Dallas was the first "Jesus music festival" of its kind, with 280,000 persons joining Bill and Billy Graham along with Johnny Cash and other Christian performers.

At the closing event of Explo '72, Joon Gon Kim, Crusade's Korean leader, made an announcement: Everyone was invited to Seoul, Korea, where three hundred thousand would gather for another weeklong event in 1974.

After the service, Bill asked Bailey, "What's Dr. Kim's plan? This is news to me."

"It's news to me, too," Bailey answered.

Explo '72 was now history. Thousands went away motivated and trained to share their faith in their communities across America with the slogan "Explo '72 Comes to You"; thousands more went away with a newfound certainty of their relationship with God through Christ. Many went back to various kinds of churches to encourage Bible study, training, and witnessing.

The event also had been financially successful. It paid for itself, and the liability insurance premium was paid, honoring the financier's fateful decision. But then came trouble. Bill had been presented with a plan for nationally televising portions of Explo '72 and seeking donations through telephone responses. The producers expected the project to pay for itself. Bill agreed to buy television time and to pay the production costs. But the revenues did not come in, and the costs—mainly the purchase of airtime—resulted in a net $1 million loss for the project and a major financial crisis that lasted for more than a year. Bill wrote to the various Campus Crusade creditors, explaining his plight and promising to pay interest on the amount owed.

Some on the board of directors were greatly concerned, and the issue came to a head at a Saturday morning board meeting about a year after Explo '72. Bill finally interrupted the somewhat heated discussion and declared matter-of-factly: "Let's just ask the Lord for the million dollars." He prayed, and that ended the discussion for that day.

On the following Tuesday, Bill was interrupted in a meeting by a new staffer with an announcement: A man named Bud Miller was on the phone, and he wanted to give the ministry $1.1 million.

Bill promptly took the call. "Dr. Bright," Miller began, "you don't know me, but I love you and Campus Crusade. You've changed my life. I have your picture on the wall of my office." He explained that a recent property sale was the source of his $1.1 million gift and added, "I assume you will know what to do with it." It was exactly the amount needed to cover not only the Explo TV debt but also the amount of interest Bill had promised to pay the creditors.

Miller, it turned out, was a Presbyterian elder in Portland who, years earlier, had been called upon to give a message at his church and didn't know what to say. He came upon the Four Spiritual Laws booklet and the Holy Spirit booklet. He prayed to receive Christ, then used those tools in what he shared at his church. Later he went to Arrowhead Springs for a Lay Institute for Evangelism, which brought new enrichment to his life. Now he was playing a strategic role in the advancement of the kingdom.

Bill loved such men, and it seemed God would send many of their caliber into his life. Bill later included Bud as part of a group of businessmen he invited to view the Crusade ministry on a monthlong tour of Crusade outposts and projects in Latin America. And there was more for Miller to do.

Joon Gon Kim was ready to apply in his own nation what Crusade had learned in Explo '72. Dr. Kim and Bill were like the two prongs of a tuning fork—when one was struck with a strategy he believed was of God, it motivated the other, right on pitch.

Kim took full responsibility for planning Explo '74 in Seoul, while turning to Bailey and Bill for financial and planning help. But Seoul was not Dallas. South Korea was a developing nation without abundant tourist lodging, fast-food restaurants, or cars. This was about rice and bicycles. How could Explo '74 provide food and shelter for such a huge gathering?

The event, a mammoth logistical operation, would stretch every ounce of Kim's faith and Bill's budget. Explo '74 would cost the equivalent of $2 million, but would have cost an estimated five times as much in the United States.

Bill faced a crisis when it became clear Kim needed more money than Crusade had to give. Bill prayed about that situation, too. He wondered if Bud Miller had any more money. He called Miller to say, "Bud, if you have any more of God's money, here's the way it can make a difference." So Miller put up a half million dollars then made plans to go to Seoul to "see what God did with his money."

Explo '74 was to be the most exhilarating experience of Bill's life to that point. But he kept his hands off the details. The event was "Dr. Kim's baby," Bailey Marks would remember. "We helped with resources, but he handled every detail." Those details would include tents, governmental permissions, the program, and the engineering of 30 huge rice cookers, never before known, each of which could prepare 5,000 meals at a time and cost $80,000 to manufacture.

An estimated 12,000 Korean churches were involved. Before the event began, a total of 160,000 Koreans took part in an all-night prayer meeting.

At the time, Explo '74 was the largest evangelistic training event in history. An estimated 330,000 Korean high-school and college students, laymen, and pastors attended the daily discipleship training sessions—offered in English, Japanese, Mandarin, and Cantonese, as well as Korean—where they were instructed in how to be filled with the Holy Spirit and in telling others how to have a personal relationship with Jesus Christ. For the largest evening session, police reported an attendance of 1.3 million.

As a result of the "personal witnessing day" held during the conference, more than 423,000 people heard the Four Spiritual Laws presentation; more than 273,000 indicated that they received Christ, and 120,000 others indicated they wanted to know more about Christ.

Kim's goal had been to train Korean Christians to become competent themselves in the training of other Korean Christians so that his entire nation could be saturated with the gospel within the ensuing two years. Kim didn't want an event; he wanted a revolution. He got it. During the next year, more than 300,000 trained Koreans took the message of Christ to nearly every city, town, and village in the nation. By the end of the century, 50 percent of the population in South Korea were Christians, compared to less than 20 percent in 1974.

A Korean newsmagazine at the time of Explo '74 reported, "Whatever its long-range effect may be, this week's convocation in Seoul has reminded people around the world that the evangelical character of Christianity is alive and well."

CHAPTER 23

Here's Life

I f Joon Gon Kim in Korea could saturate an entire nation with the gospel—why couldn't the same goal be met in America?

Bill's analysis suggested the goal would require significant outreaches in 265 cities of the United States. He asked a staff member to develop a plan. The fellow returned with a fine presentation—but for only 16 cities. Bill reminded him of the assignment and told him to make a plan for 265 cities or he would "get somebody who will."

Soon the total plan was developed, including efforts to have outposts in 18,000 smaller communities.

The total plan would include a major national marketing campaign to present the claims of Christ. Art DeMoss sent two marketing experts to Arrowhead Springs to help map it.

In a meeting with Steve Douglass, the marketing experts were telling him there wasn't time enough in the plan to do the marketing campaign right. They insisted, Steve recalled, "that this was impossible, that we couldn't test it properly, and on and on they went—the whole litany of reasons it wouldn't work. These were the top experts in the entire United States telling me it wouldn't work.

"And I remember slamming the book shut, looking them in the eye and saying, 'I am not asking you *whether* we're going to do this campaign. I'm asking you *how* we're going to do this campaign.' And at that moment I realized, Bill Bright has affected my life!"

The theme was "Here's Life, America." The advertising device was a single line: "I found it!" The principle behind it was called "suspension" marketing: repeating a simple phrase that sparked curiosity, prompting a response by phone or by direct contact that could then lead to a full presentation. The "I found it!" phrase was splashed everywhere—on billboards, bumper stickers, radio, and TV. Its success as a marketing device was remarkable. One of the hallmarks of a slogan's success, ironically, is that it's copied or mocked. Before long, someone printed bumper stickers saying: "I never lost it!" The Here's Life, America campaign had struck a chord.

The campaign from 1975 through 1977 occurred at the time the nation was slogging through the bog of defeat in Vietnam, staggering from the first resignation of a president in its history, and reeling from an oil embargo that had driven inflation and interest rates into the teens. Americans were searching for answers. "I found it!" drew responses.

The plan enlisted thousands of churches as action centers both for initiating contacts and for reaching those persons who responded to the advertising efforts. The methodology included training lay volunteers in those churches in the basics of Crusade presentation materials—the Four Spiritual Laws, the Holy Spirit booklet, and the transferable concepts as a follow-up discipleship program.

On an airplane loaned by a business friend, Bill traveled for several weeks, making multiple stops each day to kick off or encourage the campaign in various locations. Meanwhile, Crusade leaders had been searching for a mature church and pastor to step forward and embrace a saturation campaign for their city; they needed a leader and a demonstration city as a pilot for the program. Bill found it in Charles Stanley, pastor of First Baptist Church in Atlanta. From a small gathering of six persons in Stanley's office, Here's Life, Atlanta was launched on their knees. And with that success recorded on videotape, the movement marched into city after city. Stanley's endorsement and direct involvement validated the concept as a church-based plan.

At his own expense, Stanley began traveling to many cities across the nation to urge other pastors and leaders to get involved. One day in a telephone conversation with Bill, Stanley mentioned in passing that he'd spent so much time on the road that some of his deacons were wondering if they'd lost their pastor. Bill immediately volunteered to meet with the deacons. He flew to Atlanta and explained that, through their pastor, the First Baptist Church of Atlanta was helping to reach the entire country with the gospel. It was a matter of perspective. Stanley continued his travels with liberty and the support of his deacons. "I'll always be in debt to Charles Stanley," Bill would say.

Bill and his staff were attracting thousands to become involved in the ministry's concepts and projects. "We're not here to compete with the church," Bill would emphasize. "We're here to cooperate with the church to support the church in its obedience to the Great Commission." Pastors and laypersons would react, quite humanly, in one of two ways:

No, I can't do another thing. I'm exhausted. You just want our money for a show. I want nothing to do with it.

Or, *Yes, I'm so tired of the same old thing, and you seem to be genuinely offering resources as well as vision; I can't wait to get involved.*

Ultimately, 246 cities participated in Here's Life, America, including all the largest cities, except Boston and Pittsburgh. In those two cases, after host pastors had convened a citywide leadership meeting of pastors to launch Here's Life in their cities, a lone popular minister in each city stood to denounce the notion of "outsiders" being required to lead revival there.

Based on the responses witnessed by the Here's Life campaign in other larger cities, Bill would later declare, "Tens of thousands who were not reached will be in hell because of the egos of those two ministers."

Some Crusade staff saw the huge project as a distraction from what Bill and Vonette themselves had trained them to do: Stay focused on the campus and on your daily, personal evangelism—not glitz but persona, not headlines but heartlines, not big deals but big love. So Bill kept the staff inspired with his own personal enthusiasm. He would share his own witnessing experiences—from kneeling with a U.S. senator to sharing with the latest cab driver or airline attendant or hotel bellhop. He always had fresh experiences from the field.

While focusing on Here's Life, America, Bill departed from his normal practice of visiting each continent once or twice per year, although he did cross the Pacific to help launch Here's Life, Asia with its potential to train approximately seventy thousand Chinese—a strategy that was to bear immediate fruit as well as an abundant harvest decades later. It wasn't long before Bill and Bailey were moving through the nations to initiate Here's Life, Philippines; Here's Life, Malaysia; Here's Life, Singapore; Here's Life, Hong Kong; and more.

The most spectacular success in the Here's Life's movement developed in South Korea, where more than two million people took part each night in a four-day campaign. Kim did it again, with Bill's help and the support of 90 percent of the South Korean Protestant churches.

On the campaign's final night, South Korean police estimated that about three million people attended a vast open-air Here's Life meeting. It was the largest single gathering in Christian history and perhaps in all of history.

This time the event's focus was not on reaching Korea, as in Explo '74, but on reaching the world from South Korea. Bill stood to speak to the final night's audience, a lone figure standing before a sea of people. The awesome moment gripped him. He was there to draw the net of commitment to help reach the world in the fulfillment of the Great Commission. His message was what those who knew him expected it to be: a plain, bold challenge of commitment.

Bill focused his invitation for two purposes: assurance of personal salvation and commitment to allow God to set the timetable of his listeners' lives for the purpose of giving everyone on planet Earth the opportunity to respond to the love of God expressed through the life, death, and resurrection of Jesus Christ.

When he gave the appeal, an estimated 1.3 million people stood. "It was as if the earth moved," said Pakistan's Kundan Massey, who was there and in tears by the time Bill finished the invitation.

Using the Here's Life, World banner, hundreds of training centers had been established around the world. Before long, though, it grew harder to maintain the nation-by-nation efforts of Here's Life, World. The cost of training was bogging down the pace of expansion.

But for now, Bill's mind had turned a corner—into focusing on more major *partnerships* with those of like faith. As these partnerships developed, they stirred leaders in other circles to dream and develop their own plans, especially after they encountered Bill.

For example, the Southern Baptists, America's largest Protestant denomination, announced in 1976 a plan to share their faith with the entire world by 2000. With lay leadership examples such as Jimmy Carter, they gave birth to a volunteer Mission Service Corps program that was not unlike the training and sending that Campus Crusade had been doing for years.

Other churches and missions agencies also awoke to new possibilities. Bill's approach was contagious.

Meanwhile Bill encouraged the staff on American campuses to stay focused on "the campus today, tomorrow the world." Theirs was the revolutionary opportunity to bring student leaders to Christ, and that focus was the spine of the entire movement. The Here's Life movement had established Campus Crusade's relationship with many thousands of additional churches, which in the long run would mean more financial and prayer support for Crusade staff.

CHAPTER 24

The *Jesus* Film

S ince 1945 Bill had envisioned the value of a high-quality motion picture on the life of Christ. In 1974 it seemed to Bill that the right time to go forward on the project had come—but others were not convinced.

John Heyman, a British film producer with more than forty-five films to his credit, had approached Campus Crusade with the idea of producing a series on the entire Bible. He seemed to Bill to be the right person to capture the life of Christ on film. Bill also decided that the right man from Crusade to work with Heyman on such a daunting and all-absorbing project would be Paul Eshleman, who by this time had moved to the role of Crusade's U.S. director.

Heyman came to Arrowhead Springs one day to discuss the project with Bill. Eshleman at the time was on Arrowhead Mountain on a planning retreat with many of Crusade's national leaders. Bill sent word for Paul to meet with Heyman, but Paul replied through a messenger that he was too busy. Not a problem to Bill: He merely sent Heyman up the mountain to Paul.

They talked. Paul thought the project might happen if only the funding could be found. The cost was estimated at $5 million.

Several months later, Bill and Vonette were hosting Bunker and Caroline Hunt of Texas oil wealth. The Hunts had been friends and supporters of the ministry for many years, so Bill shared with them the vision of creating the motion picture. Bunker turned to Caroline and asked, "How would you feel if we financed it?" She agreed.

That was a Saturday. By Monday, the money was released.

But the project wasn't being embraced with open arms by most of the staff. For one thing, John Heyman was Jewish. As far as they knew, here was a nonbeliever trying to put the Bible on film, which just didn't make sense as part of Crusade's mission.

Then there was the matter of Eshleman's involvement. Paul had been a part of Crusade since 1966. He was popular, charismatic, visionary, organized, compassionate—a dynamic and trusted leader, someone whom the staff turned to and loved and followed. So it seemed that Bill was not only doing something beyond the framework of the ministry's mission, but he also was sacrificing one of his best people to do it.

So Bill employed one of his common leadership tactics: If the staff doesn't agree, hold another meeting. He sat down with them and explained that he had chosen Paul for the project precisely because Paul was all those things to everyone—and more. Bill knew Eshleman had the drive, the perseverance, the intellect, the energy, and the vision to wrestle such a huge project into submission and success.

Paul shifted gears and dived into the project. In time he began coming back to the staff with exciting reports of how the film was coming together. Because of his enthusiasm and the progress reports, one by one the staff began to take ownership in the project. They were catching the vision for how such a tool could help them carry out their own ministries.

The only major motion picture to be based on the literal text of the gospel of Luke, *Jesus* was filmed at two hundred sites in Israel, incorporating a cast of more than five thousand.

When Heyman completed his first version of the film, Paul and Bill found scores of things that needed changing, including some that represented theological issues. Following rounds of discussion over the course of a number of months, Heyman made the necessary changes to Paul and Bill's satisfaction. Their intense and scrupulous requirements that the movie adhere to Luke's gospel would mean that all the Christian world would have a trusted, cross-cultural tool for mass exposure of the life of Christ to anyone.

After five years of research and production, the feature-length film was ready for release in 1979. Paul had devoted the previous two years almost exclusively to working closely with Heyman in the production. Now it was time to produce another miracle: the distribution of the film into the remotest corners of the planet in the various languages of the people.

Over the next four years, the film was translated into more than 70 languages and shown to 350,000 people worldwide. After another five years, more than 640 million people had seen the film in more than 300 languages. By the end of the century, the totals were 3 billion viewers in 575 languages—figures that exceed many times over the totals for any other motion picture in history.

People responding to the film's message were further nurtured by being encouraged to study spiritual growth information in New Life Groups. Many of these groups became the nucleus for new churches.

Distribution of a video production of *Jesus* began in 1989, and in the next decade more than 320,000 video copies were distributed to American homes. Initial reports showed one salvation decision for every two videos distributed.

A special encouragement for Bill was the further measure of partnerships developed with hundreds of churches, mission groups, and other agencies in showing the *Jesus* film. Bill and his team were seeing unprecedented cooperation among Christian communities of faith. A network of collaboration was being expanded and strengthened for use in future endeavors as well.

That network would next be employed in a big way with something new called Explo '85.

With the *Jesus* film and more, the Crusade movement was starting to make a historic difference on a worldwide scale. Bill envisioned the next big international training site to be an event hosting five million people. However, the cost and logistics of such an endeavor—for food, water, sanitation, housing—ruled out the possibility. Working on a smaller scale, how could Crusade continue training the required millions to reach the world?

In the middle of a prayer session, Bailey Marks had an idea. Why not use satellite television to spread the gospel? Bill quickly asked Bailey to proceed with the project, and it was the kind of challenge Bailey loved.

It would be no easy task. At the time, satellite closed-circuit TV was a relatively untested technology. They would need downlink dishes placed strategically all over the world. Financing would be hard to find—no religious leader as yet had ever committed resources to a project of this scope. Every participating nation would have to gain permission from its national government. Some would fear that the effort was a CIA plot. And at home, there would have to be a temporary diversion of American Crusade attention for the setup period.

But what a blazing trail it promised to be! And if it worked, it would have that amazing faith-building effect: *See! The Earth can be reached with the gospel!* The short-term difficulties were nothing compared to that vision-inspiring lift it could give the global body of Christ.

Bill instantly saw the lasting value. Bailey had the bit in his teeth. Away they went.

Actually, the project was merely an extension of a long-held Crusade doctrine: Use any and every technological means to spread the gospel and, much more, to train Christians how to walk in faith-filled obedience to God, to enjoy the presence of power of the Holy Spirit, and to share this faith effectively with others to draw them into the same process.

Explo '85 was conceived as a four-day televised training conference over the last four days of December. Each day would include two hours of live transmission via satellite to close to a hundred downlink sites in auditoriums in sixty-eight countries. In nations such as Sri Lanka, Egypt, and Pakistan, the satellite dishes had to be imported. In India the downlink dishes had to be fashioned by hand in a backyard factory.

As part of Explo '85, Bill completed a globe-encircling, whirlwind tour covering forty-seven thousand miles in four and one-half days. Accompanying him were his son Brad, Bailey Marks, and key technical staff. On four consecutive nights they were in Seoul, Manila, Berlin, and Mexico City. From each location Bill spoke for thirty minutes by satellite to the worldwide audience.

In the broadcast from Berlin on December 30, Bill surprised everyone. On the spur of the moment, he said: "Before I bring my message today, I want to take a moment to wish my beautiful, adorable wife of thirty-seven years a happy anniversary." With millions looking and listening, he told her how much he loved her and appreciated her.

Vonette was watching him on-screen in a London studio where the broadcast signal was being sent via eighteen satellites to the auditoriums worldwide. The London TV director put a camera on Vonette, and the whole world watched her surprised reaction.

Explo '85 came off with only a few technical glitches. Total daily attendance at the nearly one hundred sites was more than three hundred thousand people.

Explo '85 was more than a benchmark in the innovative use of technology; it was also a huge dose of encouragement for Christians worldwide. For those believers who might have felt they were isolated in their walk of faith, seeing hundreds of thousands of other believers in live satellite feeds showed them that they actually belonged to a worldwide spiritual family. People of greatly different backgrounds and cultures could see that their common values and spiritual goals were shared by individuals of virtually every ethnic group and color. This technological tearing down of the barriers gave many a tremendous new appreciation of God's presence and purpose for today's world.

Other notable events for Bill in the mideighties included Youth Congress '85 in Washington, D.C.—where he spoke to fifteen thousand high-school students in an event sponsored by Campus Crusade's Student Venture in partnership with Youth for Christ—and Liberty '86, a Fourth of July evangelistic outreach by Here's Life, Inner City in New York that coincided with the Statue of Liberty centennial celebration.

But another dream being pushed forward at the time proved unsuccessful. Bill wanted an international Christian graduate university, where the best and brightest in all the academic disciplines would be together in one place—a "Christian Harvard or Oxford"—to build the leaders of tomorrow in government, medicine, law, engineering, technology, and more.

One day he learned that five thousand prime acres near San Diego were available. He envisioned this as the place to both build and finance the university. They would form a private for-profit corporation, buy the land, subdivide and develop it, then sell off lots and homes on a "life estate" plan, which would generously endow the university.

San Diego's mayor, city council, and business leaders were supportive. Bill was told that construction on the campus could begin within eighteen months of purchase. So he went ahead and bought the property with private funding—the contributors included Bill's friends Bunker Hunt and his brother, Herbert Hunt—although the Crusade organization was, in effect, a cosigner on the commitment.

Then politics took over. A city election brought in a new mayor and a city council majority that was more hostile to development. The council refused to grant some necessary zoning changes for the property, citing environmental and neighborhood quality concerns.

The city's business and professional leaders appealed the council's decisions on Bill's behalf. When the council still refused, the leaders tried their last resort: a referendum election seeking to overturn the council's decision.

As the election approached, the Crusade family held its breath, said its prayers, and waited for a miracle. It did not come. Despite support from business and church leaders, Bill's dream was rejected 54 percent to 44 percent.

This unexpected defeat hurt him. The project had taken a lot of time and attention, and Bill had never doubted what he thought was God's plan, although he wondered aloud if he had misunderstood the details.

The defeat brought legal and financial troubles of no small proportion. The entire project was forced into Chapter 11 bankruptcy. This allowed the organization to retain a portion of the title to the land—a potentially tremendous asset, at least—but at the time it caused a drain on Crusade finances to retain its stake in the property. That particular site was never to be used for an international Christian graduate university, but Bill continued to believe God would produce fruit from this dream.

CHAPTER 25

A Simple Little Strategy

I t seemed a fantastic thought: reaching every single person on earth with the simple message of God's love for man. Yet Bill had always felt confident he was to be personally involved in such an undertaking.

In 1986 he came up with what he later called "a simple little strategy" for bringing it about. Under his direction, Crusade developed what may be the first systematic plan with a realistic chance of providing every person in the world the opportunity of entering into a relationship with God by taking a simple step of understanding and faith.

The new strategy would be known as New Life 2000. Bill announced it in January 1987 at the annual convention of the National Religious Broadcasters, an association of Christian communicators.

To carry it out, Bill and the Crusade team aggressively sought partnership agreements with as many Christian organizations around the world as possible—nearly one thousand of them would be involved by the year 2000—while still staying true to the ministry's statement of faith.

At the core of the New Life 2000 strategy was dividing the world into Million People Target Areas (MPTAs). Campus Crusade, working together with the other organizations, mapped the world into five thousand distinct regions, each consisting of roughly one million people who shared a common language and cultural characteristics. (As the global population increased, the number of regions was adjusted upward to six thousand.) For each MPTA, a three-year plan was prepared that reflected and respected the special culture, needs, and difficulties of saturating that particular region with the message of God's love.

For all the regions, the *Jesus* film and other Crusade tools would be the centerpieces of the gospel presentation. Local church members would be recruited for training in evangelism and discipleship in programs to be known as New Life Training Centers.

Such a sweeping strategy challenged the faith of almost everyone who came into contact with it. But Bill devoted himself to sharing the New Life 2000 plan with Christian leaders in the same vigorous way he shared the Four Spiritual Laws with those who didn't know Christ.

An example of this vision-raising occurred in August 1988 when Bill invited nearly a hundred leaders and laymen from various Protestant churches and ministries to Arrowhead Springs. Those present accepted Bill's challenge for New Life 2000 and pledged themselves and their resources to seek the project's goal. One layman concluded, "It has the effect of removing your excuses. You can visualize that by following his plan, if enough shoulders were bent to the task, and God intervened, the fulfillment of the Great Commission in our lifetime would be a strong possibility."

More and more "partnerships in missions" began to form, and the methodology was put into action. An example of the project's success was in Thailand, where Boonma Panthasri, Crusade's national director in northern Thailand, documented the birth of more than twenty thousand new churches in seven years as a direct result of the New Life 2000 strategy.

Another example was in the Philippines, where metropolitan Manila and its population of 8.5 million were divided into eight sectors. Bill and Bailey went to Manila in the summer of 1990 to join a flood of more than five thousand Campus Crusade staff members and volunteers from more than a hundred countries. Their goal was to help expand existing ministries and launch new ones in an effort to saturate the entire city with the message of Jesus Christ. More than a hundred churches became New Life Training Centers after receiving Crusade's training. Bill felt like a general watching an invasion unfold, stage by stage. He and Bailey would pray, then encourage the Filipino leaders, then go with them to the streets. They had a smile and a spring in their step as they sallied forth. This was part of their manifest destiny. Bill loved it.

The campaign in Manila introduced an estimated half million people to Christ, who were then guided into partnering churches.

Meanwhile, as the Cold War ended and communist regimes in Eastern Europe crumbled, Bill went personally through the doors that were swinging wide open into Russia.

Back in 1947 at the first briefing conference at Forest Home, Henrietta Mears had placed a huge map of the world at the front of the hall. She challenged every person there to ask God what place on earth they should claim for Christ and to sign their name on the map in that location. Bill wrote his name on Russia. He had been praying for the country ever since.

Now, inside Russia himself in 1989, he found a country ripe for spiritual harvest. In a Moscow hotel one night, Bill had a "chance" meeting with two Russian scientists for dinner. Bill shared his vision for the world and how it seemed to be unfolding internationally. The scientists suggested that he tell this message to the people of Russia. Then one of them urged, "Would you appear on Russian television to report this?"

Later that night, Bill was told to be at a local television station at nine the next morning to be interviewed for a state-produced Russian news special. Bill stayed up that night preparing suggested questions for the interviewer to ask him, allowing him to give his personal testimony and to explain the gospel of Jesus Christ as well as describe the ever-widening impact of the Crusade movement.

In the rush of dramatic events in those days, it so happened that Soviet President Mikhail Gorbachev and U.S. President George Bush were to hold a summit in San Francisco later the same week. In Bill's television interview, the host asked about President Bush's disposition toward the Russian people and the coming summit. Bill, who had been at the White House only days earlier for a small gathering involving the National Day of Prayer, was able to report that President Bush was a man of prayer and that he read his Bible.

Afterward, the interviewer said that the session with Bill would not be aired immediately, but would become part of special broadcast when Bush and Gorbachev met in San Francisco. Sure enough, later in the week, an estimated 150 million viewers across the Soviet Union watched an hourlong special featuring Bush, Gorbachev—and Bill Bright. The program quoted Bill's words on Jesus, God, the Bible, faith, prayer, and the *Jesus* film. It was the largest television audience of Bill's life, and it was paid for by the Russian government!

The next year Bill was back in Moscow to give an Easter message to about five thousand people in the Palace of Congresses. Once again, his message was broadcast on national television to an estimated 150 million viewers. Bill spoke of Christ while standing in front of draperies woven with the image of Lenin. When he gave the invitation to receive Christ, about 85 percent of the people stood.

The next morning Bill encountered several Russian officials, many of whom had seen the broadcast. "Did you pray with me?" Bill asked a famous cosmonaut whom he met. "Yes, I did," the cosmonaut replied.

The next day in Saint Petersburg, he met others. "Did you pray with me?" "Of course," came the frequent reply.

When the wife of a top Russian official met with Bill, she opened her purse to show him her copy of the Four Spiritual Laws. Yes, she had prayed the prayer in the little booklet.

The following spring Bill was back once more in Moscow for another nationally televised event. On a cold and rainy Easter morning, Bill shared the platform on Red Square with Baptist pastor Adrian Rogers from the United States. The Russian police estimated the crowd in the square at 100,000 people. But the rain became so intense that a cancellation of the services was announced. Bill and others prayed for a miracle and got it. The 350-voice choir sang "How Great Thou Art" as the rain stopped and the worship and preaching went forward. Bill led the crowd in a prayer of salvation, then asked, "How many of you prayed that prayer with me?" Approximately 80 percent of the thousands there raised their hands. Then Bill invited a Russian Orthodox priest to offer the benediction.

There was more excitement to come. The country's minister of education offered to place the *Jesus* video in forty-three thousand Russian schools if

Crusade financed the project. Bill and Paul Eshleman asked if the teachers involved could be required to attend a three-day training seminar. The official agreed.

At the Moscow premiere of the *Jesus* film, nine of Russia's eleven top cabinet ministers were in the audience. When Bill gave an invitation to accept Christ, he estimated that 85 percent of those in the theater stood.

As the training seminars for the teachers began, Paul found that about 45 percent of the teachers would respond to Christ on the first day, and nearly that many more by the end of the three days.

After Paul and his team had trained some twenty-three thousand of the teachers, they realized they could not get this massive job done alone. To accelerate their efforts, they sought partners and formed CoMission, which ultimately involved more than eighty Christian organizations.

Meanwhile Bill continued to encourage urgent initiatives in Russia, fearing that the suddenly wide-open doors might someday close just as quickly.

Bill spoke of his involvement in Russia as being "among the greatest events of my life" and expressed "praise and thanksgiving to our great God and Savior that He is allowing us as a ministry to help reach this former evil empire with the most joyful news ever announced." Remembering the spiritually hungry throngs he saw in Russia, he would say, "I could not help but think back to that life-changing night in 1951 when God opened my eyes to see the multitudes of the world that would one day come into His kingdom."

CHAPTER 26

World Center

B y the late 1980s Campus Crusade had long past outgrown Arrowhead Springs and for a number of years had been leasing facilities at Colorado State University every summer for its annual staff training. Bill was thinking about selling Arrowhead Springs to move the ministry elsewhere, as had several other California-based parachurch organizations. Many among the Crusade staff resisted the idea of relocating, but Bill took the lead in demonstrating the wisdom of a move.

But move where? That took two years for ministry leaders to figure out. Extremely attractive real estate deals were offered in a number of locations. In effect, Crusade could take its pick, and a total of thirty-eight cities were considered.

In one city with a significant presence already of parachurch and mission organizations, one of their leaders advised Bill, "It could be difficult for us if you and Crusade come here. With the size of Crusade, you could squash the rest of us. There are others who feel this way but are afraid to say so lest they offend you." Bill thanked the fellow leader for a candid analysis and took his counsel as a word from God.

Meanwhile officials in Orlando had promised to meet and exceed any offer Crusade might receive elsewhere. More than five hundred city officials and business leaders turned out in Orlando not only to encourage the move but also to lay concrete packages on the table. Bill was persuaded.

He foresaw "great opportunities" in the headquarters move. Envisioning the construction of a World Center for Evangelism and Discipleship in

Orlando, he and other Crusade leaders nevertheless insisted that no money be redirected from overseas projects to build the new headquarters. Fulfilling the Great Commission was always to be the priority in Bill's plans and prayers.

Bill's vision now was admittedly driven, in part, by his own advancing years. "I'm not getting any younger," he would sometimes say in reminding a listener of the urgency of the World Center or other projects, which, of course, he saw as God's projects. More and more, "God told me" crept into his language. The phrase was a vast oversimplification of a process of perspiration—study, prayer, fasting, and planning—as well as inspiration, and the words at times made some staff uncomfortable. "I knew what he meant," an insider said, "but it always made me wince when he talked like that with visitors and newcomers." At the same time, "He really believes that" was part of the hallway commentary when staff were discussing Bill's references to God's part in his plans.

Bill became sensitive to this issue and often made clear that he "never heard an audible voice." He said that his mind and heart "were impressed" and that he "sensed" an unmistakable message which, by his measure, was in harmony with the Word and will of God. He quoted Philippians 2:13 from *The Living Bible:* "For God is at work within you, helping you want to obey him, and then helping you do what he wants." Through a person's reliance upon the promises of God, Bill would explain, "a conviction is an opinion that is carefully thought through to a defensible conclusion." With such logic, he said he was certain God was leading him through the complex and challenging projects of these years.

It was an emotional day in August 1991 when Bill and Vonette stepped out one last time from Bungalow 10, which had been their home at Arrowhead Springs for twenty-nine years. This was where their sons had grown up, and the ministry as well. And how many times had they looked at night over that San Bernardino Valley and the thousands of lights twinkling back at them, and felt as if they had a glimpse of God's view of humanity, teeming below, in need of a Friend and a Savior?

Leaving was hard. "We did shed a few tears when we left Bungalow 10 at

Arrowhead Springs," Bill acknowledged in a letter to the staff family. "But God forbid that we should ever be wed to houses and lands. Only the Lord Jesus Christ deserves our total allegiance and affection."

As Vonette sobbed, they got in the car and headed for the airport and Orlando, Florida, where Walt Disney World had a new neighbor. The Orlando community opened its arms and its hearts to the arriving Crusaders, who now could work together instead of separated at seventeen different locations.

In the fall of 1991, a celebration in an Orlando hotel marked the fortieth anniversary of Campus Crusade's founding. Part of the ceremonies included videotaped messages from key leaders in America. "I thank God for Campus Crusade for Christ," Billy Graham said. "There's nothing like it in the history of the Christian world."

Elizabeth Dole noted that Campus Crusade "has made it possible for believers of every level of maturity to be fruitful disciples of Christ.... With literally millions of others around the world, I can say that my life has been touched and my faith strengthened through the ministry of Campus Crusade for Christ."

And James Dobson declared, "You have been a role model for me, Bill, in the way that you have dedicated your life to your ministry, and in the way you have kept your integrity and lived by standards that you preached. We're living in a world of compromise where people shave the truth a little bit, or they get involved in self-serving dimensions of a ministry. But you have devoted yourself totally to the work of the Lord through all these years, and I want you to know I love you for it."

Wally Sanderlin, a top Orlando homebuilder and chairman of Orlando's Airport Authority, had joined others in giving Campus Crusade a beautiful house for the Brights in his new Brighton Woods subdivision. Bill and Vonette paid rent to Crusade and lived there for the next two years, serving as hosts over that period for more than two thousand guests. However, as Bill was returning from travel about two o'clock one morning, he noticed the occupants of a pickup truck parked in their cul-de-sac. This made him concerned about Vonette's security while he was away.

The original donors of the house then agreed that Crusade could trade it for a condominium with tighter security, and there the Brights moved next, paying a thousand dollars for their monthly rent. Their new home offered a view overlooking a lake and the city lights beyond—another reminder of the world Bill had on his heart.

Meanwhile, at the ministry site on Lake Hart near Orlando, construction began on the new World Center facilities, with more than $14 million in roads and services having been contributed by the city, county, and state governments.

In October 1999 Bill took part in the dedication ceremonies formally opening the facilities. The five-building complex was everything Bill and the Crusade leaders envisioned it to be—functional, visitor friendly, and classy but not ostentatious. One notable feature was a ground-level center area modeled after the Parthenon; on its walls, in recessed letters, were the primary words of each of the Four Spiritual Laws.

The formal dedication ceremony was nearly blown away by Hurricane Irene. The staff's original plan was for an outdoor ceremony featuring a three-thousand-voice choir. The hurricane's rains sent them to plan B: ceremonies under a tent and a three-hundred-voice choir. As Irene's winds snapped guy wires and poles in the tent, they settled on Plan C: an intimate gathering in the hallways and offices inside one of the buildings, with sing-along praise choruses and hymns. At least everyone was safe and dry. They sat in office chairs, listened as they could, and occasionally peered down the hallways to see what they could see.

Bill seized what seemed to be an awkward moment to urge everyone to celebrate the sovereignty of God and to thank Him for the inconvenience and for the inability of most of those present to see the ceremony participants. After all, Bill suggested, it was the Lord Himself whose presence could be felt there, and it was He "to whom all glory and praise for these magnificent facilities" should be given.

The program included stirring testimonies, including that of Paul Eshleman, who described the breathtaking story of a tribe of headhunters who had been converted to Christ as a result of the *Jesus* film. Nancy

DeMoss announced that the DeMoss Foundation was providing Crusade with funding for an executive ofice building in memory of her husband, Art, the former Crusade board member who had died in 1978 at age fifty-two.

After the formal activities, Bill lingered to meet new people and talk. Staff members introduced their parents to him, and one of the residents of the Lake Hart area came by; Bill took down his name because he was planning a "neighbors only" reception at the World Center. He was not too busy for anyone.

CHAPTER 27

Lessons

The relocation to Orlando raised a question: Had Bill moved to Florida only to retire, like so many others? But *retirement* was a word completely foreign to Bill. "Never," he said.

In November 1992, Bill and Vonette joined Bailey and Elizabeth Marks for a ministry trip to Australia. Returning to that continent always gave Bill a moment's pause. In the Vision back in 1951, Australia was the one specific place that had been brought to his attention. He had sensed a spiritual tidal wave emerging from this least of the inhabited continents and spreading around the globe. "That part of the Vision has not been fulfilled," Bill said. "I don't understand what or why."

So much of the Vision had, however, reached fruition. Bill described the Vision as being like a giant landscape painting in which the Artist had first sketched the outline of mountains and forests and ever since had continued to color in the details. "God has raised up an incredible group of wonderful, godly, Spirit-filled men and women by the thousands to whom He is also speaking, and together, locked arm and arm, we are taking His message of love and forgiveness, revealed in Christ, to the world.... The Vision has been unfolding all these years, and obviously it's not my doing, it's God's doing."

On Bill's first night in Sydney on this trip, five hundred staff and Crusade friends from Australia and New Zealand crowded into a hotel banquet hall. Faith-filled exuberance lit their faces as they sang, "Shine, Jesus, shine.... Flood the nations with truth and mercy."

Bill, wearing a black business suit, was introduced to a standing ovation by an Aussie who called him "an ordinary bloke" with "extraordinary faith to whom God has given this vision of helping to reach the world for Christ."

The content of Bill's message to them was familiar, but it came straight from his heart and struck motivational chords.

> Let me just say to you with every ounce of conviction I can muster that no matter how famous or powerful, no matter how popular, no how matter how great one might become in the eyes of men, there is nothing that you and I will ever be privileged to do that will compare with helping to fulfill the Great Commission.
>
> You think about it. Why did Jesus come? He came to give His life a ransom for many. He is simply giving you and me the privilege of partnering with Him. He doesn't need us. He could raise up sticks and stones to do His bidding. But He's given us the *privilege* of continuing what He came into this world two thousand years ago to do, and that is to seek and to save the lost.
>
> Now frankly, I've never known a happy Christian who was not involved in the Great Commission. When I speak of happiness, I'm not speaking of a superficial kind of thing; I'm speaking of the joy of the Lord....
>
> None of us has a long time here on planet Earth. It's kind of a staging ground. It's our split second in eternity when we have an opportunity to invest our lives, our time, our talent, and our treasure to fulfill what our Lord came into this world to do and commissioned us to do. In fact, His last words before he ascended to be with the Father were: "Be my witnesses."...
>
> By the grace of God, by the end of the year 2000, every person on planet Earth who is old enough to understand the gospel will have had a chance to say yes to Christ. At least a billion, according to our prayer target, will receive Christ. At least five million New Life groups will be started.... And we anticipate a million new churches planted. Not any of them will have the name Campus Crusade for Christ on them because we as a movement are dedi-

cated to serving the church.… The goal is to build disciples who
also will carry the message.

The next morning he switched gears. No longer a visiting statesman, he
was now a coach with a team, a low-key elder brother. He wore a white
guayabera shirt and carried his well-worn, leather-bound *Living Bible*. In a
modest brick building on a campground north of Sydney that belonged to
the YMCA of Australia, he met with sixty dedicated co-laborers, all non-
white, from Asia and the Pacific islands.

His audience sat on plain folding chairs. Bill knew that most had come
from difficult circumstances. In some of their homelands, Crusade leaders
had been beaten, arrested, jailed, and deported for sharing their faith.

After the group sang some praise choruses, Bill rose with no fanfare from
a front-row seat to begin his remarks, and the sixty listened intently.

"Holy Father," he prayed, "we're here in Your presence this morning
humbly acknowledging our total sense of dependence on You. Though I've
walked with You all these exciting and wonderful years, I still feel so totally
dependent on You. Please enable Your servants to comprehend what You
want them to know, and I pray this to Your praise and glory in the wonderful
name of Jesus. Amen."

Bill said that he recalled having once heard a profound question: "What
is the one thing you would want to teach a new believer?"

> Quick as a blister it came to me. The most important thing to
> teach a new believer or any believer is the attributes of God. Why?
> Why do we want to teach people that our God is great and mighty
> and holy and sovereign and all-powerful and wise in a loving way?
> Because the Christian life is a walk of faith, and that which is not
> of faith is sin, the Bible says. And without faith, it is impossible to
> please God…and the just shall live by faith.
>
> But faith must have an object. You've got to have faith and
> not depend on emotions and it is very important that if you and
> I are ever to become anything more than spiritual midgets, we must

understand who God is. And as we meditate on His greatness, those attributes somehow become a part of us, for "as a man thinketh in his heart so is he." The more we meditate on love and the wonder of our great God, the more our own wants are replaced.

This was crucial stuff to Bill. The mirror is no place to look unless it is angled toward the face of God. Bill believed that persons who viewed God rightly would be more likely to reach out to the world with the message of Christ.

The seed of this concept was growing that morning. Bill would later write a book on the attributes of God titled *The Character of God,* featuring a list of thirteen key attributes that had emerged from his own study:

1. Because God is a personal spirit, I will seek intimate fellowship with Him.
2. Because God is all-powerful, He can help me with anything.
3. Because God is ever-present, He is always with me.
4. Because God knows everything, I will go to Him with all my questions and concerns.
5. Because God is sovereign, I will joyfully submit to His will.
6. Because God is holy, I will devote myself to Him in purity, worship, and service.
7. Because God is absolute truth, I will believe what He says and live accordingly.
8. Because God is righteous, I will live by His standards.
9. Because God is just, He will always treat me fairly.
10. Because God is love, He is unconditionally committed to my well-being.
11. Because God is merciful, He forgives my sins when I sincerely confess them.
12. Because God is faithful, I will trust Him to always keep His promises.
13. Because God never changes, my future is secure and eternal.

Because Bill urgently wanted people to meditate on these key attributes, the Crusade ministry printed pocket-size cards containing the list, and many

Crusaders and others began using them as part of the prayer and fasting movement and in their devotional and reflective times.

Today, standing before the Asian leaders in the campground building in Australia, Bill cited other "lessons I've learned" as he continued his reflections. He spoke of the priority of loving one's spouse.

> Now I understand there's a difference in cultures, but we're all commanded by the Scriptures to love our wives no matter what the culture....
>
> You know, most of us will be married as long as fifty or sixty years; my parents were married for over seventy years. You might as well enjoy it! I mean if you're going to argue and fight, that's crazy. Enjoy each other. Laugh together. Pray together. Worship the Lord together. Serve Him together. Make it an adventure.
>
> God graciously gave Vonette a wonderful spirit as a wife and mother. I was twenty-seven years old when Vonette and I married. I had built a business and I was pretty self-sufficient. I knew what to do and how to do it. I was active in the church and was chairman of the evangelism program of the church, and I was out day and night serving the Lord, and I dragged Vonette along with me. I didn't know any better, and she seemed to enjoy it as far as I knew. The Lord God made her blind to the way I was treating her. She just fit in with my plans.
>
> I look back and recognize how dumb that was! Fortunately the Lord gave her grace...and I'm grateful for that. But I would encourage you to be more sensitive to the needs of your spouse than I was. You're going to live together as long as you live! Your spouse is far more important to you than your children. You're children come and go. They will leave home. They will live with their spouses. And they'll start their own families. And you'll always be the parent. You'll be interested in grandchildren and great-grandchildren. But the most important person in each of our lives is our spouse. So if I've learned anything, it's that Vonette is the most important person on this earth to me.

In his marriage, Bill said that he consistently practiced the use of "the twelve words." They weren't magic in the abracadabra sense, but powerful when spoken sincerely whenever he caught himself—or the Spirit caught him—slightly off-base with Vonette. Immediately, Bill would convey his heart by looking right at her: "I was wrong. I am sorry. Please forgive me. I love you." He meant those twelve words, and Vonette knew it. They were biblical and Christian in every way, and Vonette would comment, "What could you do but love a man like that?"

He cautioned the Asians against leaving family issues unconfronted, allowing them to fester: "A little pimple becomes a sore, and the sore becomes cancerous on the whole body of relationships. Teach the people where you are working to be open and honest, to admit their mistakes."

Bill also spoke to them about their duties as sons and daughters:

> I've tried to be a scriptural son. My parents are now with the Lord, and I hold fond and rich memories of them in my heart. Have courage as your parents grow old and you have the responsibility to care for them. Give special recognition to them. Your parents are important in God's eye.
>
> Concerning your children, a word to parents. Don't keep scolding and nagging your children, making them angry and resentful. Parents often are too busy to give their children time to interact, time just to talk. Listen to them. You're busy serving God and you don't have time to talk to them and so they become resentful, not only toward you but also against God. Bring them up instead with the loving discipline the Lord himself approves. Love your children. Communicate with your children. Teach them to love, trust, and obey the Lord our God above every other consideration of life.

Bill held up his Bible and said, "Another lesson I have learned is that this holy, inspired, inerrant Word is filled with power. If this is not a vital part of your daily living, if you're not feasting on the Word of God daily, you'll never be a strong Christian and you'll never really have much to say to your people."

He urged them to memorize Colossians 3:16-17, and quoted it from his *Living Bible:* "Remember what Christ taught and let his words enrich your lives and make you wise; teach them to each other and sing them out in psalms and hymns and spiritual songs, singing to the Lord with thankful hearts. And whatever you do or say, let it be as a representative of the Lord Jesus, and come with him into the presence of God the Father to give him your thanks."

Then Bill spoke about the Holy Spirit's role in our lives:

> It is impossible to live a holy life apart from the Holy Spirit. The Word of God and the Spirit of God are like wings on an airplane. You remove the Word, you remove one of the wings. You remove the Holy Spirit, you remove the other wing. We experience balance in life when we submit to the Holy Spirit and the Word....
>
> Is it any wonder that there are problems in the church when 95 percent do not understand the person and ministry of the Holy Spirit and only 2 percent are regularly sharing their faith? Sharing your faith comes from understanding the importance of the Holy Spirit.

Then he added,

> It is impossible to overexaggerate the importance of prayer: "Whatever you ask in my name I will do it." And whatever we ask according to God's will, He will hear and answer. These are promises.

Bill told them that one of the most critical decisions he and Vonette ever made was the commitment to "a life of prayer" when they started the ministry with that first round-the-clock prayer vigil at UCLA. "We saw miracles happen. Scores of students came to Christ. I must tell you that I have known liberty and joy and power and victory upon victory, which I attribute to prayer."

Finally, the coach added wise words about stifling criticism before it arises and swallowing hard and placing it in God's hands by prayer when criticism does come up.

There was a brief closing prayer, and another speaker urged everyone there to kneel for prayer.

Bill moved to the front row of folding chairs and knelt with two others to pray. In that three-gathered moment, his prayer implored God to move through Australia in revival power, to raise up the staff, full-time and volunteer, to help reach Australia and the world. He praised the Father for the love of the Son. He called upon the Holy Spirit to strengthen the other two men in his triangle of prayer.

The room of believers adjourned to a small dining area for a lunch of rice, chicken, and melon on plain tables. Then Bill and Vonette returned to their rooms for phone conversations to the United States and Europe. Bill labored as if he were in his office. In fact, as he later pointed out, a hotel room with a telephone constituted his usual "office" for nearly fifty years. One of the great joys of these later years was that now Vonette often traveled with him.

CHAPTER 28

Seeking God's Face

B y the midnineties, both of Bill and Vonette's sons were in the ministry. Zac had worked his way through Azusa University and Fuller Seminary and had accepted a call to a Presbyterian church in California—thereby fulfilling the foresight of Henrietta Mears, who had tagged him "the preacher" while he was still a young boy and had said, "Zac is special.… God's hand is upon him." Growing up, Zac almost always had a sense of being set apart by God.

Meanwhile, Brad had told Bill of his disenchantment with the pace of politics in transforming society. He had decided the best way to change society was to change people, something only Jesus Christ could do. So he chose to join the staff of Campus Crusade, a step that understandably brought joy to his parents. Bill and Vonette had never felt the freedom to openly recruit their sons for staff, wanting instead to pray that God would accomplish His perfect will for their lives, whatever that would be.

In the summer of 1994, Bill received a call for help from Brad, who with his wife, Cathy, was at this time on Crusade staff at the University of Washington in Seattle. They were living about twenty-five minutes from campus and were praying for a house much nearer as well as for something large enough to entertain students. They had found a home that fit those criteria, but it would require two thousand dollars in monthly rent, even with a steep discount.

So when he telephoned his father, Brad asked, "Dad, do you know of anybody up here who might have the financial resources and the interest to purchase a home that we would then lease from them?"

"I really don't," Bill replied. "In fact, you might be spinning your wheels and wasting a lot of time. I would encourage you to go look elsewhere."

But Brad was determined, based on what he and Cathy understood God to be leading them to do. They prayed and had the students and fellow staff praying as well.

A few weeks later, a couple whom Brad had never met heard of their need, and God led them to buy a good-sized home in the university district, which they then leased to Brad and Cathy at a very low rent. Brad described this answer to prayer as "a phenomenal experience.... God was building my faith."

He phoned Bill to tell him the news, and said, "O ye of little faith." Brad later would observe, "That was the only time in my life I believe I will ever say that" to his father. Bill, of course, was ecstatic and recounted the story of the way God honored Brad's faith to others as if it were his own experience.

That same year, God had been impressing upon Bill to fast and pray for forty days. He felt called to pray "for revival for believers and awakening among nonbelievers and for the fulfillment of the Great Commission." The world's need was great, and he believed America's resources were the key to getting the gospel to the world. But America was a mess, a moral cesspool. The nation had become largely dehumanized and desensitized to murder, mayhem, and all sorts of crime and had turned its back on the God of its Founding Fathers.

As he was meditating on 2 Chronicles 7:14, he came to see that prayer and fasting was the most effective way for most believers to fulfill all the requirements of that passage: "If my people, which are called by my name, shall humble themselves, and pray, and seek my face, and turn from their wicked ways; then will I hear from heaven, and will forgive their sin, and will heal their land." Technically, of course, the words were written to Israel thousands of years ago, but by Bill's theology, everything in the contract between God and Israel was available to believers in the God of Israel through faith in Jesus, Israel's Messiah.

Bill had fasted for a few days before, but never forty. Now he made up his mind to do it. He began on July 5. He would take nothing but water and fruit juices for forty days, following practical guidelines from secular books on the benefits of fasting, from a physician he had met from Colombia, Dr. Julio C. Ruibal, and also from Dr. Joon Gon Kim.

Bill would later say this fast revolutionized the way he understood his relationship with God: "The awareness of God's presence in my life was dramatically enhanced." It gave him new time to be alone with God and led to new inspiration to seek Him with a new passion. He now recommended fasting "unreservedly."

He reported that during his fast he began to foresee a vast awakening with "the greatest spiritual harvest in the history of the Church." The scope of this revival would depend on "how believers in America and the rest of the world respond to this call." He was convinced the Holy Spirit had given him this assurance during his fast: "I have spent fifty years studying God's Word and listening to His voice, and His message could not have been more clear."

On the twenty-ninth day of his fast, he was reading chapters 20 through 30 in 2 Chronicles and sensed that God had a special message for him there. In the record of the nation of Judah awash in sin due to the evil actions of her leaders, Bill saw a parallel with America—but Bill's focus was directed not to the behavior of America's politicians, but to that of her religious leaders.

Later, the story records how King Hezekiah came to power and reopened the doors of the temple that had been nailed shut by his evil father, Bill was captivated to see that Hezekiah wrote *letters* to be sent throughout the country calling for a return to worship in a cleansed temple (2 Chronicles 30).

When the fast was over, he realized his need to expedite a message to the whole body of American Christians by writing letters to hundreds of Christian influencers in this country. He had a plan and began to work it. First he contacted seventy-three prominent Christian pastors and organizational leaders to join him as the host committee on the invitation letter for "a time of fasting and prayer." Two dozen of them agreed. The letter would specifically *not* make any reference to Campus Crusade for Christ; Bill Bright himself was calling the cream of American evangelical Protestantism to their knees.

Then he sent the letter to about six hundred people and invited them to Orlando. He offered to provide their hotel accommodations if they would come for three days of fasting and prayer.

The letter was plain-spoken. America was in crisis. God would honor the priesthood of believers if their leaders would get on their knees and "seek God's face." No program. No performances. Just prayer and fasting for three days—December 5, 6, and 7.

He prayed for three hundred from the invited list to attend. More than six hundred showed up, giving Bill's personal staff a nightmarish logistical problem for lodging and requiring an extra run for juice.

The six hundred gathered in one big ballroom of the hotel for the sessions. There was no raised platform, only a single microphone, and Bill began with a simple prayer, asking God to touch each and every person there with the power of the Holy Spirit for individual, national, and world revival and for the fulfillment of the Great Commission.

Memphis pastor Dr. Adrian Rogers, a longtime friend of Bill's, declared: "I believe as the West goes, so goes the world. And as America goes, so goes the West. And as the church goes, so goes America. And as believers fast and pray, so goes the church."

Bill explained that he wanted each person to take a sheet of paper and write down the sins they knew existed in their lives. He urged them to do so thoughtfully, prayerfully, individually, and without comment. The room grew quiet. There was fierce and tearful scribbling. All eyes were down.

After what seemed an eternity, Bill spoke again. "Now write across your list: 'The blood of Jesus Christ cleanses from all sin.'" He reminded them of the promise of 1 John 1:9: "If we confess our sins, he is faithful and just to forgive us our sins and to cleanse us from all unrighteousness."

Then, as he had done thousands of times with Christian leaders in other parts of the world, Bill led them in seeking from God a fresh infilling of the Holy Spirit for personal revival and for reaching the world in the fulfillment of the Great Commission.

Next came a time for public confession. Bill had encouraged others there to come forward to speak, although he did not know what they would say. All in the room had successful ministries, but Bill suggested that none of them report on their accomplishments. What he was asking for, he said, was the confession of sin by the leaders of American Christianity. Without preaching, he offered a list of what some of those sins might be—loss of their "first love" for Jesus, pride, materialism, moral impurity, vanity, corner-cutting, racism, family neglect, a critical attitude toward others within Christianity, and failure to pray for "those in authority" in government.

One by one, major figures came forward to renounce their sins publicly and specifically. For those present, it was astonishing.

The president of the Southern Baptist Convention confessed that his denomination had played pat-a-cake with racist attitudes too long, that he had tolerated it, but that he had decided to target this area of racial reconcili-ation as his top priority for that year.

One of the most prominent propounders of the conservative faith ad-mitted that materialism had too often been a part of his decision-making, and he declared how embarrassed he was before God that this had been in his life. He renounced it.

A prominent Presbyterian leader confessed how the busyness of ministry was robbing him of the joy of his salvation and focus on Jesus Christ.

Up and down they came: Up to confess, down to pray. Their testimonies covered the gamut of human weakness, and their honesty, brokenness, and risk-taking faithfulness unloosed a dam-break of tears. There was not one dry eye there.

After the confession came more prayer, in groups of three. They prayed for each other, asking God to make whole, heal, and empower their brother or sister.

Over the three days there was wave upon wave of confession, session by session. There was also Scripture reading, the singing of simple, a cappella praise choruses, and much more prayer. It had the openness of a summer camp and the freshness of a baby dedication; the love of God Himself was hugging every one in the room.

Women read Scriptures telling of God's attitudes toward sin, of His for-giveness for those who genuinely turn their back on bad behavior, of His desire to bless any nation and people who sought Him early and often. The event was now a divine dialogue, a conversation between God and a few hundred of His human creations.

A lone African-American leader rose to speak. He was careful not to make more of the racism issue than had been made, and did not claim to speak for anyone but himself, but he told the virtually all-white gathering that *he* forgave the openly vulnerable leader who had confessed this problem. He also confessed the built-up bitterness that he had to deal with in coping with racist attitudes in the ministry from believers who knew better.

As the confession and prayer continued, Bill pointed them to the purpose of it all: Loving the world with the message of Christ and seeing the fulfillment of the Great Commission in this generation. But he made no specific appeals, distributed no literature, and sought no direct partnerships.

By the third day, there was fusion in the group and a complex inner explosion of confidence, purpose, focus, faith, filling. Bill urged others to take seriously his challenge to undertake a forty-day fast. He gave his own testimony of that experience.

A common note among these leaders' confessions had been their own failure to insist upon obedience to the clear command to "pray for those in authority." As a result, they drew up and signed a letter to the president, vice president, leaders of the House and Senate, Supreme Court justices, and the Joint Chiefs of Staff, pledging to be prayerful for them and urging the need for America to confess her sins, even as they had done.

After the gathering, Dr. Lloyd John Ogilvie, a pastor who would soon become chaplain of the U.S. Senate, commented that he thought Bill Bright and Billy Graham were the only persons in America who could call such a meeting and get such a tremendous turnout. They probably were the only people as well who could call such powerful, prominent leaders to their very knees in specific repentance and confession.

In the days that followed, Bill wrote and rushed into print a two-hundred-page book, *The Coming Revival: America's Call to Fast, Pray, and "Seek God's Face."* Once again he declared that America's problem was her having become disconnected from the God who gave the nation birth. He focused not only on the sins of the leaders but the sins of the citizens. "Selfishness has become a hallmark of the people," he wrote. "Americans are growing more cynical and less compassionate."

Meanwhile, Bill suggested that his staff begin planning at once to hold a much larger session the next fall, in 1995. The first fasting and prayer event had been "only a warm-up," he said. "Would God want us to stop there?"

That fall in Los Angeles, four thousand persons showed up for the second three-day convocation of fasting and prayer with Bill Bright, and it became an annual event, a movement itself in American Christendom. Satellite television was added in 1996, and by 1999, thousands of satellite sites in every state and several foreign locations would carry the eighteen-hour telecast that year from Houston, linking an estimated two million participants.

The original fasting and prayer gathering in Orlando had unleashed a movement in American Christianity. It had the effect of a one-on-one discipling experience for these Christian leaders—with the Holy Spirit as the discipler.

Bill said that he personally was praying for two million Americans to join him in forty-day fasts for revival in America and fulfillment of the Great Commission in this generation, and he predicted that one day he himself would "graduate" to a life devoted entirely to encouraging believers to fast and pray for world revival and the fulfillment of the Great Commission.

While Bill prayed and led so many others to pray, he also kept up his prophetic urgings to his nation. On July 4, 1997, he joined several American religious leaders in signing a declaration titled "We Hold These Truths—A Statement of Christian Conscience and Citizenship." It did not go quite as far as he would have liked, but it was a step in the right direction. "The bitter consequences of disordered liberty resulting from the denial of moral truth are by now painfully familiar," the signers proclaimed as they spelled out America's failures. "We cannot boast of what we have made of the experiment entrusted to our hands." In the lengthy document's conclusion, they expressed their unified vision:

> We are Catholics, Orthodox, and Protestants of differing convictions on many issues. We are conservatives and progressives of various ethnic and racial identities and with differing political views. We are agreed that we must seek together an America that respects the sanctity of human life, enables the poor to be full participants in our society, strives to overcome racism, and is committed to rebuilding the family. We are agreed that government by the consent of the governed has been thrown into question, and, as a

result, our constitutional order is in crisis. We are agreed that—whether the question be protection of the unborn, providing for the poor, restoring the family, or racial justice—we can and must bring law and public policy into greater harmony with the "laws of nature and of nature's God."

The following year Bill (with coauthor John N. Damoose) completed the book *Red Sky in the Morning,* a clear and compelling x-ray of the God-centered orientation of America's founders and another effort at helping to restore America's biblical heritage. Bill prayed that *Red Sky* would help prompt a return to the nation's spiritual roots.

CHAPTER 29

Bridge Builder

O n more than one occasion, Bill had invited the nation's African-American church leaders to take part in the activities of Campus Crusade. Some did get involved in Here's Life, America, but not to the degree he desired.

Bill's heart was to help black pastors and ministry leaders participate in the Great Commission in new ways—just as he desired that for Americans of every skin color. He was frustrated that his offers of complete leadership support, materials, and training were not accepted by the leaders of black denominations when he knew there were so many African-American individuals and churches who wanted to participate.

As with many a dream, he never gave up. Bill wanted success in this important relationship, and planned for it. Chicago '81 drew together fifteen hundred pastors, students, and laymen who accepted the challenge to influence African-Americans for Christ and for the world.

Ultimately, Bill insisted that Crusade recognize the economic disadvantages of many African-Americans who did not have access to a financial support base as large as what other would-be staffers had. He invited the entire Crusade staff to volunteer 2 percent of their own fund-raising to help support minority staff in America. Bill and Vonette set the pace, giving a total of 27 percent of their monthly income to Crusade. Eventually, this decision helped spawn the Destiny Movement, Inc., a Crusade ministry of African-Americans to African-Americans.

Increasingly, Bill made bridge-building to disaffected and disconnected groups a part of his agenda. He wasn't turning his back on his friends in evangelical America as much as he was seeking to reach out in love to others across the world.

Bill consciously aimed to make a difference by interacting with those who might have real and legitimate grievances with those who called themselves Christian. This brought him to the point where he believed, in America at least, that the word *Christian* was evoking emotional political baggage—whether it was the highly publicized moral failure of certain contemporary evangelists or the terrible things done by "the church" in the Crusades and Inquisitions of earlier centuries.

He even grew to question the helpfulness of the word *evangelical.* "Frankly, as honored as that word is—and I'm a fundamentalist when it comes to theology—I do not want to use the word *evangelical* because that means I'm not willing to reach out to the Catholics, and the Orthodox, and all the other mainline believers who love Christ as we do." In a letter to the entire Crusade staff, Bill wrote, "We would be more accurate to call ourselves 'Followers of Jesus.'"

Because of the gargantuan size of the Roman Catholic Church, Bill could not foresee fulfillment of the Great Commission in his generation without cooperating with at least some individual believers within that huge denomination of a billion persons worldwide. As early as 1969 Bill had told a reporter, "We do not attack the Roman Church. We believe God is doing a mighty work in it and will no doubt use millions of Roman Catholics to help evangelize the world."

Throughout the Here's Life, America campaign in the midseventies, Bill had found himself cooperating with Roman Catholics. It was during the seventies as well that a young Chicagoan of Polish Catholic heritage named Joe Losiak became inspired by Crusade's materials. He took an armful of them and boldly flew to Poland to discuss their value with a leading priest in the Roman Catholic Church. Of course, approval for use of such literature would have to come from higher up—and that approval came! Crusade literature soon was being used to train thousands of students and church leaders in lay renewal movements within the Catholic Church in Poland. It was a story Bill never forgot.

In the 1980s, almost annually, Bill would take a strong role in an annual Washington for Jesus event that drew Catholic priests, Pentecostal leaders, Seventh-Day Adventists, and popular televangelists like Robert Schuller. Bill was criticized among constituents of his own community of faith for associating with such people. But he just kept on cooperating, continuing to hold high the name of Jesus as Savior-God.

When Tyndale House and the Paulist National Catholic Evangelization Association decided to create a series of publications on evangelistic techniques, Bill contributed an article along with Pope John Paul II, Archbishop Joseph Bernardin, and others.

As a bridge-building initiative with both Catholics and Jews, Bill went to President Reagan with the suggestion for a "Year of the Bible" as a means of pointing people "back to the Book." The president told him that an act of Congress would be required. Bill went to work, mainly through Senator William Armstrong of Colorado and Congressman Carlos Moorhead of California, and the law was enacted with a presidential proclamation in 1983. Bill took care to see that the leadership of the event was ecumenical by including Jewish, Catholic, and Protestant leaders.

In 1986, during a plenary session at the Amsterdam '86 conference with Billy Graham, Bill said, "There was a day when Protestants and Roman Catholics would not have much to do with one another. But today the Spirit of God is doing such a great work in both the Roman Catholic and Protestant fellowships and communions that I feel very much at home wherever Jesus Christ is honored."

That same year Bill endorsed *The Mission,* a movie about Catholic missionaries "with a life-changing message that will enrich your life for years to come." About this time Bill met a prominent Catholic academician in Rome who shared that he had come across the Four Spiritual Laws and had prayed the prayer inviting Christ once and for all to come into his life. The educator liked the booklet and the Holy Spirit presentation and asked Bill if he could make liberal use of this content in his own writings. Without hesitation, Bill consented.

With these and other rich personal experiences with individual Catholics and with Catholic leaders, it was hardly surprising when Bill—along with evangelical leaders such as Chuck Colson and James Marker—signed a document entitled "Evangelicals and Catholics Together" (ECT) on March 29, 1994. He signed because ECT had so many areas of common accord between the evangelicals he knew and the individual Catholics he knew, men and women who really had trusted Jesus Christ alone for their salvation and for whom the various rituals of the Roman Catholic Church were graces rather than life-giving in and of themselves. Bill also appreciated the Roman Catholic Church's stand on issues such as abortion, as well as Pope John Paul II's focus on lifting up Jesus and his reminders to the Roman Catholic Church that the original manuscripts of the Bible served as the bedrock of Christian belief.

Those were reasons enough for Bill, but he had others. Evaluating everything in light of the Great Commission, he knew scores of Catholic leaders in foreign countries who often were the only "lighthouses" with which Crusade could interact in worship of the Lord Jesus and in trying to spread the gospel. He knew that by cooperating with Catholics, many doors could be flung open and advance bases established for making use of the *Jesus* film, the Four Spiritual Laws, and the Holy Spirit booklet. He knew that American preoccupation with religious organizations and denominations was an obstacle on the mission field to reaching people with the love of God and the Word of God, focusing on the Son of God. Therefore he viewed sitting in a conference to find topics of agreement with Catholics as a reasonable thing to do, at least for building bridges of love.

Yet Bill recognized that the issue was a hot potato. He had no doubts that salvation is exclusively a matter of grace by faith, not of works. And he was not embracing Marian worship or prayer to the saints. But the issue remained: Why was he was associating with persons in the huge Roman Catholic Church, whose established doctrines were clearly different?

Plenty of additional issues were raised as well. Had Bill forgotten how deep and wide was the rift between Catholics and Protestants? Or the teaching by many Protestant scholars that the Roman Catholic Church is the whore of Babylon in end-times prophecy?

As controversy about ECT grew, Bill accepted a face-to-face "peace meeting" set up by three national Christian leaders who said they wanted to understand his position and build bridges. However, after several minutes of discussion, some of it intemperate, one of the leaders went so far as to suggest that Bill Bright was a "heretic" and added, "you are no longer my brother." The charges hurt him, but he rested his position with the Lord and did not seek to defend himself.

The controversy continued, although most of the American Christian organizations that partnered with Crusade were unoffended; they, too, had been in missions cooperation with Catholics around the world and in political stands in Washington. Some took the offensive to defend the ECT signers. They argued that failing to seize opportunities to cooperate in the sharing of one's faith was itself a sin. They cited scriptural admonitions to work for good and not evil. They quoted Jesus' words, "He that is not against us is for us."

Bill worked with the original ECT group and others to fashion a more precise statement in 1997 that tried to be specific on the point of personal salvation. Entitled "The Gift of Salvation," it began by quoting John 3:16, and continued:

> We give thanks to God that in recent years many Evangelicals and Catholics, ourselves among them, have been able to express a common faith in Christ and so to acknowledge one another as brothers and sisters in Christ. We confess together one God, the Father, the Son, and the Holy Spirit; we confess Jesus Christ the Incarnate Son of God; we affirm the binding authority of Holy Scripture, God's inspired Word; and we acknowledge the Apostles' and Nicene Creeds as faithful witnesses to that Word.
>
> The effectiveness of our witness for Christ depends upon the work of the Holy Spirit, who calls and empowers us to confess together the meaning of the salvation promised and accomplished in Christ Jesus our Lord. Through prayer and study of Holy Scripture, and aided by the Church's reflection on the sacred text from earliest times, we have found that, notwithstanding some persistent and serious differences, we can together bear witness to the gift of salvation in Jesus Christ. To this saving gift we now testify, speaking not for, but from and to, our several communities....

The document ranged for thousands of words. The signers included such prominent evangelical leaders as Bright, Colson, and Packer again, as well as pastor and leading Christian author Max Lucado and theologians Dr. Harold O. J. Brown and Dr. John Woodbridge of Trinity Evangelical Divinity School, Dr. Os Guinness of the Trinity Forum, Dr. Kent R. Hill of Eastern Nazarene College, Dr. T. M. Moore of Chesapeake Theological Seminary, Dr. Richard Mouw of Fuller Theological Seminary, and Dr. Mark A. Noll and Dr. Timothy R. Phillips of Wheaton College. Among the many Roman Catholic signers were well-known authors Richard John Neuhaus of the Institute on Religion and Public Life, Michael Novak of the American Enterprise Institute, and Dr. Peter Kreeft of Boston College.

Meanwhile, Bill's bridge-building extended to Jews as well. In the 1970s Bill had been given an award as Churchman of the Year by the Religious Heritage Foundation, which simultaneously honored an outstanding Jewish leader who had often been critical of evangelical Christianity in general and Bill Bright in particular. As the two men stood side by side receiving their respective awards, Bill asked if they could have breakfast together. There was an unenthusiastic acceptance.

"I want to express my heart," Bill began at breakfast. "My Lord is a Jew. I love the Jews, God's chosen people. The Bible is written almost entirely by Jews. The second most powerful influence on my life, Saul of Tarsus who became Paul, was a Jew. I am a debtor to the Jewish people. And you need to know that Bible-believing Christians are among the strongest friends of Israel and of the Jewish people." Bill's words were received graciously and a mutual respect formed.

In his earlier years of ministry Bill had been ambivalent about Jewish matters, but that was no longer true. He came to understand from the Jewish perspective how terrible the persecution of Jews had been through the ages, often at the hands of so-called Christians and under nominally Christian governments. But he also wanted to be an ambassador to them of His Lord, the Jewish Carpenter and the living Christ, without any organized, denominational trappings. He consciously began to undertake initiatives behind the scenes to have dialogue with Jewish leaders and individuals. These efforts produced what he called "warm fellowship," especially with orthodox and conservative Jewish leaders.

He made known his desire for Americans to return to the Judeo-Christian principles of their roots. While he harbored no dreams of a Christocentric government, he would not give up on the need for a biblical one. Above all, he wanted to convey his love for all Jewish people, for Israel, and for its leaders.

In the 1990s a friend in Miami, Allen Morris, gave Bill a Star of David necklace containing a cross, which he chose to wear regularly thereafter. One day in the Orlando condominium complex where the Brights lived, a Jewish neighbor told Bill about a business deal in which the neighbor had a bad experience with a Christian. Bill listened and sought to sympathize, but he was rebuffed until he reached into his shirt and pulled out the Star of David necklace.

"Do you mean it?" the neighbor replied.

"My Lord is a Jew," Bill began and gave his witness for Jesus. He also found out more about the business deal and reported back to his Jewish neighbor. Not every encounter yields immediate fruit, Bill had long ago learned, but he knew he had been faithful in this one.

In 1997 a public prayer by Bill set off a firestorm regarding Jewish sensitivity after his words were incorrectly understood and the misperception reported by the news media. In the opening session of the Florida Legislature in Tallahassee, Bill was invited to pray. He began with the words, "Holy Father, Almighty God, Creator of the Universe of more than a hundred billion galaxies, we bow in reverence and in awe before You. You are holy and righteous, loving and forgiving; You are faithful and just. There is no one like You; You alone are worthy of our trust and praise.…"

He then concluded the prayer by saying, "I come to You, Father, in the name of the One whom you sent.… We worship You and we praise You and adore You, the true God, the only God. May Your blessing be upon this group of men and women in an unprecedented way."

After the prayer, one of the Jewish legislators approached Bill to say that the prayer offended him. When Bill showed him the actual written wording from which he had prayed, the legislator apologized. Nevertheless, newspaper reporters at the scene portrayed the prayer as divisive and reported that Bill had spoken of "the Lord Jesus Christ" as "the true God, the only God."

Bill wrote out his response and gave this to the media (which chose not to print it). "If I offended anyone," he wrote, "I have said that I am truly sorry and ask their forgiveness. And for the sake of a good relationship which I earnestly desire with everyone, including the Jewish community, please let me accurately tell you what I actually said." He explained:

> Even though I, as a true follower of Yeshua (Jesus), believe that He is indeed God, as He proclaimed Himself to be, you will observe that my prayer offered at the joint session of the House and Senate was a prayer clearly offered to our heavenly Father....
>
> While my prayer was not blatantly Christological...I believe I or anyone should have the liberty to pray the way they want to in any public situation. I do not believe that there would have been any controversy if a Muslim had prayed to Allah in that situation, or a Buddhist or Hindu had prayed in his customary manner, or a person of any other religion had prayed to their god, gods, goddess or goddesses. In fact, I suspect there would have been an outpouring of sympathy and support from the secular media.
>
> From my frequent travels, it is my observation that all across America the only target of these attacks is the Christian who prays in the name of Jesus. This is not right, and efforts to stop Christians from praying according to their conscience are a violation of the Constitution. Our Constitution allows people of all persuasions to pray freely according to the dictates of their beliefs and conscience, whether invited to pray before a government body or anywhere else.
>
> Equally important, I believe a generic, faithless, meaningless prayer will not go past the ceiling, and would be an insult to the God whom we worship and nothing but empty ceremonial words for human ears only, which our nation does not need. America desperately needs divine, supernatural intervention to solve the

gargantuan problems we face. It is symptomatic of our nation's problems that there are concerted efforts to stop prayers that reach the Holy of Holies—the actual throne of grace in the heavenlies.

As you probably know, Christian prayers have their roots in Mosaic Law as practiced for centuries by the ancient Hebrews before the coming of Yeshua. At that time, access to God was only through the blood atonement offered by the high priest, a symbolic act that cleansed from sin (Leviticus 16, etc.). True followers of Yeshua still believe with Moses—that blood sacrifice is a divine and eternal requisite for access to God. The Torah never changed. But we followers of Yeshua believe that those centuries of blood sacrifice were symbolic and prophetic of the perfect Lamb described by Isaiah 53 who was to come and who shed His own blood, one time, for all people everywhere, Jewish and Gentile of all nations. As with Moses, we are persuaded that it is the blood of the Lamb, in our case Yeshua, as we invoke His name, which gives us access to the Father. To deny that to us is to deny us access to God, making our prayers meaningless. To us that would be blasphemous.

No one should try to strip a follower of Yeshua of what we believe is the very key to God's heart and ear—the invocation of His own Son's name and sacrifice. To do so would be censorship of our most sacred and holy beliefs.

For Bill, the misunderstanding over the prayer was one more reason to express gratitude to His wise and sovereign Father. Thanking God, he had decided years earlier, was the best way to communicate with the living God. It was an act of faith, and Bill simply believed the Bible's statements: "Without faith it is impossible to please him.... Whatsoever is not of faith is sin.... Ask, and ye shall receive" (Hebrews 11:6; Romans 14:23; John 16:24). He seemed to have a verse for every situation, and all his circumstances seemed to be covered by "In every thing give thanks: for this is the will of God in Christ Jesus concerning you" (1 Thessalonians 5:18).

His pattern was to give God his troubles at once and expect solutions. "I learned to cast my trials and tribulation upon the Lord as soon as they are brought to my attention. For example," he would say on one occasion, "I can list at least twenty-five major problems that I've given to the Lord today—some of which would crush me and destroy my effectiveness if I tried to carry them myself…. But God's Word assures us that problems and trials are always a blessing for the trusting, obedient Christian."

CHAPTER 30

The Templeton Prize

L ong before he began to gain national and international recognition, Bill had made a conscious decision to foster humility. It clearly was a prerequisite of a Scripture passage he treasured: "If my people, who are called by my name, *shall humble themselves...*"

This requirement of humility, he reasoned, would have to be obeyed in order to expect the blessings of God.

Early in his studies he had been touched by the pen of Andrew Murray:

> Humility is perfect quietness of heart. It is to expect nothing, to wonder at nothing that is done to me, to feel nothing done against me. It is to be at rest when nobody praises me, and when I am blamed or despised. It is to have a blessed home in the Lord, where I can go in and shut the door, and kneel to my Father in secret, and am at peace as in a deep sea of calmness, when all around and above is trouble.

Having that focal discipline in his heart helped him keep the adventures of 1996 in perspective. He received an abundance of accolades within a matter of months, as he was inducted into the State of Oklahoma Hall of Fame and marked the forty-fifth anniversary of his ministry and his seventy-fifth birthday—as well as receiving the crowning tribute: winning the Templeton Prize for Progress in Religion, the world's largest annual prize, currently valued at more than $1 million.

The only honor of its kind, it was established in 1971 by Sir John Templeton, a Tennessee-born international investor who became a legend on Wall Street as founder of some of the world's largest and most successful investment funds. Templeton was concerned that religion—particularly progress in religion—was unrecognized on the world scale. "The purpose of the Templeton Prize," he stated,

> is threefold. The first is to recognize a living person who has done something unique and original to increase humankind's love and/or understanding of God. Second, the Prize is intended to inspire others to learn about the work of each recipient and to undertake similar or new spiritually related endeavors. Third, the Prize is designed to encourage a mindset in which the world as a whole looks in expectation to progress in spirituality and spiritual information.

Taken collectively, the panel of judges for the 1996 award seemed hardly prone by their background to select a missionary-evangelist. Besides former American President George Bush, they included businessman and Jewish activist and philanthropist Norman E. Alexander; Unity Church leader James Dillet Freeman, who was also a poet and lecturer; Nichiko Niwana, leader of a Tokyo-based Buddhist international lay organization with 6.5 million members worldwide and head of the World Conference on Religion and Peace; Winfred Crothers, a registered nurse from Toronto; Robert John Russell, founder and director of the Center for Theology and the Natural Sciences in Berkeley and a member of the Society of Ordained Scientists; Anne D. Zimmerman, a physician and surgeon from Casper, Wyoming; the duke of Abercorn, a member of the British Parliament and trustee of the Winston Churchill Memorial Trust; and Viscount Brentford, a member of the House of Lords who was active in the Church of England and in Third World issues.

The nomination they contemplated included something unique: A full statement by the spouse of the nominee. Vonette had been reluctant to prepare it, but those nominating Bill felt her special perspective could overcome any unspoken objections. No one else knew Bill Bright better. Further, her own credibility as cofounder of Campus Crusade and as a leader in the effort to establish a specific day for America's National Day of Prayer, in the Great Commission Prayer Crusade, and on the Lausanne Committee for World Evangelization made her fully qualified to comment on Bill's career.

Among her written remarks were these:

> His character has always spoken as loudly as his words.… Bill is a bridge builder. Without compromising his convictions, he has always built friendships and partnerships with people of all religions and nationalities. He has taken the initiative time and again to bring denominations together, to encourage people to work together, to pursue peace.…
>
> There is no question about integrity. He has not been untested, but there has never been a time he has compromised on principle. He so lives what he believes and demonstrates trust. What most people regard as problems, he sees as an opportunity to trust God.… He has a wonderful sense of humor that has helped us both keep our perspective.
>
> I know we are in an era where it may be distinctive to know without any doubt that this Christian leader has been a faithful husband and father. Our shared prayer for years on our knees has been that we would never do anything to bring disgrace to the name of our dear Lord. And He has given us the grace to have an unwavering commitment to each other. In fact, Bill has prayed that God would take his life before He would allow him to be unfaithful to me.
>
> Although a man of rare vision and drive, one of the qualities I constantly observe is his heart of compassion. When people are in need, whether he knows them personally or not, his heart is easily moved and he seeks to meet that need.… This man is not only my lover and best friend, but also my minister.

In May 1996 Bill Bright was announced as the twenty-sixth winner of the annual prize (previous winners had included Mother Teresa, Billy Graham, and Aleksandr Solzhenitsyn). The official statement included these words:

> He is perhaps God's supersalesman who has utilized the technology of his day to "go and make disciples of all the nations." The number of people that Bill Bright and his coworkers in Campus Crusade have reached with the gospel would be the envy of any advertising agency's report to a client. Yet Bill Bright is not fully satisfied: hence he strives to share the gospel with every person on earth by the end of the year 2000. And if his past and current achievements are anything to go by, who is to doubt his intention and desire to fulfill his stated aim in five short years?
>
> A detailed strategy marshaled from a lifetime of experience in marketing, coupled with a strong commitment entrenched in the Christian faith, sets Bill Bright aside from many others. He is a convinced layman whose abundant energy for the cause of the faith has been richly rewarded. A preacher who has no pulpit of his own but who, to paraphrase John Wesley, has the world as his parish.
>
> Some may be critical of Bill Bright, but no one can surely doubt the genuine nature of this man who has denied himself the luxuries of life for the gospel of Jesus: who did forsake corporate success for the relentless task of telling the "ever new" story of the babe from Bethlehem.

Sir John Templeton himself said privately, "He's just the kind of man I had in mind when I started the program twenty-five years ago, because he's an example to everybody of all religions that it's possible to have progress in religion."

The prize ceremonies included a presentation in London and his formal acceptance of the award in Rome, where Bill's introduction by a

Roman Catholic cardinal included recognition of his contribution to the Evangelicals and Catholics Together document.

In his acceptance remarks, Bill was himself: gracious, visionary, Christ-centered, diplomatic, and bold.

"Dear friends," he said, "the driving force of my life is to live and walk and work in the same reality and in the same power and vitality of the New Testament Christians, and to help complete the Great Commission given by our Lord—and do it by December 31 of A.D. 2000."

In prophetic voice he warned: "Nuclear and biological weapons are available to terrorists who will not hesitate to use them. New strains of diseases are epidemic, and scientists predict more. The interdependent world economy is a house of cards built on debt, electronic monetary transfers, and computer entries, which could collapse with one major disaster."

He spoke of America's decay and how he revered George Washington, among all American heroes, for his faith and perseverance. He quoted Abraham Lincoln on national fasting and prayer. He contrasted the godless former Soviet Union's economy with the godly majority of South Korea to illustrate the importance of a nation's obedience to God.

He emphasized Christ: "You will observe that I purposely do not speak of religion, or the church, which I love, but I speak of a personal relationship with Jesus Christ as God incarnate. This relationship is available to all people, everywhere, in every country and in every culture, regardless of race, age, or gender.

"Unfortunately, there is much skepticism about the church on the part of many nonbelievers and believers alike. They fail to see the power of Christ in much of the twentieth-century church because all too often they are exposed to a Christianity that is impotent and fruitless."

People "lack an understanding of who God really is," he said, reiterating one of his life themes. "They need an understanding of His attributes. The God who created the universe is totally sovereign; He is omnipotent... omnipresent...omniscient.... He is all-wise, holy, perfect, loving, and merciful. We are commanded to love God with all our heart, soul, and mind. We are commanded to obey and trust Him. But without an understanding of who He is, we are trying to trust someone whom we have not yet experienced to be trustworthy. Therefore, to truly love, obey, and trust God, we must know who He is."

He portrayed the sweeping experience of his call and vision:

> An unseen hand, whom I discovered has a name, became the driving force in my life—an inextinguishable fire in my bosom that will not go out, but just keeps burning and burning and burning all the more brightly—a spiritual flame that has started brushfires, then raging conflagrations all over the world.
>
> As a young man, I was a materialist and humanist. So I can identify with multitudes of men and women, young and old, throughout the world, who have little knowledge of God. I was committed to whatever it took—hard work and long hours—to accomplish the materialistic goals I had set for myself, to build my own business and financial empire. I was the center of my universe....
>
> I discovered the amazing truth that this magnificent Creator, this all-powerful Almighty God, not only created the universe, but He loved me—little, insignificant me, less than a nameless speck in space—and He devised and through His prophets revealed an elaborate plan to redeem me and all mankind by personally visiting this planet as the God-man, Jesus of Nazareth, the only begotten Son of God. He even declared that He will share His eternal kingdom with me and all people of the world who will accept His free gift of love and forgiveness.
>
> The sheer strength, power, love, and majesty of this Man, the Holy One of Israel, the Son of God, totally captivated me. I was drawn to know Him better and personally. This began a lifelong quest and inquiry, an exciting spiritual journey, which continues to this day....
>
> In the lengthening shadows of my life, I am preparing to pass the torch to you and others. I speak to you after fifty years of ministering to the intellectual world—students and professors—and

other segments of society. In thousands of lectures and in some fifty books and booklets, I have endeavored to communicate spiritual truths that will inevitably change the lives of men and women who respond. They, in turn, continue this process of spiritual multiplication, resulting in changed societies and countries....

Will you accept that torch and join me and millions of others who are already committed to following Christ, proclaiming "the most joyful news ever announced," to help populate the kingdom of heaven, and to help build a better world here on planet Earth? Over half the people who have ever been alive are alive today. Those who do not know Him desperately need to meet and know our great Creator God and heavenly Father, who "so loved the world that he gave his only begotten Son, that whosoever believeth in Him shall not perish but have everlasting life."

Bill received a standing ovation for his forty-five-minute oration. In a reception afterward, he accepted the congratulations of several hundred persons, including evangelical leaders from around the world.

As Bill made his way through the jam-packed reception room, he met Zac and Brad, one by one. To each he said: "You realize that none of this would have happened without your sacrifice."

On the flight back to America from Rome, Bill's reflections were not on Campus Crusade's latest accomplishments and growth but on his distant past—on the string of "coincidences" in his early years that so clearly showed God's hand in answering prayer, especially those of his mother. He thought of her dedicating her unborn son to God; of his football injury that kept him from military service but created in him a hunger to be part of an army changing the world; of his first night in Los Angeles, when he picked up a hitchhiker who took him to meet a few of the most visionary Christian leaders of the century; of his trying out a church down the street that happened to have an extraordinary ministry to people of his age and interests as well as an education director who was Spirit-filled, sought-after, fruitful, respected, able, and with a heart's focus on training young men for ministry to the world. He thought of his experience at Princeton Theological Seminary and the connections and circumstances that prompted him to enroll in the fledgling Fuller Seminary, where academic quality blended with an emphasis on world evangelization—scholarship and salesmanship, to put it bluntly, education and evangelism, intellect and spirit. He thought of the scientifically oriented Vonette Zachary from his Oklahoma hometown, who had a minor in chemistry and planned to teach but who happened to be confronted with the claims of Christ by a former chemistry teacher who was mentoring the man Vonette wanted to marry.

These were the "coincidences" that had launched his life—and on that airplane ride home, he remembered them with a vividness as if he were reliving them all over again.

CHAPTER 31

Keeping Score

Bill never lost the wonder of the unusual in his life—the Contract, the Vision, knowing the constant love of God and of Vonette and the boys, watching the ministry grow and encircle the globe. He would just shake his head and say, "Thank You, thank You, Holy Father!"

He now had more reasons than ever to be grateful for his decision to leave the business of trying to make money for the Lord's work. If he had continued being successful as a businessman, in his lifetime he might have been able to give as much as $1 million or even—with a few miracles—$100 million toward the fulfillment of the Great Commission. But by dedicating his life to helping thousands of others work to fulfill the Great Commission, Bill was seeing hundreds of millions of dollars, even billions, flow into the kingdom's work through thousands and thousands of people who influenced millions of others.

In the fall of 1998, a supporter and longtime friend had included these words in a letter to Bill and Vonette: "In this life, I trust the Lord will never allow you to know how many lives you two have directly and indirectly touched for Jesus." He no doubt was thinking of having the privilege of that discovery reserved for when the Brights met the Lord in heaven.

But Bill aimed high...and kept score.

As a matter of stewardship, Bill was interested in getting the greatest return on time and dollars invested, and he pursued the collection of reliable reports and statistics. "You can expect only what you inspect," he would quote, and "you can't manage what you can't measure."

He also believed in the value of making public the numbers that accurately reflected ministry results. For the glory of God, he would say, it's worthwhile to tell what you know and can reasonably assess, even when it's impossible to know precisely.

To this end, staff members were required to file reports on the fruitfulness of their ministries. By 1990, Bailey Marks had directed the development of a "standard ministry tracking" system, including a regular data report titled *Vital Signs,* a publication subject to review by the Evangelical Council for Financial Accountability.

In 1999 the *Vital Signs* data below demonstrated just how far the movement had developed since Bill and Vonette set out in obedience to the Vision. At that point in time, the statistics for Crusade showed the following:

- 20,514 full-time staff worldwide, plus 663,612 trained volunteer staff. This did not include the millions of other laypersons who had been trained across the world in previous years and who were putting their training to work day by day. By any reasonable projection, God had multiplied Bill and Vonette into a mighty worldwide witness.

- Full-time staff or a ministry presence in 181 countries, representing 99.2 percent of the world's population. There was an active Crusade ministry in 390 strategic urban centers around the world and on 1,085 priority university campuses.

- More than 852 million "exposures" to the gospel in the previous year (including 720 million through Crusade staff efforts and 132 million by partnership organizations). These "exposures" came mainly through the various methods of showing the *Jesus* film. Since the Crusade ministry began in 1951, there had been approximately 4.5 billion exposures to the gospel worldwide through Crusade and its ministry partners.

- More than 54.5 million salvation decisions for Christ in the previous year in "live" evangelism situations through Crusade and its partners' efforts. That definition meant that a trained Crusade person was physically present in counseling with these persons after a presentation of the gospel; the total excluded responses to electronically broadcast presentations.

- More than 100,000 churches which Crusade had helped plant worldwide in the twentieth century, in cooperation with other partners, who were for the most part indigenous churches.

The New Life 2000 strategy was bearing fruit. With its many partners, Crusade had established approximately 3,200 training centers in million-person-target-areas worldwide, with "active ministry presence" in training, mass evangelism, and spiritual multiplication.

How accurate were the numbers? The evidence seemed to be that, if anything, they were too small. For example, records of Christian conversions in communist and other tyrannical countries often could not be conveyed, lest the lists produce targets for state police harassment or imprisonment of believers.

"We have been so very conservative," Bill said, quickly adding that "only the Lord knows who is making sincere commitments."

To qualify as an "indicated decision," an individual voluntarily fills out his or her own name and records the decision made. The *Vital Signs* publication reported other clarifying definitions. For example, an "exposure" occurs "when a person hears a clear presentation of the gospel and has an opportunity to respond by trusting in Jesus Christ as Savior." A "live" exposure occurs when there are trained persons presenting the gospel and calling for a decision. This excludes, therefore, a television program's total audience. But it would include instances when viewers of the television presentation make a telephone call to talk with trained counselors or when they mail in a response.

What did all these big numbers mean? They meant essentially that every person counts with Bill Bright. His desire for data was to help everyone in the Crusade movement keep a daily focus on influencing individuals for Christ. To him, this was no marketing contest; this was eternal business. The once-a-week staff prayer sessions, occurring throughout the movement and sometimes lasting hours, were filled with celebration as reports were registered from around the world.

Those reports also pointed to areas of need for greater prayer and planning and effort. While there were 4,852,830 "decisions" recorded in Sudan in 1998, along with 2,491,425 in India, 764,075 in Nigeria, and 420,606 in

Mexico, the numbers were only 38 in Morocco and 21 in Algeria—two countries where such choices in the face of militant Islamic forces can mean certain death.

As for ministry structure, there were 6 leaders reporting directly to Bill at the end of the twentieth century. Together they supervised the more than 20,500 staff and 663,000 volunteers. Of the ministry's team of international leaders, 14 of the 20 were non-Americans and 13 were non-Caucasian. The Crusade international ministry was divided into 13 major regions of the world. In 11 of them the ministry was led by an indigenous spiritual leader exercising responsibility for both the advancement and administration of Campus Crusade's goals.

And what was to come in the twenty-first century?

The recruitment and management themes in Bill's plan for Crusade's future were the familiar ones from the ministry's past, and the same ones Jesus and Paul had used. Bill's strategy worked like this: Identify leadership qualities in certain individuals in various countries and cultures. Share the vision of the movement. Recruit someone. Invest yourself in mentoring them. Train them in the basics. Give them an area of responsibility. Encourage them to use the talents they have to reach their own peoples. Help them wherever possible. Supply them with literature and materials and leadership. And let them go for it. In effect, multiply yourself through others.

For Bill this strategy came from meditation on the Scriptures and from "simply obeying" 2 Timothy 2:2 (NKJV)—"The things that you have heard from me among many witnesses, commit these to faithful men who will be able to teach others also."

Bill foresaw that the tactics for following those strategies would increasingly involve new technologies—the Internet, interactive CD-ROM, DVD, and much more—so that every generation of Christians on the planet in the future can reach and teach its own generation with the message of God's great love and forgiveness through Jesus Christ as Savior and Lord.

Was this not the goal Jesus had in mind when He gave the Great Commission? "The Great Commission was not my idea," Bill said. "It's God's idea. To simply love, trust, and obey Him is our responsibility." That was the essence of his approach in the past and in the future.

Consistent with the ministry's heightened focus on technology was the establishment of the International Leadership University (ILU). Long after the failure of the plan for a university in San Diego, God had given a better idea—and it was working. Classes were offered in the Empire State Building beginning in the fall of 1999, but the ILU was being developed primarily as an Internet-based learning experience capable of educating millions of students at a time.

With the benefit of the years, Bill came to believe he was on the right track all along with his higher education dream—he'd just had the wrong timing and a too-narrow focus on a place rather than a process. He now was praising God for being denied permission to build in San Diego. A defeat was being recycled into a victory, which he claimed by faith even before all the details of ILU's electronic education were worked out. Somehow, one day, God would vindicate his thinking. So he plunged himself into recruiting the "best" Christian leaders at the turn of the century to place their best work in electronic interactive format to be consumable for generations to come.

He was also raising a billion dollars to create—over the next decade— twenty thousand hours of instructional video and interactive CD-ROM and DVD products to be used at ten thousand "extensions" of the university worldwide. They would provide a Christian world-view education for professionals of all kinds, especially those in government, education, liberal arts, theology, and the media.

This was a capstone project for him—among many. There was the Freedom Train to cross America over a five-year period and establish Freedom Centers in each state as it went, lighthouse points for the gospel. And he wanted to help Vonette on her idea of promulgating the Golden Rule in all its cultural expressions throughout the world.

And there was always his own personal witnessing—to the woman he'd just met on the airplane, the taxi driver on the drive from the airport, the business executive in the elevator, the member of Congress at the meeting, the custodian while he was waiting. By now, they'd all heard of the Four Spiritual Laws.

Bill could think of nothing more important than communicating the gospel to these and other living souls. And he imagined what the world would be like if every follower of Jesus truly obeyed His commands to be a holy, living, faithful witness. It would mean that everyone on earth would have a chance, in a very short period of time, to say yes to Jesus!

And to that end, Bill and Crusade had a plan.

Meanwhile, as CEO of what had become the largest movement of its kind in history, Bill had already placed in a safety deposit box the name of the person whom he would recommend to the board of directors to succeed him in a corporate sense in the event of his death. That name had changed from time to time over the years, as Bill himself pondered which person among many should become president.

Already in 1991 Bill had delegated almost every major responsibility to someone else on his capable team. He had trained his leaders and he trusted them. "This organization is operating without my hands-on, day-to-day direction right now," he said in 1999, "and it can go on just fine without me in the years ahead…. These men don't need me looking over their shoulders." He spoke of dedicating his remaining years to promoting "a life of prayer and fasting for world evangelism and discipleship."

After speaking to the opening session of a gathering of international ministry staff leaders in the late 1990s, Bill met with four of his key leaders: Paul Eshleman, Bailey Marks, Steve Douglass, and his executive assistant, Syd Wright. As was his custom, Bill invited criticism. "How was it?"

The message had been good, they said. But Bailey Marks challenged Bill for more. He suggested the international directors in attendance needed a greater challenge, a higher call. Bill nodded.

Eshleman nudged in the same direction with a brief reference to the kind of trumpeted message that had conquered him in Minnesota decades earlier. The others offered small tweakings of their leader's message.

Bill listened patiently. They were urging a sharper edge, a specific challenge. He listened.

In later messages to the international staff at the conference, he gave that challenge. Consistent with one of his life themes—"the best is yet before us"—he plotted a twenty-year course: A staff size by the year 2020 of more than one hundred thousand; an associate trained volunteer staff of more than ten million; an annual budget of three billion dollars.

"I am praying," Bill told them, "that all the major ministries of U.S. Campus Crusade for Christ will be saturating every country and culture of the world under the leadership of nationals in a partnership arrangement with hundreds of mission groups and tens of thousands of churches of all denominations."

He envisioned the creation of a children's version of the *Jesus* film. "Since over half the world's population is teenager or younger, can you imagine the impact that film will have? Then we'll go back to the same villages and tribes, we'll go back to the universities, we'll get on the networks, and we'll have the opportunity to reach additional billions with the gospel."

Then he strongly cautioned "the troops" against pride, carnality, lack of faith, lack of vision, satisfaction with mediocrity, presentation fatigue, and departure from the basics as developed by Crusade itself.

Bill spoke "without apology" of their need to continue using proven Crusade tools. "In my back pocket, I have the Four Spiritual Laws, I have the Holy Spirit booklet, I have the card of thirteen attributes of God—I am equipped for battle." He specifically cited inadequate staff use of his booklet on the Holy Spirit: "Some of you don't use the little booklet—is it because it's beneath your dignity?"

He warned of disunity: "We cannot have conflicts among us. Dear ones, there's no place for that. We are at war. When you go into the front lines of battle, soldiers know their very lives depend on harmony and unity and cooperation; they protect each other, and unfortunately, that doesn't happen with Christians as it ought."

And then his final challenges: "At least two or three times a day, remember that the God who created the heavens and the earth, a couple of hundred billion galaxies, is the One who so loved the world, He gave His only begotten Son. He came personally, visibly—Jesus of Nazareth died for us, was raised from the dead, and now lives within us. Meditate on that; because, you see, the Great Commission is His idea. It has not been rescinded."

As the year 2000 dawned, Bill and Vonette Bright had just celebrated their fifty-first wedding anniversary on December 30. He was scheduling another forty-day fast—his seventh—something that always recharged him, he felt, for national and world revival. He was wrapping up the writing of several new books. He and Vonette were plenary and seminar speakers at Billy Graham's Global Consultation on World Evangelization in Amsterdam.

He had slowed some, but not measurably. He was mature enough to know he needed to change gears, but he was not changing course. It was now a matter of timing. Every day that went by, more human beings were becoming accountable to God. Would they worship the Creator as God or would they fashion their own gods? Would they learn of a loving Father who sent His own Son to die for the failures of humanity?

He would keep working to see the truth disseminated, with only two determinative factors on his horizon—the return of the same Jesus who had ascended approximately 1,970 years ago or his own demise. If he died before Christ returned, he was still insisting on an unmarked grave, and Vonette was still insisting she would have nothing to do with such talk. They needed God to settle this one—but then, what was new about that?

CHAPTER 32

Where the Action Is

I t's a snowy Thursday evening in Philadelphia, just three days after
Christmas.

Out of the cold, a man walks through a hotel door with an energetic
stride, an obvious sense of purpose, and jut-jawed determination.

Hours earlier he had left his wife and a holiday reunion in sunny California with their two sons and their wives and three grandchildren. He's
beginning a three-day, three-city, three-state speaking tour. It's a sacrifice, but
he knows, in obedience to God, that this is where he belongs.

He wears a navy trench coat, a dark blue suit, white shirt, and color-
splashed tie. He isn't tall, but there seems to be a sort of aura around him so
that he stands out in a crowd.

With an effusive smile he raises his arm in greeting and is met by a man
in his midforties. Across the lobby stands a huddle of teenagers. One of them
whispers, "Is that Dr. Bill? Oh yeah, it *is!*"

Bill Bright has come to a Crusade conference for young students to challenge them to join the Crusade movement. It's the kind of thing he does in
various cities almost every year. It was in a conference of this kind twenty-
four years earlier that the man meeting Bill in the lobby was recruited to join
the movement, and he's been on Crusade staff ever since. Bill wraps his arm
around him and asks about his family.

Bill is accompanied by an aide, a young man whom he instructs to get
their room keys. Moments later they're on an elevator with the host staffer,
speaking pleasantries.

Immediately after entering the hotel suite, Bill takes off his coat, drops to his knees at a coffee table, and urges the others to pray with him.

He coughs. Up close, the others can see his watery eyes. He acknowledges that he has a raw throat, a runny nose. He knows he has every symptom of bronchitis ready to become pneumonia. He tells the others he's counting on echinacea and cough drops to deal with the symptoms and the Good Lord to take care of the rest.

His color is wan, and age spots are starting to change his complexion. There are bags under his eyes. He's overweight—despite his strongest efforts, including fasting and various diets; it's a reality that frustrates him.

"Dear Blessed Lord," he begins, "'nothing in my hands I bring, only to Thy cross I cling.'" The phrase from an old hymn flows easily, quickly. The words are, in fact, the sum of his substance for this hour. He has lived most of his life with the words of Paul emblazoned on his heart: "I am crucified with Christ: nevertheless I live; yet not I, but Christ liveth in me, and the life which I now live in the flesh I live by the faith of the Son of God, who loved me, and gave himself for me."

"Use this earthen vessel," he prays, "to make a difference in Your kingdom…in Jesus' name. Amen and amen." The others pray for Bill and for the gathered students.

The time is 6:45. "We'll be going down at seven," his aide, Louis, reminds him. The young man's job is to help make Bill efficient. He'll direct the handling of countless details every day of this trip—making calls, screening callers, collecting faxes, coordinating travel and meeting plans.

There have been dozens of such young men who, over these many years across literally millions of miles of journeys around the globe, have accompanied Bill as personal assistant and secretary. Never a female traveling secretary; in fact, never a female alone in his quarters.

Fifteen minutes later, Bill is eight stories below, approaching one of the hotel banquet rooms. Music, loud music with a beat, pummels his eardrums. A half-dozen college-age musicians are doing their warmup while the young people crowding the room clap, sing, shout, jump, and smile, smile, smile.

The music continues as Bill enters the room, right at seven o'clock, and comes down the center aisle. Many in the audience rush toward him. He shakes hands, recognizes some by name, and presses through the crowd.

Patiently, he makes his way to the front row, soaking in the youthful activity as the program gets underway. Occasionally, as he's struck by a speaker's phrase or a song's words, his head tips to the right, then he looks up, as if to the heavens, and acknowledges a joyous conviction. "Isn't that something?" he says to the person next to him. "God is so good!"

Finally, at 8:40 P.M., Bill is introduced. An intelligent, articulate, engaging, and suitably humble emcee says a word of personal testimony about Bill's influence on his own life, then brings on the president of Campus Crusade for Christ.

"I greet you in the name of our risen Lord," Bill begins.

> In Him dwells all the fullness of the Godhead bodily. He is the visible expression of the invisible God. To Him God has given all authority in heaven and earth.
>
> I fell in love with Him fifty-one years ago. I was a happy pagan when I was your age, doing my own self-centered thing. Then I met Jesus, and He changed everything—so I greet you in that wonderful name.
>
> We're here tonight because Jesus is that One who is truly great. Forty-four years ago, along with my beloved wife, Vonette—and she sends her greetings to you—we literally took sheets of paper and signed a contract with Jesus to be His slaves for life...relinquishing everything we had to Him. I want to tell you now: As I have walked with Him all these years as a deliberate slave, I have had opportunity to see His faithfulness; He *is* God; and the more I know Him the more I love Him and want to serve Him.

The voice is bass in its range, though crackling and raspy. It conveys an authenticity of experience, but his speaking style is not particularly charismatic, as he races off whole paragraphs of information as if he were in a hurry to finish, only to pause for slow, emphatic pronouncements of truth.

Jesus came for one purpose—to seek and save the lost. He came to pardon our sins. He came to give us meaning and purpose to life.

He created everything. Astronomers tell us there are more than one hundred billion galaxies. Our planet is no more than a grain of sand in the vastness of space. Yet the One who created us all has come to dwell within the heart of every believer. God became man and dwelt among us, took upon Himself our sins at the cross and three days later was raised from the dead. The greatest truth my little finite mind has ever tried to comprehend is this: That this loving, great Creator God, this holy heavenly Father and mighty Savior, has come to live within me and every believer.

For forty-five minutes, Bill barely pauses except for breath. Along with his ringing declarations of truth there are also touches that bring laughter from the young crowd—his self-deprecations and occasional pungent criticisms of those who would ostracize Christianity.

He finishes with a flourish of superlatives about Christ and a challenge to their commitment to the Great Commission.

"It can be done, you know. In our strategy…we will be able to give every one on planet Earth a chance to say yes to the claims of Christ, if we commit now."

The room grows quiet. Minds and hearts are churning.

"We serve an amazing God. He doesn't ask us to do it. He asks us to let Him do it through us! Isn't that something? Partners with the Creator of the universe!" This is not wandering rhetoric. Bill knows where he is going, and he expects many to go with him.

"Let me ask you: Would you stand, if you are willing to say to God, 'Use me. I am available. You can change my plans. I want to be part of fulfilling the Great Commission.'"

Nearly every person in the crowded room stands.

"Only a couple of sinners here on the front row didn't stand," Bill half jokes. Then he concludes, "Now if you believe the Lord wants you to consider Campus Crusade for Christ, please join us in the next room after this meeting."

All remain standing in an ovation as Bill resumes his seat on the front row.

About twenty minutes later, there are fourscore young adults, virtually all college-age, who have gone on to the "next room," an adjoining hotel conference room. There is again a word of testimony from another young man introducing Bill. This time as Bill speaks, he becomes even more transparent, describing his personal search for God, his marriage, and the ministry he says God gave the two of them.

He evidences no energy drain; he takes cough drops and occasionally wipes his eyes. He speaks of matters this audience cares about—the future, love and marriage, sex, God, a needy world that can be grappled with and changed, and a worldwide ministry in which one can exercise one's own talents, but only if the heart is right, the motives are godly, and the behavior is righteous. And he speaks of money—the funds that must be raised by each individual's solicitation.

Bill the recruiter finds dozens in Philadelphia who want to "join the team," "become a part of the movement," and "let God use you." They get further instructions on forms to fill out, future interviews, future training, and raising support. Then it will be off to help change the world.

Bill is still energized, enjoying the evening. Not until shortly before midnight does he close the door of his hotel room and telephone Vonette. He reports on his day and hears her report. He speaks a prayer for them, and on the other end so does she.

He turns to his well-worn Bible and begins a study time by reminding himself of Psalm 25:14, that God will reveal His secrets to those who reverence Him. As usual, his study, no matter the passage, is a search for more understanding of God's attributes.

By one o'clock in the morning Bill sleeps. Not long after six, he is up for a morning devotional and time on his knees by the bed in prayer, his physical and mental preparation for the day. This is his best time. "The most precious hours of my day," he has said, "are when I'm alone with Jesus; He is with me all day, of course, but when just the two of us are there, I can say: *Now* I can be with Him *alone*." It's during these moments that he prays, "Lord, I'm just Your slave; You are the Master. Here is my body. Wear me like a suit of clothes today. Move around in my life however You want to move.

Help me be sensitive to Your leading. May I not say or do anything that would bring discredit to Your dear name. Lead me only to bring worship, glory, and praise to You."

Bill arises from his knees and goes to meet the morning. He leads an inspirational breakfast meeting, then strategizes in a meeting with key Crusade leaders from the northeast region. He takes time to talk to several individuals, one by one, who want a few brief minutes with him.

Later in the morning he's off to catch a plane to Indianapolis for another conference appearance tonight.

It's a pace the weak would not keep up with.

If it were solely up to Bill, he wouldn't be such a traveler. "I would try to acquire a home by the beach or in the mountains; I would probably be a recluse; I love books, I love music, I enjoy being alone with Vonette and the Lord."

Once when someone said to him, "You must love to travel," Bill replied, "By that logic, the apostle Paul must have loved being in prison. No, I don't love to travel. I'd rather be home with my family listening to Handel or an old hymn or Steve Green." But he explains that he's been called by God to serve Him in this way. "The reality of His presence is what motivates me to travel." And since obeying God "is the greatest privilege of life," he adds, "I don't ever want to tell Him I don't want to travel."

On the hour-and-forty-minute flight to Indianapolis, Bill signals he intends to rest. He naps for a while. Immediately as he awakens, he engages the flight attendant in a conversation about God, then Christ, then conversion. "I know the Lord," she says, "and I love Him!"

"Wonderful!" Bill exclaims.

The flight attendant, an African-American, carries on an animated conversation with him as if they had known each other for years.

In Indianapolis, Bill gives a wide smile and a warm greeting for those who've come to meet him. "Beloved brother, it's so good to see you. What is God up to here?" The conference is in its second day, and the hotel is jammed with people, pulsing with energy.

In his room the message light is lit on Bill's telephone. There are calls to return to executives of the organization. They want his counsel. He gives it, pointedly, often suggesting that confirmation of the decision lies in the counsel of others and much prayer.

He lies down for a quick nap. Before an hour passes, someone comes to his mind. He calls upon Louis to track down the telephone number for that person and get him on the line.

When they're connected, Bill greets him by name and adds, "Beloved friend, greetings from our wonderful Lord." A moment later he asks, "Tell me, why has the Lord put you on my heart today? What can I pray for?"

After listening, Bill prays for him over the telephone.

That night in front of a thousand students, Bill seems sharper. The cold and bronchitis seem to be lessening. Although his message is essentially the same as in Philadelphia, the delivery is more precise, more staccato. He's a lawyer before a jury, bringing out the evidence. First, his own testimony of a life changed from hedonism to being in love with Jesus Christ. Then the irrefutable facts: This Christianity business didn't start in a corner. The resurrected Lord was seen by many individuals and at one gathering by more than five hundred persons. Were they all hallucinating?

And look at the claims of Christ. "Jesus said: 'I and the Father are one.... No man comes to the Father but by me.'"

He reads much of the first chapter of John's Gospel from *The Living Bible.* "Before anything else existed, there was Christ, with God...." He reads several verses from Colossians 1. "Christ is the exact likeness of the unseen God...." And the opening verses of Hebrews: "Long ago God spoke in many different ways to our fathers through the prophets [in visions, dreams, and even face-to-face], telling them little by little about his plans. But now in these days he has spoken to us through his Son to whom he has given everything, and through whom he made the world and everything there is. God's Son shines out with God's glory, and all that God's Son is and does marks him as God. He regulates the universe by the mighty power of his command. He is the one who died to cleanse us and clear our record of all sin, and then sat down in highest honor beside the great God of heaven" (1:1-3).

Bill drives home his point. This same Jesus, as He left the earth, delivered the greatest challenge of history to a handful of men; it is known as the Great Commission: "Go into all the world and make disciples of all nations."

Bill uses an exacting logic that demands a decision about not only the person of Christ but also about this Great Commission and of personal obedience to it. He recounts the Sound Mind Principle: If Jesus is God, and the greatest thing in the world is to know God, then what is the best thing you can do for another? Introduce that person to Jesus Christ!

It logically follows that since Jesus commanded His followers to make disciples of other nations, every Christian should be engaged in some exercise carrying out that command.

"I believe the Great Commission can be fulfilled in our lifetime," he tells them.

Soon, another invitation. This time every person in the auditorium is standing, and they remain standing and applauding as the speaker descends the platform.

Minutes later the gathering in the adjoining room is greater than in Philadelphia. The recruiting goes well.

The next morning it's off to Minneapolis, where Bill is greeted at the airport by two couples whom he recruited more than a decade ago. With open arms, he says to one, "Beloved, greetings, greetings." And to the second couple: "Hello, dear ones," as he remembers them from a decade before. To all of them he adds, "Vonette sends her love."

Outside it's foggy and spitting snow on this fifth day after Christmas. They crowd into a Volvo for a twenty-five-minute drive from the airport to the hotel, where sixteen hundred students are gathered. Bill uses the time to ask questions and to listen—what to celebrate, what to pray for, strategic developments, new possibilities. How goes the movement, really?

There is candor in their replies. The staff members are mostly positive. Even concerns are cast in a context of prayer. *Disappointment* is as negative a word as Bill receives. They remember common experiences, laugh, and celebrate God's goodness.

At the hotel downtown, they dash inside and press into a crowded elevator. Most of those inside are under twenty-five, including one clear-eyed male about fourteen. As Bill moves to the back of the elevator, the boy's eyes follow him. "This is Dr. Bill," someone says to him.

"Yo," says the student matter-of-factly, looking Bill directly in the eye. "I've seen your stuff."

"Really," says Bill. "What have you read?"

"No, I mean I saw one of your videos…it was great!"

Touching this next generation with the message and call of Christ is why this grandfather and veteran leader is in this hotel on this wintry night—by the will of God. There is no place Bill would rather be.

"I've lived with one purpose," he so often has said. "To help fulfill the Great Commission in our lifetime. This is where the action is—the battle for young minds."

CHAPTER 33

The Way to Go

_____

Time and again Bill has been asked, "How did you do it?" Here, at the close of 1999, is Bill's own answer:

"I discovered that the awesome Creator God and loving Savior loved this one little depraved termite. Ever since, it has been my desire to love Him supremely, as Father, Son, and Holy Spirit, Three in One. He led me to sign a Contract with Him to be His slave throughout this life. He gave me a Vision for helping reach the world with the word of His love and forgiveness. In obedience to His plain word, I devoted myself to seeking to help fulfill the Great Commission in this generation.

"As I went, I practiced spiritual breathing, confession of sin, and being filled by His Spirit. I discovered there is room for only One on the throne of my life, and my goal has been to stay in tune with Him twenty-four hours a day.

"On my knees, as an act of worship, I read His Word, the Holy Bible, every morning and evening, as if He were speaking directly to me, and I seek to obey what He tells me. On my knees, my prayers are that He would keep me from sin as well as empower me for service, and we share moments when I feel especially enveloped in His presence. On my knees with my precious and adorable, loving partner, Vonette, we pray specifically for our priorities: our first love, the Lord Jesus; marital love and strength; family faithfulness; and fruitful ministry.

"Out of the overflow of these disciplines and of His love, I have wanted to share my faith every day, faithfully making known the claims of Christ in the power of the Holy Spirit and leaving the results to God.

237

"He has led me to faith-filled partners, wonderfully talented men and women. Our hearts and minds and hands are woven together in common bond to serve God. Helping fulfill the Great Commission is our aim, nothing less. We focus on evangelism and discipleship, nothing more and nothing less. We readily admit that we're only a part of the vast body of Christ. We see ourselves as only a leaf from a twig from the branch of the Vine.

"Whether or not we are believers, we are going to have problems in this life. Believers or not, we will one day die. If I'm going to be a follower of Christ, I want all that God has for me—and I want to be all that He wants me to be. If I'm going to suffer at all and one day die, why not suffer and die for the highest and best—for the Lord Jesus Christ and His gospel?

"This is the way to go! I have enjoyed this life beyond measure. Business success I once knew. Worldly ambitions and possessions I once had. But they seem so hollow and vain, so pitiful compared to the exciting adventure of walking in harmony with our risen Lord, the great God of Abraham, Isaac, and Jacob, and of Peter, James, and Paul, the God and Father of our Lord Jesus Christ—He who spun more than one hundred billion galaxies in space and reached down to touch little ol' me. What a Savior! I love Him more than life."

And what will be Bill Bright's place in history?

One of the nation's foremost church historians, Dr. John Hannah of Dallas and Westminster theological seminaries, has said, "Most assuredly, Dr. Bill Bright will go down in history as one of the great Christian men who has ever lived."

Opinion research specialist George Gallup Jr. wrote, "He has reached people in a depth and in numbers matched by few others in history."

As someone who has known of Bill Bright since 1971 and focused on him as a subject for the past eleven years—having had countless opportunities, public and private, to witness his interaction with hundreds individually and thousands assembled—I offer the following assessment.

At a California church growth seminar in 1998, a speaker with no relationship to Bill Bright declared, "As D. L. Moody was to growth of the church in the nineteenth century, so Bill Bright has been to the twentieth century." That may have been an understatement as to numbers of persons affected, but it's an accurate account of Bill Bright's spiritual leadership impact on our times.

Like Moody, Bill's ministry has attracted devoted laymen. Like the Wesleys, Bill started a movement built on the Christian education of those laypersons. Also like them, the heart of his message is assurance of salvation solely through faith in Jesus Christ. Like Martin Luther, Bill emphasizes faith alone for salvation and is unafraid of confronting the religious establishment of his day.

Like pioneer missionaries William Carey, Hudson Taylor, and many others, he traveled far in delivering the gospel in remote corners of the world. Like Watchman Nee, he found "life in the Spirit" to be the empowering and peaceful presence in his life and took time alone with God to grow in that presence.

Like George Mueller, Bill is sensitive about any praise or credit given to him. He is always giving "honor, glory, and praise to our great God and Savior." (It took four years of prodding, prayer, and appeals to persuade him to allow this biography to be written.)

Bobb Biehl, a friend to Bill and to Campus Crusade, once told me, "I've had the privilege of being with Bill Bright many times all alone, after the cameras were all turned off, the stage lights gone, the crowds had gone home. I've watched him share his faith with a waitress at eleven o'clock at night after everyone is bone tired and we're alone in a restaurant. I've watched him in the crunch of ministry crisis. I've also watched him nearly bent double laughing, and I've watched him weeping with compassion." From that perspective, he offered this judgment: "There are only a few men and women who actually have played a role in the eternal destiny of billions of men and women worldwide. Bill Bright is authentically one."

Bill Bright is about quality living—life with a capital *L,* full of meaning and purpose, confidently linked to a living Lord. For Bill, ultimately, it's about simply being an obedient follower of that Lord. Bill Bright isn't perfect—far from it—but how many in all of history have focused more faithfully on the God they knew and, as a result, reflected His attributes, character, and program?

He still signs his letters, "Yours for fulfilling the Great Commission in this generation." And that's what he's still doing. Having given himself completely, totally, and irrevocably to the One who declared that commission, he spends himself in harness with others to seek to reach the entire planet with "the most joyful news ever announced." Clearly he has done this not for wealth, power, or fame; his objective has been to keep his heart right and his motives pure, as near as humanly possible. Humanly speaking, he gets the job done as he goes forward, joyfully and faithfully following Jesus—in such contrast to the dull and boring among us who focus on the temporal instead of the eternal.

Someone has said that most Christians are so subnormal that when a normal one comes along, he or she seems abnormal. By that measure, Bill Bright is merely one normal, authentic follower of Jesus of Nazareth. To claim more would be to ignore his testimony of faith in the promises of his God.

Appendixes

In Sum

Bill Bright's 77 Key Decisions

His name was Todd—a young man of twenty-two who was working for the summer at a Campus Crusade for Christ conference center in California. He knew about some of Bill Bright's feats of faith. I asked him, as I had many others, what he really wanted to know about Bill Bright.

Todd's reply: "How'd he *do* all that?"

As best I can tell, the answer has to do with the following key decisions that Bill made in life, the same choices any of us can make:

1. He chose to think about and meditate on the existence and presence of God as a way of life.

2. He decided Jesus Christ is the most extraordinary, absolutely unique Person in the universe.

3. He received Christ as his Savior and Lord, then devoted everything he had to the cause of Christ.

4. He majored on the attributes of God in his Bible study.

5. He chose a wife of character and intelligence and made honoring her a daily priority.

6. He consciously chose to be a godly example to his sons.

7. He loved his parents and did not lose touch with them or with his hometown.

8. He stopped letting money motivate him.

9. He decided to make a difference in his world.

10. He and his wife signed a literal contract with God, relinquishing ownership of all they had, purposing to live their lives in submission to God as their Full and Major Partner—He as Master, they as slaves.

11. He decided to be a daily learner.

12. He decided never to be satisfied with mediocrity.

13. He decided to circulate with movers and shakers—persons in public and private positions of authority and success—without losing contact with the poor and needy.

14. He asked God questions and listened expectantly for His answers.

15. He sought the advice of experts.

16. He made his wife his full partner.

17. He saw the role of women as crucial to the success of ministry.

18. He looked for ways to practice the principles of God; he tried to do everything to the glory of God.

19. He tried to weigh every attitude, every action, every motive, every desire, every word, by the Bible's standard.

20. He listened when others spoke.

21. He read volumes and took notes.

22. He got organized and stayed that way.

23. He studied hard with an eye toward passing on what he was learning.

24. He loved by faith when he did not feel like loving.

25. He worked when he did not feel like working.

26. He labored to communicate clearly.

27. He sought to communicate concepts *transferably*, in ways that others could communicate them equally clearly and effectively.

28. He invited constructive criticism.

29. He confessed his sins and believed God forgave them.

30. He asked God's help and expected it.

31. He sought to glorify God by attempting great things for God.

32. He never thought small when he had the option to think big.

33. He consciously chose to relate to leaders in different fields.

34. He learned from the successes of others and from his own mistakes.

35. He invited others to be involved in his work.

36. He sought to do those things that needed to be done, yet no one else was doing.

37. He honored his mother and father.

38. He took responsibility for the development of his children.

39. He focused on training, training, training. He trained his family; he trained his friends; he trained his colleagues. He trained his colleagues how to train their families, friend, and colleagues.

40. He developed leadership qualities among his followers.

41. He chose to view staff as one big family.

42. He wrote down his ideas, and, when sure they were of God, he never gave up on them.

43. He made lists of ways to implement his ideas.

44. He worked those lists until the ideas were realities.

45. He communicated by every means possible—especially through writing (first in letters, then booklets, treatises, speeches, and finally books) but also through records, tapes, radio, television, satellites, and the Internet.

46. He built a personal mailing list and wrote to his friends and supporters regularly.

47. He envisioned major events involving others but also including an appropriate place for himself.

48. He envisioned publications, recordings, and books involving others but also including an appropriate place for himself.

49. Though naturally shy, by faith he never flinched from asking key questions: Where are you on your spiritual journey? Do you want to know Jesus as your Savior? How would you like to be involved? I'd be interested in your opinion; what do you think? Would you like to contribute to this cause?

50. He made it clear there was room in his organization for talented, visionary, committed people.

51. He trusted his trained followers.

52. He also inspected what he expected from others.

53. He communicated high standards and usually lived up to them.

54. He took risks—on technologies, projects, and methods—to advance the cause.

55. He practiced hospitality with his wife's support and made it a key feature of the ministry God gave him.

56. He tried not to offend in lesser things.

57. He was willing to offend when the cause of Christ was at stake, although this occurred rarely.

58. He handled criticism patiently and learned from it, but mostly he let God defend him against the attacks of others.

59. He looked for ways to cooperate with those who love Jesus Christ.

60. He reached out to those inclined to build walls and sought to love them anyway.

61. He never compromised on the person and principles of Christ.

62. He never compromised the message of the Bible as God's Word.

63. He committed to seek the fulfillment of the Great Commission in his lifetime out of love for the Savior and his desire to demonstrate that love by obedience.

64. He changed methods to be relevant to the culture in focus.

65. He developed a positive lifestyle and attitude.

66. He looked for God's hand in everything, especially in tragedy.

67. He shared his faith faithfully—with those of high and low estate, both when he felt like it and when he did not.

68. He did not hold grudges.

69. He never let the critic discourage him but used the critic's words as fuel to further his efforts.

70. He tested almost every action by whether it advanced his life's goal: the fulfillment of the Great Commission in his lifetime.

71. He prayed a lot, alone.

72. He made gatherings for prayer a part of his schedule and of his organization.

73. He adjusted to the seasons of his life.

74. He "faithed" his way through life, believing the promises of God.
75. He never gave up.
76. He never lost the wonder of being loved by the infinite, incomprehensible God of Creation, of Calvary, and of the empty tomb.
77. And he concluded that he is not at all special but rather ordinary, and only microscopic in comparison to an infinite but loving God.

Because of that last conclusion, to Bill Bright's way of thinking anyone else who happens to be willing to live like this can have the same degree of impact Bill has had.

Best wishes, Todd.

Chronology

_____

Major Events in Bill Bright's Life

1921 William Rohl Bright is born on October 19 near Coweta, Oklahoma, to Forrest Dale Bright and Mary Lee Rohl Bright.

1935 Playing high-school football, sustains ear injury that will later block his acceptance into the military.

1939 Graduates from Coweta High School; enrolls in Northeastern State College (now University) in Tahlequah, Oklahoma.

1943 Receives a bachelor of arts degree from Northeastern State College; denied entry into military because of ear injury; takes job as assistant county agent in Muskogee County for Oklahoma's state university system.

1944 Moves to Los Angeles; enters business; visits Hollywood Presbyterian Church for first time.

1945 Commits his life to Christ; begins receiving discipleship training under Dr. Henrietta Mears at First Presbyterian Church of Hollywood.

1946 Enrolls at Princeton Theological Seminary in New Jersey.

1947 First "Briefing Conference" at Forest Home Conference Center in California; enrolls at Fuller Theological Seminary in California.

1948 Marries Vonette Zachary, December 30.

1950 Chosen as deacon, First Presbyterian Church of Hollywood.

1951 Writes and signs the "Contract with God"; experiences "the Vision";

Bill and Vonette Bright launch Campus Crusade for Christ on the campus of UCLA.

1952 Staff members serve on four campuses in three states; "God's Plan," forerunner of the "The Four Spiritual Laws," developed for staff to memorize.

1954 Son Zachary adopted.

1956 Campus Crusade staff numbers 62, serving on 23 campuses in 10 states.

1957 "Four Spiritual Laws" now complete with inclusion of first law— "God loves you and offers a wonderful plan for your life."

1958 Son Brad adopted; international ministries of Campus Crusade established in South Korea by Joon Gon Kim.

1959 Campus Crusade's ministries in Pakistan and the Middle East begin; Bill begins speaking at Lay Institutes for Evangelism (LIFE), which later develop into the Here's Life, America ministry.

1960 Campus Crusade active on 40 U.S. Campuses in 15 states; 109 staff members.

1961 Weekly radio broadcasts air; 154 staff members serve on 45 campuses; purchase of Arrowhead Springs property and hotel complex as Campus Crusade headquarters and staff training site.

1962 Latin America ministry begins in Mexico.

1963 Illusionist Andre Kole joins staff.

1965 First published copies of *Have You Heard of the Four Spiritual Laws?*

1966 Several new ministries begin: Athletes in Action under leadership of Dave Hannah; high-school ministry (now known as Student Venture) under Carl Wilson; military ministry established under retired Air Force Colonel John Fain; music ministry with pioneering group, the New Folk.

1967 Canadian and European ministries begin; Berkeley Blitz at Berkeley campus of University of California results in commitments to Christ by 700 students.

1968 African ministry begins; Bill publishes *Revolution Now,* evangelistic book; Campus Crusade ministries in 32 nations.

1971 The Great Commission Prayer Crusade officially established under leadership of Vonette Bright.

1972 Explo '72 in Dallas–Fort Worth.

1974 Explo '74 in Seoul, Korea.

1975 Here's Life, America ministry launches "I Found It!" campaign in 246 major American cities by 1977; continues with international Here's Life campaigns through 1980.

1977 Christian Embassy begins in Washington, D.C.

1978 Here's Life Publishers founded as ministry of Campus Crusade.

1979 The *Jesus* film premieres after 5 years of research and production.

1980 Here's Life, Korea world evangelization crusade draws more than 2 million people to each of 4 night sessions, with South Korean media reporting 3 million persons at largest session—the largest Christian gatherings in recorded history.

1980 Bill co-hosts Washington for Jesus, drawing one million people to pray together in nation's capital; Arrowhead Springs property miraculously withstands a major forest fire, the Panorama fire.

1981 Chicago '81, Campus Crusade conference for African-Americans.

1983 Kansas City '83 evangelism and discipleship training conference for U.S. college students; the *Jesus* film now being viewed in 72 languages by total audiences averaging 350,000 people per night.

1985 Explo '85, a video satellite evangelism and discipleship conference, first of its kind; Youth Congress '85 in Washington, D.C., for high-school students.

1986 Liberty '86, Fourth of July evangelistic outreach of Here's Life, Inner City in New York City.

1987 New Life 2000 campaign announced with prayer target of at least 1 billion people receiving Jesus Christ as Lord and Savior by the end of the year 2000; Destiny '87 world missions conference in Atlanta for African-Americans.

1988 The *Jesus* film now shown in 120 languages, with more than 30 million recorded decisions for Christ to date; National Day of Prayer established, largely through efforts of Vonette Bright.

1991 International headquarters moves to Orlando, Florida; Campus Crusade for Christ celebrates fortieth anniversary.

1994 First annual Prayer and Fasting gathering draws 600 U.S. Christian leaders to Orlando.

1995 Bill's book *America's Coming Revival* is published.

1996 Bill receives Templeton Prize for Progress in Religion and dedicates $1,050,000 prize for prayer and fasting for world revival; first use of satellite television for annual Prayer and Fasting conference.

1997 *Worldchangers* radio program begins with Steve Douglass and Bill Bright; number of *Jesus* film viewers reaches 1.1 billion.

1998 Campus Crusade operates 50 different ministries involving full-time staff of 17,000 (including 9,000 overseas), plus trained volunteer staff of more than 200,000.

1999 Dedication of Campus Crusade's new international headquarters in Orlando, Florida.

2000 The cumulative audience for the *Jesus* film reaches 4.5 billion people; total distribution of the Four Spiritual Laws presentation reaches 2.5 billion copies, representing every major language.

For of him, and through him, and to him, are all things:
to whom be glory for ever.
Amen.
ROMANS 11:36

Trusting God for the Adventure

Excerpts from Bill Bright's Writings on Faith

FOCUS OF FAITH

For me, the Christian life is an exciting, joy-filled adventure. You start by getting to know God—who He is, what He is like, and the benefits we enjoy when we belong to Him. Your view of God influences all the rest of your relationships. Scripture says the righteous shall live by faith. Faith must focus on an object, and the object in which we have our faith is God and His inspired Word.

But how do we acquire that kind of faith? "Faith comes by hearing, and hearing by the word of Christ" (Romans 10:17, NASB). It is as simple as that. You are building up your storehouse of faith every time you read the Word of God, every time you hear the Word of God, and every time you memorize the Word of God.

Our view of God determines the quality and degree of our faith. A small view of God results in a small faith. Great faith is the result of a correct biblical view of God—recognizing Him as great, mighty, all-wise, and worthy of our trust.

Our view of God as sovereign, holy, loving, righteous, just, and compassionate will produce these same qualities in our lives. If we view Him as a God of love and forgiveness, we are prompted to love and forgive others also.

Nothing is so important in the Christian life as understanding the attributes of God. No one can ever begin to live supernaturally and have the faith to believe God for "great and mighty" things if he does not know what God is like, or if he harbors misunderstandings about God and His character. Would you like to live a joyful, abundant, and fruitful life—every day filled with adventure? You can!

What is God like to you? Is He a divine Santa Claus, a cosmic policeman, a dictator, or a big bully? Many people have distorted views of God and as a result are afraid of Him because they do not know what He is really like.

Our heavenly Father yearns for us to respond to His love. It is only as we respond to a scriptural view of God that we are able to come joyfully into His presence and experience the love and adventure and abundant life for which He created us and which He promised us.

God's power to live a holy life and be a fruitful witness is released by faith, based on His faithfulness and the authority of God's Word.

On the basis of His command to be filled (Ephesians 5:18) and His promise that if we ask for anything in accordance with God's will, He will hear and answer us (1 John 5:14-15), we know that we can be filled with the Holy Spirit by faith—as a way of life

By Faith

By faith you can become a gentle person. By faith you can confess your sins and know that they have been forgiven. By faith you can appropriate the filling of the Spirit of Christ. By faith you can practice tender-hearted mercy and kindness to others.

The Lord has commanded us to be gentle people, so by faith we can ask for that portion of the fruit of the Spirit, gentleness, and love, and know that He is changing us for the better. This usually develops over an extended period of time, usually through the nurturing process that comes only with time and trials and sometimes tribulation. Pray that God will give you patience with yourself as you mature into the gentle and humble person He wants you to be.

The law of God is clear: When we disobey Him, He disciplines us as a loving father and mother discipline their child, and when we obey Him, He will bless us.

FAITH AND WORKS

We become spiritual and experience power from God and become fruitful in our witness as a result of faith and faith alone.

The Bible clearly teaches that "the just shall live by faith" (Romans 1:17). However, it is equally important to know that good works are the result of faith—"trusting in the Son of God"—and unless there are "good works" there is not faith, for "faith, if it hath not works, is dead" (James 2:17).

Many Christians are confused on this point. They think of works (Bible study, prayer, and other spiritual disciplines) as the means to, rather than the results of, the life of faith. They spend much time in these activities, seeking God's favor and blessing.

They may even attempt to witness for Christ and to obey the various commands of God, thinking that by these means they will achieve supernatural living. But they remain defeated, frustrated, powerless, and fruitless.

As you are filled with the Holy Spirit—"Christ living in me"—and walk in His power by faith, the Bible becomes alive, prayer becomes vital, your witness becomes effective, and obedience becomes a joy.

GROWTH IN FAITH

At one state of my spiritual growth, I was able to trust God for a soul—and He answered that prayer by leading me to one person whose heart He had prepared. Through the years God has increased my faith to trust Him for 6 souls, then 20, 50, 100, 1,000, 1 million, 100 million souls! Always He has honored my faith and obedience. Now I pray for a billion souls and, by faith, I believe that a billion will be harvested for the glory of God.

God has not changed; I have changed.

I believe that God deals with us in a similar way with regard to spiritual fruit. As we continue to trust God to develop in us all the various love traits, He honors that faithfulness because we are obeying Him by doing what He commands us to do.

Faithfulness is that trait of the Holy Spirit that makes faith a living reality every day in the life of the believer who is living supernaturally. As we continue to walk in the power, love, and wisdom of the Holy Spirit, we learn to develop greater confidence in the Lord Jesus Christ, in His Word, in our rights as children of God, and in the ability of the indwelling Holy Spirit to empower and control our lives.

Faithfulness can be compared to an athlete's conditioning. A marathon runner does not begin training by running great distances. Instead, he starts with short runs. Then, as his body becomes more conditioned, he increases the distance of his runs until he reaches the full distance of the marathon.

Faithfulness in the life of a Christian also develops over an extended period of time spent in "conditioning." As we learn to trust God in small things, our faith grows and grows until we are able to trust Him in greater things.

God rewards us for our faithfulness, and each time we see Him respond favorably, He reaches out to us through His Holy Spirit and increases our faith to trust Him for even greater things.

SHARING FAITH

To be unwilling to witness for Christ with our lips is to disobey His command just as much as to be unwilling to witness for Him by living holy lives is to disobey His command. In neither case can the disobedient Christian expect God to control and empower his life.

There are those who say, "I witness for Christ by living a good life." But it is not enough to live a good life. Many non-Christians live fine, moral, ethical lives.

According to the Lord Jesus, the only way we can demonstrate that we are truly following Him is to produce fruit, which includes introducing others to our Savior as well as living holy lives. And the only way we can produce fruit is through the power of the Holy Spirit.

SUFFERING FAITH

James writes that the trying of our faith is to be expected, and Peter adds that it is a purifying experience. You and I may be called upon to suffer for the cause of Christ. By faith, we are not to fear, knowing that an "unending, glorious future" awaits us.

This promise might apply equally to the physical suffering we encounter from time to time as a part of the natural order of things. If we can accept such suffering as part of God's plan for us—one of the "all things" of Romans 8:28 that is working together for our good—we will be among those victors who are able to "count it all joy."

Paul wrote (in Romans 5) that tribulation merely starts a process that creates in us more godly love for others as we experience His love for us. As we consider these possibilities, we may be optimistic, even cheerful, knowing that we are already on the winning side—more than conquerors. And we need not be afraid, for "God has not given us the spirit of fear, but of power, and of love, and of a sound mind."

"There Is Nothing Too Big"

More Excerpts from Bill Bright's Writings

BIG IDEAS

I have come to the conclusion, after many years of serving our wonderful Lord, that there is nothing too big for us to attempt for the glory of God. If our hearts and motives are pure, if what we do is according to the Word of God, He hears and is able to do more than we ask or even think.

For example, is it God's will that the Great Commission be fulfilled? Of course. It is His command. We read further in 2 Peter 3:9 that God is not willing that any should perish but that all should come to repentance, and according to verse 15 of this chapter He has delayed His return in order that more people might have a chance to hear.

WITNESSING

I have never led anyone to Christ, and I never shall. However, I have had the privilege of praying with thousands of people who have received Christ as a result of my witness.

When a person receives Christ, it is the work of the Holy Spirit. That is why I cannot boast over much fruit or be discouraged over little fruit. The responsibility for fruit belongs to the Holy Spirit who works in and through the believer, producing fruit and changing the lives of those who respond favorably to our witness.

FALSE TEACHERS

How can you recognize false teachers? The test is threefold:

1. What is their view of the Lord Jesus Christ? Is He truly the Son of God? Did He die on the cross for our sins? Was He raised from the dead?
2. Do they profess that the Bible is the authority of God, divinely inspired?
3. Do they live lives that are consistent with the teachings of Scripture? Or do they condone practices that are contrary to the Word of God? If they do the latter, beware, for they will rob you of the supernatural resources of God that are available to you.

TITHES AND OFFERINGS

The importance of tithing is one of the first lessons I learned as a new Christian. Now I realize that that is only the beginning, because everything that I enjoy has been entrusted to me by a gracious, loving Father who expects me to maximize all that He has put into my hands; therefore, tithing must be followed by offerings, based on the clear Word of God that as we sow, we reap. The more we give back to God, the more He will entrust to us, but we are to give with a cheerful heart out of a deep sense of gratitude for all that God has given to us.

A PURE LIFE

I can live a pure life as I follow God's Word. And if that is true—and I have no doubt it is—then certain things surely should follow. I will begin today by determining to know His Word and to obey it. Simple logic would dictate that I cannot and will not obey His Word if I am not familiar with it.

A WISE PERSON

In God's economy, the truly wise person is that one who is redeeming the time, buying up every opportunity to share his faith, refusing to put off that which he knows should become a natural, everyday, moment-by-moment part of his life. Wonder of wonders, God even promises to put the very words in our mouths, if we ask Him, as we go in His name.

THANKS AND PRAISE

One of the greatest lessons I have ever learned about the Christian life is the importance of praise and thanksgiving. The greater the problem or crisis, the more difficult the circumstances, the more important it is to praise God at all times, to worship Him for who He is: for His attributes of sovereignty, love, grace, power, wisdom, and might, and for the certainty that He will fight for us, that He will demonstrate His supernatural resources in our behalf.

NOT HOARDING

The New Testament makes clear that everything belongs to God. We are custodians, stewards, of that which is entrusted to us for only a brief moment of time. Threescore and ten years (or possibly a little more), and then all that we possess will pass on to another. We are not to hoard, nor are we to pass on large estates to our heirs. That which is entrusted to God's children is given to them to be used while they are still alive. We are to care for our own and make provision for their needs, but all that is entrusted to us beyond that amount should be spent while we are still alive, while we can guarantee proper stewardship.

THE CHRISTIAN LIFE

The Christian life is the process of becoming in our experience through the enabling of the Holy Spirit what we already are in God's sight, in order to bring maximum glory, honor, and praise to His name. It is His supernatural life, in all of its resurrection power, released through the ministry of the Holy Spirit, that enables us to live supernatural lives for the glory of God. Only then can we be free, for the Son alone can liberate us.

LEGALISM

The greatest heresy of the Christian life is legalism, and yet it inevitably seems to attract dedicated, committed Christians. They are happy to accept salvation as a gift of God by faith. But like the Galatians, they insist on earning their way thereafter.

We must never forget that salvation is a gift of God, which we receive by faith. Nothing can be earned. If we believe God, we will want to work to please Him, not to earn His favor.

TRUE EDUCATION

We seem to be preoccupied with the accumulation of knowledge, to the neglect of that wisdom which alone can save us from the misuse of knowledge.

William Lyon Phelps, famous English professor at Yale University and a godly statesman, once said, "If I could choose between a knowledge of the Bible and a college education, I would readily choose the knowledge of the Bible."

HUMILITY

"Humility is not thinking meanly of yourself; it is not thinking of yourself at all." Under that rigid definition, not many of us would qualify as being truly humble. Nevertheless, the statement contains a great deal of truth, for it is a goal toward which we should all strive.

No real progress is made toward God in any person's life—believer or unbeliever—without this special characteristic of humility. One proof of that is found in the familiar verse: "If my people, which are called by my name, shall humble themselves, and pray, and seek my face, and turn from their wicked ways; then will I hear from heaven, and will forgive their sin, and will heal their land"(2 Chronicles 7:14). Even before we pray, before we seek His face, before we turn from our wicked ways, we must humble ourselves. Why? Because we are in no position to meet any of these other three criteria without first humbling ourselves.

Every Christian who seeks to advance in a holy life must remember well that humility is the most important lesson a believer has to learn. There may be intense consecration, fervent zeal, and heavenly experience, yet there also may be an unconscious self-exaltation. True humility must come from God.

PRIORITY FOR CHRISTIANS

The most important truth that I or anyone else could share with Christians is to help them understand the person and ministry of the Holy Spirit. My own life was dramatically transformed when by faith I claimed the fullness and power of the Holy Spirit.

We shall see a resurgence in evangelism and a zeal unparalleled in church history as we endeavor—in the power of the Holy Spirit—to help fulfill the Great Commission.

VICTORY EVERY DAY

1. As an act of your will, decide that you're going to be full of the joy of the Lord. You are the one who decides whether you're going to rejoice or be discouraged and sad.
2. Demonstrate before all men an unselfish, considerate attitude.
3. Remember that the Lord can come at any moment, and be prepared.
4. Do not worry about anything.
5. Pray about everything.
6. Thank Him in faith for His answers.

THE UNIQUENESS OF JESUS

Jesus has done more good for mankind than anyone else who has ever lived. He is the greatest person of the centuries. Compare Jesus, even as a man, with any other person—Muhammad, Buddha, Confucius, Socrates, Plato, Aristotle, anyone else in any country at any time in history—and it would be like comparing a giant with a midget.

Though he lived two thousand years ago and changed the course of history, though He was the greatest leader, the greatest teacher, the greatest example the world has ever known, He is infinitely more than these. He is God.

The omnipotent Creator God visited this little planet Earth and became a man, the God-man, Jesus of Nazareth. He was perfect God and perfect man, and as perfect man He understands our weaknesses, since He had the same temptations we do—though He never once gave way to them and sinned.

INTIMACY WITH GOD

In my own life, as I have come to know God better and to live more fully in the power and control of the Holy Spirit, my daily devotional Bible reading and study is not a duty or a chore, but a blessing; not an imposition on my time, but an invitation to fellowship in the closest of all ways with our holy, heavenly Father and our wonderful Savior and Lord.

Remember, God delights to have fellowship with us. The success of our studying God's Word and of prayer is not to be determined by some emotional experience which we may have (though this frequently will be our experience), but by the realization that God is pleased when we want to know Him enough to spend time with Him in Bible study and prayer.

Here are some important, practical suggestions for your individual devotional reading and study of the Bible:

1. Begin with a prayer. Ask the Holy Spirit to give you an understanding of God's Word.
2. Keep a Bible study notebook.

3. Read the text slowly and carefully; then reread and take notes.

4. Find out the true meaning of the text. Ask yourself:

   (a) Who or what is the main subject?

   (b) Of whom or what is the writer speaking?

   (c) What is the key verse?

   (d) What does the passage teach you about Jesus Christ?

   (e) Does it bring to light personal sin that you need to confess and forsake?

   (f) Does it contain a command for you to obey?

   (g) Does it give a promise you can claim?

5. List practical applications, commands, promises.

6. Memorize the Scriptures—particularly key verses.

7. Obey the commands and follow the instructions you learn in God's Word.

OBEDIENCE AND BLESSING

If we obey His commands, we are blessed. If we disobey them, we must suffer the consequences. His hand of blessing will remain upon our worldwide efforts. If we disobey Him, He will not only withhold His blessings, but will discipline us as individuals and as a movement.

Statement of Faith

Campus Crusade for Christ

We believe in the Trinity as being God the Father, God the Son, and God the Holy Spirit; and these three are one God, creator of heaven and earth.

We believe in Jesus Christ as our Savior and Lord, the only virgin-born Son of God. We accept Him in His sinless life and ministry, His vicarious atonement, His resurrection from the tomb, His present intercession in heaven, and we believe that His visible and bodily return to the earth may occur at any time.

We believe in the Bible as God's infallible Word, uniquely inspired, the Spirit's supreme and final authority for man in all matters of faith and conduct, His sustenance for every believer.

We believe in the Great Commission of our Lord Jesus Christ as a command to live a life of abandonment to Him who loved us and gave Himself for us; surrendering His personal ambitions in an unreserved commitment to the task of proclaiming the gospel throughout the world and discipling men of every nation.

The sole basis of our beliefs is the Bible, God's infallible written Word, the sixty-six books of the Old and New Testaments. We believe that it was uniquely, verbally, and fully inspired by the Holy Spirit and that it was written without error in the original manuscripts. It is the supreme and final authority in all matters on which it speaks.

We accept those large areas of doctrinal teaching on which, historically, there has been general agreement among all true Christians. Because of the specialized calling of our movement, we desire to allow for freedom of conviction on other doctrinal matters, provided that any interpretation is based upon the Bible alone and that no such interpretation shall become an issue which hinders the ministry to which God has called us.

We explicitly affirm our belief in basic Bible teachings, as follows:

1. There is one true God, eternally existing in three persons—Father, Son, and Holy Spirit—each of whom possesses equally all the attributes of Deity and the characteristics of personality.

2. Jesus Christ is God, the living Word, who became flesh through His miraculous conception by the Holy Spirit and His virgin birth. Hence, He is perfect Deity and true humanity united in one person forever.

3. He lived a sinless life and voluntarily atoned for the sins of men by dying on the cross as their substitute, thus satisfying divine justice and accomplishing salvation for all who trust in Him alone.

4. He rose from the dead in the same body, though glorified, in which He lived and died.

5. He ascended bodily into heaven and sat down at the right hand of God the Father, where He, the only Mediator between God and man, continually makes intercession for His own.

6. Man was originally created in the image of God. He sinned by dis-obeying God; thus he was alienated from his Creator. That historic fall brought all mankind under divine condemnation.

7. Man's nature is corrupted, and he is thus totally unable to please God. Every man is in need of regeneration and renewal by the Holy Spirit.

8. The salvation of man is wholly a work of God's free grace and is not the work, in whole or in part, of human works or goodness or reli-gious ceremony. God imputes His righteousness to those who put their faith in Christ alone for their salvation and thereby justifies them in His sight.

9. It is the privilege of all who are born again of the Spirit to be assured of their salvation from the very moment in which they trust Christ as their Savior. This assurance is not based upon any kind of human merit, but is produced by the witness of the Holy Spirit, who confirms in the believer the testimony of God in His written Word.

10. The Holy Spirit has come into the world to reveal and glorify Christ and to apply the saving work of Christ to men. He convicts and draws sinners to Christ, imparts new life to them, continually indwells them from the moment of spiritual birth, and seals them until the day of redemption. His fullness, power, and control are appropriated in the believer's life by faith.

11. Every believer is called to live so in the power of the indwelling Spirit that he will not fulfill the lust of the flesh but will bear fruit to the glory of God.

12. Jesus Christ is the Head of the Church, His Body, which is composed of all men, living and dead, who have been joined to Him through saving faith.

13. God admonishes His people to assemble together regularly for worship, for participation in ordinances, for edification through the Scriptures, and for mutual encouragement.

14. At physical death, the believer enters immediately into eternal, conscious fellowship with the Lord and awaits the resurrection of his body to everlasting glory and blessing.

15. At physical death, the unbeliever enters immediately into eternal, conscious separation from the Lord and awaits the resurrection of his body to everlasting judgment and condemnation.

16. Jesus Christ will come again to the earth—personally, visibly, and bodily—to consummate history and the eternal plan of God.

17. The Lord Jesus Christ commanded all believers to proclaim the gospel throughout the world and to disciple men of every nation. The fulfillment of that Great Commission requires that all worldly and personal ambitions be subordinated to a total commitment to "Him who loved us and gave Himself for us."

Have You Heard of the Four Spiritual Laws?

Bill Bright's Classic Evangelism Tract

Just as there are physical laws that govern the physical universe, so are there spiritual laws that govern your relationship with God.

LAW 1

*God **loves** you, and has a wonderful **plan** for your life.*

God's Love

"God so loved the world that he gave his one and only Son, that whoever believes in him shall not perish but have eternal life" (John 3:16, NIV).

God's Plan

[Christ speaking] "I came that they might have life, and might have it abundantly" [that it might be full and meaningful] (John 10:10).

Why is it that most people are not experiencing the abundant life?
Because...

LAW 2

*Man is **sinful** and **separated** from God.*
Therefore, he cannot know and experience God's love and plan for his life.

Man Is Sinful

"All have sinned and fall short of the glory of God" (Romans 3:23).

Man was created to have fellowship with God; but, because of his own stubborn self-will, he chose to go his own independent way, and fellowship with God was broken. This self-will, characterized by an attitude of active rebellion or passive indifference, is an evidence of what the Bible calls sin.

Man Is Separated

"The wages of sin is death" [spiritual separation from God] (Romans 6:23).

This diagram illustrates that God is holy and man is sinful. A great gulf separates the two. The arrows illustrate that man is continually trying to reach God and the abundant life through his own efforts, such as a good life, philosophy, or religion—but he inevitably fails.

The third law explains the only way to bridge this gulf...

LAW 3

*Jesus Christ is God's **only** provision for man's sin.*
Through Him you can know and experience God's love
and plan for your life.

He Died in Our Place

"God demonstrates His own love toward us, in that while we were yet sinners, Christ died for us" (Romans 5:8).

He Rose from the Dead

"Christ died for our sins...He was buried...He was raised on the third day, according to the Scriptures...He appeared to [Peter], then to the twelve. After that He appeared to more than five hundred...." (1 Corinthians 15:3-6).

He Is the Only Way to God

"Jesus said to him, 'I am the way, and the truth, and the life; no one comes to the Father but through Me'" (John 14:6).

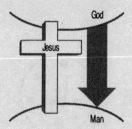

This diagram illustrates that God has bridged the gulf that separates us from Him by sending His Son, Jesus Christ, to die on the cross in our place to pay the penalty for our sins.

It is not enough just to know these three laws...

LAW 4

*We must individually **receive** Jesus Christ as Savior and Lord; then we can know and experience God's love and plan for our lives.*

We Must Receive Christ

"As many as received Him, to them He gave the right to become children of God, even to those who believe in His name" (John 1:12).

We Receive Christ Through Faith

"By grace you have been saved through faith; and that not of yourselves, it is the gift of God; not as a result of works, that no one should boast" (Ephesians 2:8-9).

When We Receive Christ, We Experience a New Birth
(Read John 3:1-8.)

We Receive Christ Through Personal Invitation

[Christ speaking] "Behold, I stand at the door and knock; if anyone hears My voice and opens the door, I will come in to him" (Revelation 3:20).

Receiving Christ involves turning to God from self (repentance) and trusting Christ to come into our lives to forgive our sins and to make us what He wants us to be. Just to agree **intellectually** that Jesus Christ is the Son of God and that He died on the cross for our sins is not enough. Nor is it enough to have an **emotional** experience. We receive Jesus Christ by **faith,** as an act of the **will.**

These two circles represent two kinds of lives:

Self-Directed Life

S—Self is on the throne.

†—Christ is outside the life.

•—Interests are directed by self, often resulting in discord and frustration.

Christ-Directed Life

†—Christ is in the life and on the throne.

S—Self is yielding to Christ.

•—Interests are directed by Christ, resulting in harmony with God's plan.

Which circle represents your life?

Which circle would you like to have represent your life?

The following explains how you can receive Christ:

YOU CAN RECEIVE CHRIST RIGHT NOW
BY FAITH THROUGH PRAYER

Prayer Is Talking with God

God knows your heart and is not so concerned with your words as He is with the attitude of your heart. The following is a suggested prayer:

Lord Jesus, I need You. Thank You for dying on the cross for my sins. I open the door of my life and receive You as my Savior and Lord. Thank You for forgiving my sins and giving me eternal life. Take control of the throne of my life. Make me the kind of person You want me to be.

Does this prayer express the desire of your heart?

If it does, I invite you to pray this prayer right now, and Christ will come into your life, as He promised.

HOW TO KNOW THAT CHRIST IS IN YOUR LIFE

Did you receive Christ into your life? According to His promise in Revelation 3:20, where is Christ right now in relation to you? Christ said that He would come into your life. Would He mislead you? On what authority do you know that God has answered your prayer? (The trustworthiness of God Himself and His Word.)

The Bible Promises Eternal Life to All Who Receive Christ

"The witness is this, that God has given us eternal life, and this life is in His Son. He who has the Son has the life; he who does not have the Son of God does not have the life. These things I have written to you who believe in the name of the Son of God, in order that you may **know** that you have eternal life" (1 John 5:11-13).

Thank God often that Christ is in your life and that He will never leave you (Hebrews 13:5). You can know on the basis of His promise that the Christ lives in you and that you have eternal life from the very moment you invite Him in. He will not deceive you.

An important reminder…

Do Not Depend upon Feelings

The promise of God's Word, the Bible—not our feelings—is our authority. The Christian lives by faith (trust) in the trustworthiness of God Himself

 and His Word. This train diagram illustrates the relationship among **fact** (God and His Word), **faith** (our trust in God and His Word), and **feeling** (the result of our faith and obedience) (John 14:21).

The train will run with or without the caboose. However, it would be useless to attempt to pull the train by the caboose. In the same way, as Christians we do not depend on feelings or emotions, but we place our faith (trust) in the trustworthiness of God and the promises of His Word.

NOW THAT YOU HAVE RECEIVED CHRIST

The moment you received Christ by faith, as an act of the will, many things happened, including the following:

- Christ came into your life (Revelation 3:20, Colossians 1:27).
- Your sins were forgiven (Colossians 1:14).
- You became a child of God (John 1:12).
- You received eternal life (John 5:24).
- You began the great adventure for which God created you (John 10:10; 2 Corinthians 5:17; 1 Thessalonians 5:18).

Can you think of anything more wonderful that could happen to you than receiving Christ? Would you like to thank God in prayer right now for what He has done for you? By thanking God, you demonstrate your faith.

To enjoy your new life to the fullest…

SUGGESTIONS FOR CHRISTIAN GROWTH

Spiritual growth results from trusting Jesus Christ. "The righteous man shall live by faith" (Galatians 3:11). A life of faith will enable you to trust God increasingly with every detail of your life and to practice the following:

G—*Go* to God in prayer daily (John 15:7).

R—*Read* God's Word daily (Acts 17:11); begin with the gospel of John.

O—*Obey* God moment by moment (John 14:21).

W—*Witness* for Christ by your life and words (Matthew 4:19; John 15:8).

T—*Trust* God for every detail of your life (1 Peter 5:7).

H—*Holy Spirit*—allow Him to control and empower your daily life and witness (Galatians 5:16-17; Acts 1:8).

Fellowship in a Good Church

God's Word instructs us not to forsake "the assembling of ourselves together" (Hebrews 10:25, KJV). Several logs burn brightly together, but put one aside on the cold hearth and the fire goes out. So it is with your relationship with other Christians.

If you do not belong to a church, do not wait to be invited. Take the initiative; call the pastor of a nearby church where Christ is honored and His Word is preached. Start this week and make plans to attend regularly.

Special Materials Are Available for Christian Growth

If you have come to know Christ personally through this presentation of the gospel, helpful materials for Christian growth are available to you. For more information, write Campus Crusade for Christ, 100 Sunport Lane 2100, Orlando, FL 32809.

If this booklet has been helpful to you, please share it with someone else.

—

How You Can Be Filled with the Holy Spirit

From Bill Bright's "Transferable Concept" Booklet on This Topic

Most Christians live in self-imposed spiritual poverty because they don't know how to appropriate from God the spiritual resources that are already theirs.

During the Depression a man named Yates owned a sheep ranch in West Texas. Because he did not earn enough money to make his ranching operation pay, Mr. Yates was in danger of losing his ranch. His family, like many others, had to live on government subsidy.

Day after day, as Mr. Yates grazed his sheep over those rolling West Texas hills, he was greatly troubled over how to meet his financial obligations. Then a seismographic crew from an oil company came into the area and informed Mr. Yates that they felt there might be oil on his land. They asked permission to drill a wildcat test well, and he signed a lease contract.

At 1,116 feet they struck a huge oil reserve. The first well came in at 80,000 barrels a day. Many subsequent wells were more than twice as large. And Mr. Yates owned it all.

The day he purchased the land he received the oil and mineral rights. Yet, he had been living on relief—a multimillionaire living in poverty. The problem? He did not know the oil was there. He owned it, but he did not *possess* it.

I do not know of a better illustration of the Christian life than this. The moment we become children of God through faith in Christ we become heirs of God, and all of His divine supernatural resources are made available to us. Everything we need—including wisdom, love, power—to be men and women of God and to be fruitful witnesses for Christ is available to us. But most Christians continue to live in self-imposed spiritual poverty because they do not know how to appropriate from God those spiritual resources that are already theirs.

It is useless to try to live in our own power the kind of life God has commanded us to live. Our strength must come from the Lord! The Holy Spirit came to enable us to know Christ. When we receive Christ into our lives, we experience a new birth and are indwelt by the Spirit. The Holy Spirit enables us to live and share the abundant life that Jesus promised to all who trust Him.

LACK OF FAITH

Many Christians are not filled, controlled, and empowered with the Spirit because of a lack of knowledge. Unbelief keeps others from experiencing the abundant life. There are still other Christians who may have been exposed to the truth concerning the person and ministry of the Holy Spirit but who, for various reasons, have never been able to comprehend the love of God. They are afraid of Him. They simply do not trust Him. Suppose, when my two sons were young, they had greeted me with these words: "Daddy, we love you and have decided that we will do anything you want us to do from now on as long as we live." What do you think would have been my attitude?

If I had responded to their expression of trust in me as many believe God will respond when they surrender their lives to Him, I would have taken my sons by the shoulders, shaken them, glared at them sternly and said, "I have just been waiting for this! I am going to make you regret this decision for as long as you live. I am going to take all the fun out of your lives—give away your toys and make you do all the things you do not like to do." Many people believe this is the way God will respond when they say, "Lord, I surrender the control of my life to You." They do not understand how much God loves them.

Do you know what I would do if my sons came to me with such a greeting? I would put my arms around them and say, "I love you, too, and I deeply appreciate this expression of your love for me. It is the greatest gift which you could give me, and I want to do everything in my power to merit your love and trust."

Is God any less loving and concerned for His children? No, He has proved over and over again that He is a loving God—our heavenly Father who cares deeply for His children. He is worthy of our trust.

FILLED BY FAITH

How can one be filled with the Holy Spirit? We are filled with the Spirit by faith. We received Christ by faith. We walk by faith. Everything we receive from God, from the moment of our spiritual birth until we die, is by faith.

You do not have to beg God to fill you with His Holy Spirit. You do not have to barter with Him by fasting, weeping, or pleading. For a long time I fasted, prayed, and cried out to God for His fullness. Then one day I discovered from the Scriptures that "the just shall live by faith" (Galatians 3:11, KJV). We do not earn God's fullness. We receive it by faith.

Suppose you want to cash a check for a hundred dollars. Would you go to the bank where you have several thousand dollars on deposit, place the check on the counter, get down on your knees, and say, "Oh, please, Mr. Teller, cash my check"? No, that is not the way you cash a check. You simply go in faith, place the check on the counter, and wait for the money that is already yours. Then you thank the teller and go on your way.

Millions of Christians are begging God, as I once did, for something that is already available and just waiting to be appropriated by faith. They are seeking some kind of emotional experience, not realizing that such an attitude on their part is an insult to God and a denial of faith, by which we please God. In Hebrews 11:6 we are told, "Without faith it is impossible to please God" (NIV).

HEART PREPARATION

Though you are filled with the Holy Spirit by faith and faith alone, it is important to recognize that several factors contribute to preparing your heart for the filling of the Spirit.

First, you must hunger and thirst after God and desire to be controlled and empowered by His Holy Spirit. We have the promise of our Savior: "Blessed are those who hunger and thirst for righteousness, for they shall be filled" (Matthew 5:6, NKJV).

Second, be willing to surrender your life to Christ in accordance with Paul's admonition in Romans 12:1-2—"And so, dear brothers, I plead with you to give your bodies to God. Let them be a living sacrifice, holy—the kind he can accept. When you think of what he has done for you, is this too much to ask? Don't copy the behavior and customs of this world, but be a new and different person with a fresh newness in all you do and think. Then you will learn from your own experience how his ways will really satisfy you" (TLB).

Third, confess every known sin which the Holy Spirit brings to your remembrance and experience the cleansing and forgiveness which God promises in 1 John 1:9: "But if we confess our sins to him, he can be depended on to forgive us and to cleanse us from every wrong. [And it is perfectly proper for God to do this for us because Christ died to wash away our sins]" (TLB).

COMMAND AND PROMISE

There are two very important words to remember. The first is *command*. In Ephesians 5:18, God commands us to be filled: "Be not drunk with wine, wherein is excess; but be filled with the Spirit" (KJV). Not to be controlled and empowered by the Holy Spirit is disobedience. The other word is *promise*—a promise that makes the command possible: "This is the confidence which we have before Him, that, *if we ask anything according to His will, He hears us. And if we know that He hears us in whatever we ask, we know that we have the requests which we have asked from Him*" (1 John 5:14-15, NASB).

Now, is it God's will for you to be filled, controlled, and empowered by the Holy Spirit? Of course it is His will—for it is His command. Right now, then, you can ask God the Holy Spirit to fill you—not because you deserve to be filled, but on the basis of His command and promise.

When you receive Christ, the Holy Spirit comes to dwell within you. Therefore, you do not need to invite Him to come into your life. The moment you received Christ, the Holy Spirit not only came to indwell you, but He imparted to you spiritual life, causing you to be born anew as a child of God. The Holy Spirit also baptized you into the body of Christ. In 1 Corinthians 12:13 (KJV), Paul explains, "For by one Spirit we are all baptized into one body." There is but one *indwelling* of the Holy Spirit, one *rebirth* of the Holy Spirit, and one *baptism* of the Holy Spirit—all of which occur the moment you receive Christ. There are many *fillings,* as is made clear in Ephesians 5:18. In the Greek language in which the New Testament was originally written, the meaning is clearer than in most English translations. This command of God means to *be constantly and continually filled, controlled, and empowered with the Holy Spirit as a way of life.*

If you wish to be technical, you do not need to pray to be filled with the Holy Spirit, as there is no place in Scripture where we are told to pray for the filling of the Holy Spirit. *We are filled by faith.* However, since the object of our faith is God and His Word, I suggest that you pray to be filled with the Holy Spirit as an expression of your faith in God's command and in His promise. You are not filled because you pray, but because by faith you trust God to fill you with His Spirit in response to your faith.

Have you met God's conditions? Do you hunger and thirst after righteousness? Have you confessed every known sin in your life? Do you sincerely desire to be controlled and empowered by the Holy Spirit, to make Jesus Christ the Lord of your life? If so, I invite you to bow and pray a prayer of faith right now. Claim the fullness of the Holy Spirit by faith:

"Dear Father, I need You. I acknowledge that I have been in control of my life and that, as a result, I have sinned against You. I thank You that You have forgiven my sins through Christ's death on the cross for me. I now invite Christ to take control of the throne of my life. Fill me with the Holy Spirit as You commanded me to be filled and as You promised in Your Word

Bill Bright's
Published Writings

FOR PERSONAL EVANGELISM

A Man Without Equal: Jesus, the Man Who Changed the World
Good News Comic Book
Have You Heard of the Four Spiritual Laws?
Jesus and the Intellectual
Would You Like to Belong to God's Family?
Would You Like to Know God Personally?
Your Life Can Become a Great Adventure
Your Most Important Investment

FOR PERSONAL GROWTH AND DISCIPLESHIP

As You Sow: The Adventure of Giving by Faith
Beginning Your Journey of Joy (with Vonette Bright)
Believing God for the Impossible
Building a Home in a Pull-Apart World: Powerful Principles for a Happier Marriage—Four Steps that Work (with Vonette Bright)
Come Help Change the World
The Coming Revival: America's Call to Fast, Pray, and "Seek God's Face"
Five Steps of Christian Growth

Five Steps to Discipling New Believers

Five Steps to Fasting & Prayer

Five Steps to Knowing God's Will

Five Steps to Making Disciples

Five Steps to Sharing Your Faith (also published as *How to Reach Your World*)

God: Consider His Character

Have You Made the Wonderful Discovery of the Spirit-Filled Life?

The Holy Spirit: The Key to Supernatural Living

Kingdoms at War (with Ronald Jenson)

Love's Not Enough

A Movement of Miracles

Preparing for the Coming Revival

Promises: A Daily Guide to Supernatural Living

Quiet Moments with Bill Bright

*Red Sky in the Morning: How You Can Help Prevent America's Gathering
Storms* (with John N. Damoose)

The Secret: How to Live with Purpose and Power

Ten Basic Steps toward Christian Maturity (booklet series; their content is
also published in one volume as the *Handbook for Christian Maturity*):

Introduction—The Uniqueness of Jesus

Step 1—The Christian Adventure

Step 2—The Christian and the Abundant Life

Step 3—The Christian and the Holy Spirit

Step 4—The Christian and Prayer

Step 5—The Christian and the Bible

Step 6—The Christian and Obedience

Step 7—The Christian and Witnessing

Step 8—The Christian and Giving

Step 9—Highlights of the Old Testament

Step 10—Highlights of the New Testament

The Transferable Concepts Booklets (also published in one volume as
Transferable Concepts for Powerful Living):

How You Can Be a Fruitful Witness

How You Can Be Filled with the Holy Spirit

How You Can Be Sure You Are a Christian

How You Can Experience God's Love and Forgiveness

How You Can Experience the Adventure of Giving

How You Can Fulfill the Great Commission

How You Can Introduce Others to Christ

How You Can Love by Faith

How You Can Pray with Confidence

How You Can Walk in the Spirit

The Transforming Power of Fasting and Prayer: Personal Accounts of Spiritual Renewal

Witnessing Without Fear

Acknowledgments

Untold stories stir me. Societies without heroes worry me. The rarity of modern American concern for posterity troubles me deeply. So, when I discovered there was no formal biography of the life and times of Bill Bright (my mind had first met his in 1971 through his writings), I naturally ventured forth. Dr. Bright declined my requests for four years. I did keep asking, and we came to agreement on the grounds that the matter was to be handled especially for a rising generation of leaders who might benefit from his story. I asked for extraordinary and exceptional access to Bill's life, his office, his home, his family, and his records, and I made quite an impertinent presence in and out of his life for more than a decade.

Anyone who writes of such broad endeavors knows the utter implausibility of telling such a story in a single volume, and the actual impossibility of it without the scores and scores of good people who oblige your intrusion into their lives. I am forever grateful to each one. They know who they are, and so does the good Lord who allowed us to meet and talk about the things His Providential hand has been doing in and through Bill and Vonette Bright for more than five decades.

My great regret is that space did not allow, in this telling, the stories of so many nationals throughout the earth who decided to follow on Bill Bright's great world adventure. They, in so many ways, are the secret story of the astonishing reach of this man's multiplied ministry. Perhaps, on another day.

I owe so much to my family for the sacrifices they made, the prayers they prayed, and the shoulders they offered when the going got tough. Michele

Peek, Mark Richardson, and Mindy Barmer are precious to their Mom, Margaret, and me. My mother, Ruth, once wrote a college paper on "word choice" and made my childhood a place of reading the best. My father, W. R., made leadership and politics and strategic thinking important to me.

I want to thank each of the following pastors and their flocks—Dr. George Billings, Dr. Charlie Martin, Dr. Roland Barrington, Dr. Billy Cruce, the late Dr. Earl Edington, Dr. Charles Stanley, and Ben Haden.

I owe such a great debt to Elizabeth and Bailey Marks, who, as my mentor Eugene Patterson used to say, "told it with the bark off" so that I could have a frame of reference, a portal for focusing on such a complex person as Bill Bright. In like manner, Annie and Sid Wright never gave up on me.

Then the listing ranges so widely, from fleeting interviews of Crusade's top leaders, and on to wonderful staff assistants like the late and beloved Erma Griswold, Bill's personal secretary for more than two decades, and Mary Canada, Paula Marolis, and a string of Dr. Bright's personal assistants whose candid asides helped me fill in the picture of the humanity and the reality of this man.

My appreciation goes to interviewees on five continents, not the least of whom, Sir John Templeton, really took time to discuss the global implications of Bill's ministry.

Finally, it is amazing to me that Bill and Vonette Bright spent so many hours with me out of their schedules—usually when they were supposed to be truly taking a break—all of it quite beyond what any journalist deserves.

Although Dr. Bright and I had a few moments of disagreement, I came to see those as something of a badge of courage—like running a tribal gauntlet for initiation into a family that debates the means of message-telling as if it were sport. He was never demanding, but he was not without his opinions. In the end, it was easier to focus on acres of documented agreeable and controversial territory. There are, in fact, many disclosures herein never before printed.

I especially thank Zac and Brad Bright and their families for their willingness to be brought into these pages with candor and vigor.

The very special agent in all of this is Robert Wolgemuth, the best. Of course, without publisher Dan Rich none of this would be possible. His vision and patience and hard-working staff are Bright-like.

My goal was to leave something for the next generation—the beginning of an empirical history of an intellect big enough to tackle all comers, a heart big enough to hug the world, and a hand willing to nudge or spank it. On the last page of the book, you are invited to a dialogue about the degree to which such a goal may have been reached. I trust by now it is clear: With Bill Bright, what you see is what you get.

Michael Richardson
Dunedin, Florida
November 1999
Romans 11:36

www.amazingfaith.net

You are personally invited to visit the author's Web site, **www.amazingfaith. net**, where you can:

1. Write your comments about this book or about Dr. Bright.
2. Tell your own story of interacting with Dr. Bright.
3. Share an anecdote about the Bright family or their ministry.

By so doing you may be contributing to a further publication chronicling the ministry of Bill Bright.

You can also contact me by e-mail at mlrusa@aol.com.

Thank you for your interest.

Sincerely,
Michael Richardson